Contemporary Thought

The Tenth Anniversary Commemorative Volume
of the Trinity College Biblical Institute 1966 - 1975

TRINITY COLLEGE BIBLICAL INSTITUTE
Burlington, Vermont

GREENO, HADDEN & COMPANY, LTD.
SOMERVILLE, MASSACHUSETTS

Copyright © 1975 by Trinity College Biblical Institute
All Rights Reserved
Printed and Bound in the United States of America

Distributed by Greeno, Hadden & Company, Ltd.
Library of Congress Catalog Card Number: 75–17036
International Standard Book Number: 0–913550–07–8

To The memory of the late
George Ernest Wright
for his unfailing loyalty to the
Trinity College Biblical Institute

Contents

FOREWORD

Nowhere in this century has so much real progress been made in religious studies as in the area of the Bible. For Catholics the impetus has come from different sources, the greatest of which was DIVINO AFFLANTE SPIRITU of Pope Pius XII, issued in 1943. Stemming from that major encyclical on Biblical Studies, and embodying its principles, the Dogmatic Constitution on Divine Revelation, DEI VERBUM, was promulgated by the Second Vatican Council in November, 1965.

Inspired by Vatican II, and encouraged by the developing climate of ecumenism, Trinity College, Burlington, Vermont, initiated a series of annual Biblical institutes. In the sixth chapter of DEI VERBUM, entitled "Sacred Scripture in the Life of the Church", the Council Fathers urge the faithful to study the Sacred Scriptures toward a deeper understanding of the Word of God. The Trinity Biblical Institute was founded to help to implement these directives. In a spirit of ecumenism the Trinity Institute has presented from its inception in 1966 the highest level of Catholic and non-Catholic Biblical scholarship. The internationally recognized faculty has included both American and European scholars who are active participants in current trends shaping the future of Biblical studies.

This volume commemorates the Tenth Anniversary of the Trinity College Biblical Institute. Its intent is to reflect the nature and scope of topics explored during the annual sessions by a representative selection of subjects.

In the area of Biblical hermeneutics, *T. A. Collins, O.P.,* and *P. G. Duncker, O.P.,* examine different aspects of the problem of the truth of the Bible. With the advances in textual criticism and related disciplines, the possibility of error in the Bible becomes very real. In his essay entitled

"The Truth of the Bible Debate", Father Collins surveys the present state of the debate on this delicate question. A former member of the Pontifical Biblical Commission, Father Duncker, traces the genesis and evolution of Vatican II's formulation of the statement on the relation between Scripture and Tradition. The author reveals the human side of the agonizing process in the decision that has had such an impact on scriptural study and on ecumenical relations between Catholics and Protestants.

Although the Trinity institutes have never suffered from the 'relevancy hang-up', nevertheless, they have not neglected the relation between the Bible and modern living. In his essay entitled "Human Dominion Over Nature", *Bernhard Anderson* responds to those who indict Christianity for the modern disastrous ecological situation. On quite a different note, *Eugene B. Borowitz* and *Raymond E. Brown, S.S.*, examine concerns of modern Judaism and Christianity, respectively. Rabbi Borowitz, with Biblical Judaism as his point of departure, spans a wide range of Jewish history and literature in treating the question of Jewish religious experience in a changed social situation. Father Brown, on the other hand, confronts a problem of concern particularly to Catholics. He treats the impact of modern Biblical studies on theology and on the teaching of Catholic doctrine.

Kevin J. Cathcart and *Carroll Stuhlmueller, C.P.* present representative studies on the Old Testament. Professor Cathcart examines a problem in a too-little known part of the Bible, the book of Nahum, a Minor Prophet. Father Stuhlmueller lends a liturgical bent as he examines the way the Bible reflects life, with the particular emphasis on the Psalms.

Our New Testament essays reflect a diversity of topic and approach. *Peter F. Ellis, C.SS.R.* examines the literary aspects of Mark's gospel underlying the author's theology; *Eugene H. Maly* explores the new meaning that Jesus Christ has given to creation; *M. Lucetta Mowry* discusses the Pauline charismatic gifts with special reference to the modern Pentecostal movement; Monsignor *Jerome D. Quinn,* in his essay toward a history of ministry, offers a paper highly significant in ecumenical discussion today.

With the directive of Pius XII concerning the importance of discovering the literary genre, and his stress on archaeology and allied sciences in mind, the Trinity institutes have given special recognition to the revolutionary advances in archaeology and its impact on Biblical studies. The Jewish scholar *Cyrus H. Gordon,* presents a lucid account of the significance of one of the century's greatest discoveries — the Ugaritic tablets — to Biblical studies. *George Ernest Wright,* the late Dean of American archaeologists, exemplifies in his article the painstaking and scientifically accurate kind of work characteristic of this relatively new science in the last several decades. As Dr. Wright points out in his preliminary footnotes, this report on the Biblical city of Ai was written prior to completion of the proposed expeditions, but with three sessions as a basis for his conclusions.

Grateful to all who have made these ten years so rewarding an experience, The Trinity College Biblical Institute hopes to continue to assist in opening up more lavishly the treasures of the Bible, "so that richer fare may be provided for the faithful at the table of God's Word."*

Miriam Ward, R.S.M.
Director
Trinity College Biblical Institute
June, 1975

* (*Constitution on the Sacred Liturgy,* Chapter II, Section 51)

Thomas Aquinas Collins, O.P.

THE TRUTH OF THE BIBLE DEBATE

The debate over the nature of the Bible's truth is a fairly recent one. Within the last decade, well-known scholars such as Oswald Loretz, Pierre Benoit, Norbert Lohfink, Louis Alonso-Schökel, and Heinrich Schlier have focused attention on the question: "What do we mean when we say that the Bible is true"? Are we necessarily thinking in terms of the familiar *adaequatio rei et intellectus* of our philosophy courses? Or should we not be thinking in terms of the conception of biblical truth as proposed by Oswald Loretz, who insists that the above-mentioned concept of truth is a Greek, not a Semitic one. Loretz protests that such a Greek concept of truth has no place in the Bible, at least no primary place. As we shall see below, Loretz proposes that the concept of God's faithfulness to his promises is the principal idea signified by the Hebrew term for truth, *'emet.*

In the course of the truth of the Bible debate other problems have been laid bare, especially those concerned with proper hermeneutical procedures, as well as those concerned with the nature of Biblical theology itself. It is well-known in biblical circles that there is serious disagreement among outstanding scholars over just what constitutes a biblical theology. The late Roland de Vaux, for example, vigorously protested that Von Rad's OLD TESTAMENT THEOLOGY was not really a biblical theology. If the description of biblical theology as "the fruit of exegesis and the germ of systematic theology" be accepted, any precision the truth of the Bible debate gives to the exegetical process will be welcomed by biblical theologians. We turn now to the details of the debate.

A.   Oswald Loretz

We begin with the work of Oswald Loretz. Loretz states clearly his intention: ". . . what I am speaking of is the *truth* of the Bible, not its inerrancy or freedom from error."[1] What does Loretz mean by the expression "Truth of the Bible"? He insists that the answer to the question, "In what sense does the Bible claim to be true?", must come from the Bible itself. Loretz proceeds to (1) investigate the biblical modes of conception and understanding of truth, (2) examine the biblical terms used to express the concept of "truth", especially the term *'emet* and (3) compare

THOMAS AQUINAS COLLINS, O.P., is Professor of Hebrew and Old Testament at Providence College Graduate School, Providence, Rhode Island.

1 Oswald Loretz, DIE WAHRHEIT DER BIBEL (Freiburg: Herder and Herder, 1964); revised version of the original edition translated by David J. Bourke, under the title THE TRUTH OF THE BIBLE (N.Y.: Herder and Herder, 1968), p. viii.

the results of his investigations with what is known of the Ancient Near East and Semitic concept of truth. He concludes that the Old Testament speaks primarily "of God being 'true' to his words, and not of the truth of the words themselves". The term *'emet* means primarily not 'truth' but 'firmness, stability, reliability, certainty, sureness, integrity, faithfulness'." Loretz grants, as he must, that the Old Testament does also state that God's words are true but he insists that "for the Old Testament the 'truth' of God is primarily bound up with his faithfulness." Loretz argues that the Old Testament reveals Yahweh as a covenant God who not only demands faithfulness from his chosen people, but also promises faithfulness on his own part.[2] From his study of *aletheia*, the Greek term used most often in the Bible to translate *'emet*, Loretz concludes that *aletheia*, like *'emet*, can signify many different things depending upon the context: "truthfulness", "reliability", "uprightness", and the like.[3] Loretz's position on the question of the Bible's truth can be summarized as follows: (1) The truth of the Bible consists not in the adequation between the mental word and the extra-mental reality, but rather in God's faithfulness to his promises made to Israel. The Bible would be untrue, according to Loretz, not because it presented something erroneous but because it made God to be a liar. (2) For the most part, Loretz based his thesis on the results of linguistic investigations of the Hebrew word *'emet*, which signifies not only the hellenistic concept of truth as the adequation between mental word and extra-mental reality, but more principally the concepts of "faithfulness", "firmness", "reliability" and the like. (3) Finally, Loretz claimed that this is the way the Bible speaks of itself with respect to its truth. Biblically speaking, says Loretz, to teach without error means to teach without lies: "Since the truth of God is manifested in his faithfulness to his covenant people, Scripture could only be charged with error if God broke his faith with Israel."[4]

Sharp and severe criticism of Loretz's proposal was not long in coming. On linguistic grounds came challenges from James Barr (in THE SEMANTICS OF BIBLICAL LANGUAGE [London: Oxford University Press, 1961], pp. 161-205), from Luis Alonso-Schökel (in his review of Loretz's

2 *Ibid.*, pp. 82, 83.
3 *Ibid.*, p. 85. For the derivation of the Johannine concept of truth, cf. I. De La Potterie, "L'arrière-fond du thème johannique de vérité", STUDIA EVANGELICA: Papers Presented to the International Congress on the Four Gospels in 1957, held at Christ Church, Oxford, 1957, edited by K. Aland, F.J. Cross, J. Danielou, H. Riesenfeld, and W.C. Van Unnik, found in TEXTE UND UNTERSUCHUNGEN 73 (Berlin: Akademie-Verlag, 1959), pp. 277-294. For the notion of Jesus as the Truth in Ep 4:21, cf. I. De La Potterie, "Jésus Et La Vérité D'Après Eph 4,21", STUDIORUM PAULINORUM CONGRESSUS INTERNATIONALIS CATHOLICUS (Rome: Pontifical Biblical Institue, 1961), Vol. II, pp. 45-57.
4 Loretz, p. 89.

THE TRUTH OF THE BIBLE in *Biblia,* Vol. 46, 1965, pp. 378-80), from P. Benoit (in his review of the same work in *Revue Biblique,* Vol. 75, 1968, pp. 132-3), from B. Brinkmann (in his review in *Theologie Und Philosophie,* Vol. 41, 1966, pp. 115-118), and from E. Gutwenger (in his article "The Inerrancy of the Bible" in *Zeitschrift für katholische Theologie,* Vol. 87, 1965, pp. 196-202). Barr, for example, insists that *'emet* should be translated as "truth" and not primarily as "firmness", "steadfastness", or "reliability":

> But for *'emet* also it is excessively etymologizing to offer 'firmness' as the 'basic meaning'. 'Truth' is already the right translation as early as the only occurrence in Ugaritic literature.[5]

J. R. Driver translates this Ugaritic evidence as follows:

> "Lo! truly, truly, I have wasted (my) life,
> "truly I get mud (grasping it)[6]

Gutwenger questions Loretz's linguistic methodology in placing too great an emphasis on the frequency of the meaning of *'emet* rather than on the meaning of the word derived from a given context. Brinkmann and Alonso-Schökel agree that *'emet* signifies not only God's faithfulness and fidelity, but also objective truth. Alonso-Schökel argues that there are clear examples in the Bible (e.g., Dt 13:15) where *'emet* can only mean objective truth. In Dt 13:14-16, involving a legal case, clear instructions are given concerning the certainty of the evidence to be used against the accused: "You must inquire carefully into the matter and investigate it thoroughly. If you find that it is true (*'emet*) and an established fact . . ." Alonso-Schökel further criticizes Loretz for failing to make proper distinctions when speaking of the relationship of fidelity to covenant and promise.

Loretz's position that all truth of the Bible must fall under the "fidelity" concept has also occasioned strong objections. Alonso-Schökel asks about those truths which do not pertain directly to the fidelity of God. He cites the preachings in Deuteronomy, or the texts which proclaim the oneness of God, his primordial cosmic action, his universal knowledge.[7]

Benoit also questions whether Loretz has given sufficient attention to the element of intellectual knowledge or understanding which is involved in revelation. He, too, recalls that "fidelity" is not the only sense of the word *'emet.* In the Bible we find manifestations of truth in the ordinary

---

5 Barr, p. 187.
6 G.R. Driver, CANAANITE MYTHS AND LEGENDS (Edinburgh: T. & T. Clark, 1956), Baal I* i. 18f, p. 103.
7 *Ibid.,* p. 379. Alonso-Schokel has in mind such a text as the discourse put into the mouth of Moses (Dt 1:5-4:40); the explicit monotheism of Isaiah: ". . . and I, I am your God, I am he from eternity" (Is 43:13). Cf. also Is 41:4, 21-24; 42:8-13; 44:6-8; or a text which refers to God's creative action and wisdom such as in the speeches of Yahweh in the book of Job: "Where were you when I laid the earth's foundations? . . . Who decided the dimensions of it?" (Jb 38:4-5).

sense of the word. Benoit means those religious truths to which we adhere by faith but which do not pertain solely or totally to the idea of trusting in God's fidelity.

J. Jensen asks:

> Granted that Scripture does not normally formulate doctrine as we do, does it not teach truths — truths not immediately identifiable with God's fidelity nor immediately derivable from it — that we must formulate (e.g., the personal nature of the Holy Spirit) and hold as taught inerrantly (even in the western sense) in Scripture? In fact, the Church does so formulate her doctrines and proclaims them to have been revealed.[8]

Brinkmann offers strong objections to the very basis of Loretz's concept of biblical truth, namely, that of the faithfulness of God to his covenant with Israel. What Brinkmann urges against Loretz's argumentation really amounts to this: before we can speak of biblical truth as being God's faithfulness to his promises, we must first establish that the Bible, which is claimed to have presented this testimony of God's faithfulness, is itself without error when it presents it.

In his review, quoted above, Alonso-Schökel raises a pivotal question concerning the "fidelity" concept:

> Is it true because it treats of fidelity simply? — the content would be the basis for the truth, or is it true because it gives testimony of a fidelity that in fact is realized? — the truth consists in a relationship. Clearly it treats of the second alternative, because the author tells us that the Bible would not be true if God were unfaithful to His people (p. 379).

Alonso-Schökel sees in this response a truth which cannot be reduced simply to the idea of "fidelity." The question he raises is pertinent: Is the Bible true because its content treats of fidelity or is the Bible true because it testifies to a fidelity that in fact is realized?

In his article mentioned above, Gutwenger raises an objection similar to that of Alonso-Schökel. He maintains that "We can only speak of the fidelity of God if his words correspond to facts. Even fidelity in this case is concerned with agreement of word and actuality" (p. 198). The interpretation itself of Scripture by Loretz has drawn criticism from Benoit, who claims that Loretz has failed to take into account the uniqueness of the New Testament in the evolution of words, from Jensen, who thinks that the summary of the New Testament use of the Old Testament is inadequate, and from Alonso-Schökel, who takes Loretz to task for the way he uses the Fourth Gospel.

---

8 Joseph Jensen, O.S.B., review of Loretz' THE TRUTH OF THE BIBLE in *Catholic Biblical Quarterly* (Vol. 27, 1965), pp. 276-277.

How are we to evaluate Loretz's concept of biblical truth as God's faithfulness in the face of such criticisms against some of his linguistic, theological, and hermeneutical positions? Firstly, in spite of the hermeneutical problem aggravated by the fact that the dialogue is between opposing western and semitic cultures, in spite of the heavy criticism launched against the basic thesis of Loretz, and in spite of the shortcomings of Loretz's argumentation, I should like to insist that Loretz has made an important contribution to the truth of the Bible debate in calling attention to the primary sense of 'emet in the Bible as "faithfulness." It is true to say that the biblical sense of 'emet is mostly, though not always, that of "faithfulness." To my knowledge no one has seriously challenged that fact. To call attention to this sense of 'emet as primary in the Bible is important, however faulty one may judge the hermeneutic, the argumentation, and the projection of Loretz to be.

Secondly, I suggest that the two great weaknesses in the thesis of Loretz are (1) his failure to convince his critics that all truths in the Bible must be seen in the light of the one great truth, the faithfulness of God to his promises, and (2) his seemingly over-preoccupation with the difference between the biblical and the Greek term for truth. Regarding the first of these weaknesses, Loretz admits that the Bible does, indeed, contain truths which cannot simply be reduced to the concept of "faithfulness", but he insists: "While we cannot, and indeed do not dispute this, we must at the same time observe that sacred Scripture sees these truths in their connection with a single great truth, namely, the faithfulness of God to his people" (p. 90-91). The response gives no argumentation to support the position and appears to be quite gratuitous. With regard to the preoccupation with the difference between the Semitic and Greek concept of truth, I find myself in complete sympathy with Gutwenger who writes:

> There is no point in making much of the difference between the biblical and Greek term truth, for the person, be he semite or Greek, would like to know whether a report telling of facts corresponds to actuality or not. This is a prevalent human response. To make an exception for semites sounds as if they have been excluded from the species *homo spaiens* (p. 198).

Loretz responded to Gutwenger by saying that "This may apply to an *a priori* approach, but not to modern research into the real position based on historical and philological grounds" (p. 82, n. 23). Unfortunately Loretz says nothing further on this rather important point so pertinent to his thesis. He gave no really satisfactory response to Gutwenger's objection.

B.   The Proposal of Norbert Lohfink

Whereas Loretz looked for the truth of the Bible in the concept of

God's faithfulness, Norbert Lohfink insists that the truth of the Bible must be derived from the study of the Bible as a whole. He first examines the older formulae which enshrine the belief in the inspiration of Holy Scripture. He then compares these with the more recent formulae. Aware of the newly acquired knowledge concerning the multiple authorship of even a single biblical book, and aware also of the problems arising from this multiplicity in the area of inspiration, Lohfink attempts to give some direction to the as yet unsolved problem of the relationship between the results of critical scholarship and the determination of the meaning of the Bible as a whole. The problem as Lohfink sees it may be fairly posed as follows: what does a careful study of the historical meaning of successive layers of biblical texts really contribute to our determining the final meaning of a given biblical truth, a final meaning which has been derived from the study of the Bible as a whole?

In his examination of the older formulae which enshrine the belief in the inspiration of Holy Scripture, Lohfink states clearly his purpose:

> The purpose of the following considerations is very modest. They are not intended to lead to radically new formulae, but for the most part only to exclude those among the traditional formulae which today inevitably lead to misunderstanding, and to commend the one which is still true today.[9]

He recalls that in the standard treatises on inspiration, inerrancy was predicated of (1) the Bible as a whole, (2) the individual books of the Bible, (3) the inspired writers of the sacred books. In the nineteenth century, the preferred expression in both ecclesiastical documents and in theological treatises was "the inerrancy of the sacred writers", an expression which won out over the expression "the inerrancy of the biblical books" and "the inerrancy of the Bible". Lohfink recalls that theologians and exegetes of the past century thought of biblical authorship as the work of a small, easily identifiable group of inspired individuals such as Moses, who wrote the Pentateuch, David, who wrote the Psalms, and Isaiah, the prophet who wrote the entire work which bears his name. In like manner, the New Testament was attributed to eight sacred authors. This idea of biblical authorship, Lohfink claims, is part of the background of the encyclical *Providentissimus Deus* (1893) but later ecclesiastical documents modified substantially the above-mentioned ideas of biblical authorship:

> It is commonly acknowledged that the "Letter to Cardinal Suhard" (1948) and various official pronouncements of the Biblical Commission on the occasion of the second edition of ENCHIRIDION BIBLICUM (1954) enabled Catholic exegetes to depart, even in public pro-

---

9 Norbert Lohfink, S.J., "The Inerrancy of Scripture" in The CHRISTIAN MEANING OF THE OLD TESTAMNET, translated by R.A. Wilson (Milwaukee: Bruce, 1968), p. 25.

nouncements, from the theses on questions of biblical authorship which the Biblical Commission has propounded at the beginning of the century (p. 27).

According to the "one author, one book" theory, a book was considered to be a finished product when it came from the hand of its inspired author. The task of an exegete was to attempt to understand the work and, consequently, to determine what the single author had intended to say. The nineteenth century Catholic formulation was made and stated within the limits of the understanding of inerrancy which was current among most Catholic scholars of the period. Contemporary scientific biblical scholarship has benefited enormously from the studies of archaeologists and philologists working in the field of Ancient Near Eastern literary remains hitherto unknown. It is now abundantly clear to present day biblical scholars that the received text of most of our biblical books was not the work of a single author. Critical studies of the Pentateuch, of the prophetical books, and of the Gospels indicate beyond a reasonable doubt, that these works are the end product of a long and complicated process of composition, alterations, the question: "What do we understand by the phrase 'author of a biblical book'?" Lohfink realizes that in view of this new understanding of the concept of author certain modifications have to be made with respect to the understanding of the formula "the inerrancy of the sacred writer". Not one, but many authors are now known to have participated in the composition of even a single book. Lohfink carefully delineates the relationship of multiple authors to the finished biblical work as follows:

> It was accepted that God might have inspired several human collaborators, working either in parallel or succeeding each other. No single person was responsible for the whole book, and perhaps in carrying out what would emerge centuries later as the final product of the process of composition. Therefore the intention of what is said by individual sacred writers and what is in fact said by the books of the Bible were in many cases not the same. But these sacred writers were all supposed to be inerrant. The consequence was that in the light of the new knowledge, the old formula of the "inerrancy of the sacred writers" no longer meant the same as that of the "inerrancy of the books of the Bible," but far more (p. 29).

We can appreciate how differently the phrase "inerrancy of the sacred writer" must now be understood in the light of the new concept of biblical authorship if we become aware that the concept of multiple authors means that every phase in the growth of the composition of a given biblical book shares in the inerrancy of the sacred writer. Each addition, each gloss and editorial comment, each adaptation results in a new and inerrant totality taught by the inspired book. The end result of this process of composition has been compared to an archaeological dig: each layer of inerrant material is in danger of being piled upon its predecessor. If many hands during many stages of composition actually enjoy inerrancy, then it follows that whatever content these stages exhibit now becomes part of the matter of revelation, and consequently of our faith. The dogmatic theologian would then be required to include as an intrinsic element in his study the results of the cirtical study of these early stages.

In the light of this new conception of authorship, how should the inerrancy formula be rephrased? Two solutions have been proposed. The first suggests the adoption of the formula, "inerrant final author." This is rejected because the formula does not seem to do justice to all those prior authors who seem to have contributed substantially to the composition of a work but did not have a hand in its final editing.[10] Lohfink prefers the second solution which urges the adoption of the formula "inerrancy of the books of the Bible" in terms of proportionate inspiration:

> Thus the inerrancy consequent upon the inspiration could not be predicated directly of all the individuals who worked on the book and their particular intention, but only upon the book which finally resulted. The inspiration of the many individuals whose work formed a book could then be regarded as a unity, which manifested its effect of inerrancy only once, in the final result of the collaboration (p. 31).

Lohfink thinks that proportionate inspiration preserves the divine influence on the sacred writers and upholds the inerrancy of the book as finally composed. In the previous solution only the last man who worked on a biblical book in the course of its gradual evolution would have enjoyed the charism of inspiration. In the second solution all writers who have been involved in the composition of the sacred book share in the unity of the book's inspiration. Moreover, if God is the principal author of sacred Scripture, as faith teaches, it would seem more appropriate that God should have guided "the process of composition as a whole, and above all its main phases" (p. 32-33). The question now arises how are the "inerrant books" related to the truth of the whole Bible?

Lohfink answers with an interesting description of the growth of the Canon. He begins with the analogy of a scholar who begins to fill a new bookcase with books:

> Whenever a book was added, or another taken away, no part of the total meaning or of the statement contained in the other books which stood on the shelves was altered. Thus, according to the views of that

---

10 An application of this conception of "final author" to the question of the authorship of the Fourth Gospel would mean that the only inspired author of the Gospel would be the final redactor. Current critical scholars deny that the final redactor was John, son of Zebedee. For the details, cf. Raymond E. Brown, THE GOSPEL ACCORDING TO JOHN I-XII (Garden City: Doubleday, 1966), Introduction, pp. xxiv-xxxix.

period, books of the Bible which already had been accepted into the canon remained the same when another book was taken into the canon. They said exactly the same thing as before. They had long received their final form (p. 34).

In further describing the nineteenth century view of the Canon, Lohfink calls attention to the following characteristics: (1) the unity of Scripture was assured by its divine author; (2) this divine author preserved the sacred books from the appearance of contradictions; (3) each book came into the Canon as an independent entity and enjoying its own inerrancy. Obviously, such a view of the nature and growth of the Canon precluded any question of the fundamental unity inherent in the Bible itself. As a result of the new critical studies on the growth of the Canon, the above somewhat static conception has ceded to a conception more evolutionary in character. Lohfink writes: "The growth of the Canon seems to be no more than a further stage, somewhat different in form, of the process which brought the individual book into being" (p. 34). He offers a detailed and informative treatment of how recent studies on the relationship of the Prophets to the Pentateuch reflect the new understanding of the unity of the Canon. These studies, particularly those concerned with examples of prophetic influence on the Book of Deuteronomy, support Lohfink's position regarding the interrelationship of the canonical books: "This shows that no book of the Bible was read except through the *analogia scripturae* — within the unity of meaning of the whole scripture" (p. 36).

The Canon, says Lohfink, was considered to be a single book. Any addition to it altered the total statement of the previous parts. The Old Testament Canon, as it grew, was constantly moving toward a final meaning. As long as the Canon continued to grow, no single book within the Canon had attained its ultimate meaning. Lohfink describes this process of taking a book into the Canon as an act of authorship, affecting the growth of each book and, consequently, of the Bible as a whole. The growth of the Old Testament Canon attained its full stature and, consequently, its fixed and final meaning at the moment when the Old Testament as such was received into the New Testament. By "New Testament" he means "not the collection of New Testament books, which was still to have its own history, but the reality itself which is reflected in these books." Lohfink notes that Jesus, the Apostles, and the primitive Church decided that the Old Testament Canon was to form "the enduring background history and document of the New Testament which had come in Christ." This was the final addition made to the Old Testament. Lohfink thinks the addition made the New Testament a sort of sacred writer:

Like every previous addition, this once again changed the pattern of meaning in the Old Testament as a whole. Thus, to use paradoxical language, one could say that in the sense of the dogmatic doctrine of inspiration the New Testament was one of the 'sacred writers' of the Old Testament (p. 38).

What is the unifying force of the Old Testament? Lohfink answers: the Christological interpretation of the Old Testament given by Jesus and the New Testament writers. He sees in this Christological intention the unitive force which makes the Old and New Testaments a single book. He maintains that "only within this all-embracing unity is the sense of each individual statement finally determined" (p. 39).

Turning his attention to the interpretation of the biblical text itself, Lohfink describes clearly what he understands by the term "literal sense." It is not confined to that sense obtained by the use of the historical and critical method but must be extended to the traditional theological concept of the literal sense.[11] Lohfink describes the "fuller sense" of the Old Testament as the one intended both by God and by the New Testament, the final author of the Old Testament, as we saw above. He claims that this concept of the fuller sense is similar to the hermeneutic principle of the Fathers and of the Scholastics also. Nowadays this doctrine of the "spiritual sense" is exemplified especially in the writings of Henri De Lubac.[12] Lohfink is careful not to deny the validity of "purely historical exegesis, as it is now carried out at the present day with such vigor." Considered as an initial and transitional phase of the process of exegesis, historical exegesis is admitted to be "an irreplaceable necessity."[13] However, he finds the scope of historical criticism incomplete when it limits its study to the layers of meaning within the Old Testament itself. Here he must face the critical question: what does the careful study of the historical meaning of successive layers of biblical texts really contribute to the final meaning derived from the study of the Bible as a whole? It is a problem as yet unsolved. Lohfink agrees that he himself cannot determine just what form his intended exegetical process should take. He concedes that in practice the inerrant sense of scripture will be reached in the study of biblical theology, that is, in the study of the theology of the Bible as a whole. He admits that at the present time no such adequate work exists. He suggests that perhaps we should look towards the construction of a more biblically oriented dogmatic theology. What Lohfink has done is (1) to insist upon the study of the doctrine of the Bible as a whole and to ex-

---

11 Cf. p. 43, where Lohfink writes: "This 'theological' sense means nothing other than the meaning of the scripture read as a whole and in the *analogia fidei*. When theological tradition refers to the 'literal sense' as inerrant, it is always assuming this 'theological' understanding of the concept."

12 Henri de Lubac, EXÉGÈSE MÉDIÉVALE: LES QUATRE SENS DE L'ÉCRITURE, two parts in four volumes (Paris: Aubier, 1959-64).

13 Lohfink, p. 148.

plain why this must be done, (2) to lay bare the problems arising from historical and critical exegesis when it is related to the study of the Bible as a whole, (3) to urge scholars to work towards the construction of an adequate biblical theology along dogmatic lines. He has left unsolved the role to be played by historical and critical exegesis in contributing to the final meaning of the Bible.

C. Reflections of Pierre Benoit

Pierre Benoit has been preoccupied with the problems of biblical inspiration and hermeneutics for a long time.[14] Hhis writings on these subjects range over more than a quarter of a century. I present here some of his reflections drawn from the address which he gave to the International Congress of Theology of Vatican II in September 1966.[15] In this address Benoit commented on four major poionts of the *De Divina Revelatione* Constitution bearing on the truth of the Bible:

1. The truth of the Bible is not purely speculative but addressed to the whole man, not to his intellect only.

2. Biblical truth is communicated to men for the sake of salvation (*salutis causa*). It does not teach the truth of all sciences.

3. Biblical truth is communicated to men by men. It is necessary to appreciate fully all that this implies.

4. Biblical truth in its fullness is to be found in the whole Bible, not in any particular passage or book.

Benoit makes a valuable contribution to the truth of the Bible debate

---

14 Listed here are Benoit's more important works on the subject of biblical inspiration and hermeneutics. Benoit, with Paul Synave, LA PROPHÉTIE (Paris, 1947), English translation by A. Dulles and T. Sheridan: PROPHESY AND INSPIRATION (N.Y., 1961). "L'inspiration biblique selon Mgr Florit", *RB* (Vol. 57, 1951), pp. 609-610. "La Septante est-elle inspirée?", VOM WORT DES LEBENS, Festschrift für Max Meinertz (Munster: Aschendorffsche Verlagsbuchhandlung, 1951), pp. 41-49; reprinted in *Exégèse et Théologie* (Paris, 1961), pp. 3-12. "Inspiration", INITIATION BIBLIQUE, A. Robert and A. Tricot, editors (Paris, 3rd ed., 1954), pp. 6-45; English translation: A GUIDE TO THE BIBLE, trans. E. Arbez and M. McGuire (N.Y., 1960), I, p. 9-64. "La doctrine de Newman sur la Sainte Écriture", *RB* (Vol. 61, 1954), pp. 603-605; reprinted in *Exégèse et Théologie* (1961), pp. 15-19. "La sensus plenior de l'Écriture", *RB* (Vol. 63, 1956), pp. 285-287; reprinted in *Exégèse et Théologie* (1961), pp. 19-21. "Notre complémentaire sur l'inspiration", *RB* (Vol. 63, 1956), pp. 416-422. "Les analogies de l'inspiration", SACRA PAGINA: MISCELLANEA BIBLICA CONGRESSUS INTERNATIONALIS CATHOLICI DE RE BIBLICA, J. Coppens, A. Descamps, E. Massaux, editors (Gembloux) vol. I, pp. 86-99; reprinted in *Exégèse et Théologie* (III, 1968), pp. 17-30. "La Plénitude de sens des Livres Saints", *RB* (Vol. 67, 1960), pp. 161-196; reprinted in *Exégèse et Théologie* (III, 1968), pp. 31-68. "Inerrance Biblique", CATHOLICISME HIER, AUJOURD'HUI, DEMAIN, G. Jacquemet, editor (Paris, 1963) V., col. 1710-1721. "Inspiration Biblique", *Idem.,* cols. 1539-1549. "L'inspiration des Septante d'après les Peres", L'HOMME DEVANT DIEU, Melanges H. de Lubac (Paris: Aubier, 1963), I., pp. 169-187; reprinted in *Exégèse et Théologie* III, pp. 69-89. "Révélation et inspiration selon la Bible, chez saint Thomas et dans les discussions modernes", *RB* (Vol. 70, 1963), pp. 321-370; reprinted in *Exégèse et Théologie* (III, 1968), pp. 90-142.

15 Benoit, *Exégèse et Théologie* (III, 1968), pp. 143-156. Originally given in Latin, the French title is "La Vérité dans la sainte Écriture".

in his comments on the fourth point. He uses as his point of departure this conciliar text: "These books [of the Old Testament] though they also contain some things which are *incomplete and temporary,* nevertheless show us true divine pedagogy."[16] Benoit examines the phrase "incomplete and temporary."[17] He notes that Israel made only slow and gradual progress in her understanding of God's revelation:

> In the Bible we notice a progress of revelation from the first generations to the end of the New Testament, and that not only in the scientific domain, which does not directly affect the message, but even in moral or in dogma.[18]

In the words "incomplete and temporary" Benoit sees also the way opening for a new conception of inerrancy. He sees God as accommodating himself to the Israelites' inability to learn profoundly everything at the beginning. The early Israelites could not be expected to receive in every text all of God's revelation on a given subject. God does not reveal the whole of any given truth in every phrase of the Bible. Benoit holds that God will even allow his partial truth to be clothed in a word or expression which God may have to "correct" later by replacing it with a more proper expression:

> 'Corriger,' ai-je-dit. En effet la pédagogie divine n'a pas procédé seulement par mode de compléments et de perfectionnements; elle a opéré aussi de corrections, voire des suppressions. Ceci est important et doit être clairement vu.[19]

Benoit thinks that in the unfolding of divine revelation we must admit not only a progression from the imperfect to the perfect (which no one would deny) but also from erroneous views to corrected ones. God never taught such errors, Benoit insists, but he permitted, for a time, his own truth to be clothed in elements which were sometimes deficient. These deficient expressions would be replaced in God's good time by more perfect expressions of his truth. Benoit spells out this divine pedagogy with respect to the Old Testament doctrines of *sheol* and *herem.*[20] To the question what is inspired and inerrant in sacred Scripture Benoit replies that the word of God is inspired and inerrant not in isolation but only in relationship to the ensemble of inspired truth which assumes into a final synthesis what is not "incomplete and temporary." This assumption into a final synthesis will take place when what is erroneous or deficient will have been replaced by other and more perfect revelation. God in his wise providence took many centuries to unfold his divine truth. To attain this

---

16 *Acta apostolicae sedis* (Vol. 58, 1966) p. 825, #15: "Qui libri, quamvis etiam imperfecta et temporaria contineant, veram tamen paedagogiam divinam demonstrant."
17 Benoit, *Exégèse et Théologie* (III) p. 153.
18 Benoit, "La Verite Dans La Bible" in *La Vie Spirituelle* (April, 1966, no. 526), p. 410.
19 *Exégèse et Théologie,* III, p. 153.
20 "La Verite Dans La Bible", p. 411.

truth, Benoit writes, we must study the whole work, that is, we must re-trace all the steps from the first imperfect gropings to the full revelation in Christ.[21] No stages of the full revelation should be neglected. To accomplish this task the exegete-theologian must study each text in the light of the whole Bible and be guided by the analogy of faith and by tradition. This process must be followed in the interpretation of the New as well as the Old Testament.

Benoit's reflections on the "incomplete and temporary" elements in the Old Testament, as well as his description of how a given biblical truth ought to be traced from its early stages to its full revelation in the New Testament as interpreted within the Church, constitute, it seems to me, a significant clarification and a specific contribution to the truth of the Bible debate. The last word of this debate has not yet been spoken, but I suggest that before it is ever spoken, P. Benoit must be heard.

---

21 *Exégèse et Théologie* (III), p. 154.

Peter Gerard Duncker, O.P.

TRANSMISSION OF DIVINE REVELATION
ACCORDING TO VATICAN II*

Our subject has been dealt with authentically in the second chapter of the Dogmatic Constitution on Divine Revelation *Dei Verbum,* issued by the Second Vatican Council. The composition of the text of this Constitution extended over a long period of time. This was due to the strong diversity of view shown even before the Council, and in evidence up to the final written document. A first Schema presented to the Council by 'the Preparatory Theological Commission' was rejected as an inappropriate basis for discussion by the vast majority of the Fathers, who found it not up to date in view of present biblical and theological studies, and lacking that pastoral concern the Council had so much at heart. A second Schema, drawn up by the Theological Commission of the Council, with the aid of the then 'Secretariate for Christian Unity', was to be thoroughly revised into a third, and this one to be retouched and emendated into a fourth. Finally, a fifth Schema with still some very important ultimate corrections became the text voted upon at the Council and accepted with 2081 *placet* (ayes), 27 *non-placet* (nays), and 7 *voids* (abstentions). By a new voting, resulting in 2344 'placet' and only 6 'non-placet', the text was officially declared to be the Dogmatic Constitution on Divine Revelation, whereupon Pope Paul VI promulgated *Dei Verbum* on November 18, 1965.

The second chapter 'On the Transmission of Divine Revelation' is the centre and heart of this whole Constitution and divided into four sections: (I) On the Apostles and their Successors; (II) On Sacred Tradition

PETER GERARD DUNCKER, O.P., is Professor of Hebrew and Old Testament at the Pontifical Biblical Institute, and the Beda College, Rome, Italy.

* This study is based on: 1) the original latin text of this Dogmatic Constitution in *Acta Apostolicae Sedis,* 58, 1966, pp. 818-830, translated by R.A.F. MacKenzie, S.J. in: THE DOCUMENTS OF VATICAN II (New York: Guild Press-America Press-Association Press, 1967); 2) *La Constituzione Dogmatica Sulla Divina Rivelazione, Collana Magistero Conillare*[4], 3, (Turin, ELLE, DI, CI, Leuman, 1967), in which U. Betti, O.F.M., one of the *periti* or experts, who were constantly consulted by the drawing up of the text of the Constitution, tells the story of its coming about, gives the latin text of its first Schema, and that of the following four, in parallel columns, as also of the main reports by which the third Schema was presented and explained at the Council; 3) "Dogmatische Constitutie over de Cjoddelyke Openbaring," in: *Constituties en Decreten Van Het Tweede Vaticaan Oecumenisch Concilie,* 12, (Katholiek Archief, De Horstink, Amersfoort, Olanda), which contains, apart from the Latin text and corresponding Dutch translation of the Constitution and of the main reports, also other supplementary reports; 4) Giovanni Caprile, S.J., *"Tre emendamenti allo Schema sulla Rivelazione,"* La Civilta Cattolica, 117, I 1966, pp. 216-223, who deals with the final addition to the text we are concerned with; 5) Joseph Ratzinger, "Dogmatische Konstitution über die Göttliche Offenbarung," in: DAS ZWEITE VATIKANISCHE KONZIL, LEXIKON FUR THEOLOGIE UND KIRCHE[2], II, (Freiburg-Basel-Wein: Herder, 1967), pp. 497-583.

and Sacred Scripture; (III) On the Relation of Sacred Tradition and Sacred Scripture; and (IV) On the Relation of Sacred Tradition and Sacred Scripture to the Whole Church and its Teaching Authority.

It is only by going into the difficulties the composition of this second chapter encountered, that we will be able to understand its docrine and realize the problems that were at stake.

Linking up with the preceding chapter on divine revelation itself, the first paragraph affirms: 'Christ the Lord in whom the full revelation of the supreme God is brought to completion (cf. 2 Cor 1:20; 3:16; 4:6), commissioned the apostles to preach to all men that gospel, which is the source of all saving truth and moral teaching, and thus impart to them divine gifts.' This is, from the outset, a very important and illuminating statement, for divine revelation is here presented, not as something of a law to be observed, but as a continuous, gratuitous and generous gift of God to have all men — and we may note here not only the pastoral but also the ecumenical concern of the text — share in his own fullness, made known to us in Christ. It is moreover to be noted that nowhere in this whole Dogmatic Constitution, except in that sentence, and precisely in that part which is a quotation from the Council of Trent, the word 'source' is used, here referring to divine revelation as a whole.

The text continues by pointing to the fact that Christ's commission was indeed faithfully fulfilled, as well by the apostles who in their oral preaching handed on all they, in whatever way, had learned from Christ himself or through the prompting of the Holy Spirit (Tradition), as by those apostles and apostolic men who, under the inspiration of the same Holy Spirit, committed the message of salvation to writing (Scripture). Thereupon, the apostles transmitted their teaching role to the bishops as their successors, "in order to keep the gospel forever whole and alive in the Church."

This latter, twofold, aspect in the transmission of the gospel, of divine revelation as a whole, is enforced by these concluding words of the paragraph: 'This Sacred Tradition, therefore, and Sacred Scripture of both the Old and New Testament are like a mirror in which the pilgrim Church on earth looks at God, from whom she received everything, until she is brought finally to see Him as He is, face to face (cf. 1 Jn 5:2).' 'Looking at God like in a mirror' implies that, in spite of the 'everything' the Church received through divine revelation, there is still something defective, imperfect in it, to become completed only when the Church will have fully attained what she is striving after.

Although this first paragraph concerns divine revelation as contained and transmitted in both Tradition and Scripture (the former in a certain way includes the latter), it did not encounter difficulties worth mentioning. Rather, it was exclusively the question of Tradition as oral preaching and transmission of divine revelation that aroused severe criticism. Inserted into the text from the third Schema on, this question appears in the second paragraph which we shall now consider.

Tradition as oral preaching and transmission not only comprises the official teaching office of the Church, but just as well the constant putting into practice of the teaching by the faithful, and the devout expression of all that the Church believes, in its worship, its liturgy. All this taken together as transmitted by the apostles, is handed on further by the Church, by the entire People of God on the way, till the end of time, and in its full integrity. Hence, by this Tradition the Church perpetuates what she herself has always been, always believed from the very beginning.

By insisting on the apostolicity of Tradition the Council wanted to exclude all sorts of purely ecclesiastical traditions which cannot be traced back to the apostles. Precisely because they do not belong to the divine apostolic Tradition concerning only divine revelation, those merely ecclesiastical ordinances, usages, devotions, religious practices have but a relative value, and as such, can be changed and be abolished, as, in fact, many have been.

On the other hand, as a Church to be kept alive, she, like every living reality, still grows, progresses, increases. There was much debate at the Council to make it unequivocally clear in the text that this growth is not to be understood, as if new truths in the course of time could have been added to those handed on by the apostles, (and thus Tradition itself would increase), but merely as a progress in the understanding of the revealed truths.[1]

This progress is then said to come about "through the contemplation and study made by believers who *treasure these things in their hearts* (Lk 2:19, 51), and through the intimate understanding of the spiritual things they experience." This latter part of the sentence had to replace the former redaction: 'and through the intimate experience of spiritual things', which could be mistaken as insinuating that by experience of spiritual things new revealed truths might be discovered. However, even in its somewhat miti-

---

1 The latin text of the third Schema read: *"crescit enim tam rerum quan verborum traditorum intelligentia"*, which is ambiguous, for it can be understood as meaning either: "for it (Tradition) grows by the understanding of the realities and words that have been handed on", or: "for the understanding grows of the realities and words handed on". The reason for this ambiguity lies in the latin word *intelligentia*, which can be taken as an ablative as well as a nominative. In order to make it clear that the nominative is intended, as in the latter of the two possible translations, the latin word *perceptio*, which like *intelligentia* means *understanding*, but becomes in the ablative *perceptione*; cf. DOGMATISCHE CONSTITUTIE . . . , p. 92.

gated form, and in spite of a still further attenuation, presently to be indicated, this text expresses something quite new. Nowhere to be found in any former authentic ecclesiastical pronouncement is the notion that the growth in the understanding of revealed truths is attributed to the contemplation, the study, the increasing knowledge and experience of the faithful at large, of the whole Church as People of God. Though, of course, the teaching authority is implicitly included, quite a number of Fathers wanted it to be explicitly mentioned. The Theological Commission refused to change the text in this regard. However, through the insistence of those Fathers wanting a change,[2] and by use of their *placet iuxta modum,* their demands were finally met in the form of an addition: "and through the preaching of those who received through episcopal succession the true gift of truth." The faithful's own essential and important share as to the growth in understanding of revealed truths is thus maintained. It is, in fact, plainly borne out by the true and profound knowledge and experience of God and his designs with man. The lives of a great many — often illiterate — saints and holy people have constantly given witness through the ages. However, the added clause puts it all under the control of the teaching authority of the Church.

This section of the second paragraph is then concluded by these words; "For as centuries succeed one another, the Church constantly moves toward the fullness of divine truth, until the words of God reach their complete fulfillment in her (cf. 1 Cor 13:10; Ap 17:17)." From the voting *placet iuxta modum,* it also appeared that several Fathers were not satisfied with this assertion either. They, moreover, kept on urging that in this whole section it should be more patently stated that in no way Tradition itself could ever increase, but only the understanding of the revealed truths transmitted by it. This time, however, the Theological Commission maintained its decision not to alter the text in this point, convinced that the text could not be misunderstood in this respect. There is no question of a development, as though something substantially new could be added, but merely that things obscurely, implicitly contained in it, are brought to a clear and explicit expression. An inner development is meant, proper to every living reality, keeping the substance unaltered, yet making it more perfect by a continual growth, which is something intrinsic, an integral part of it. The Church thus really strives after the fullness of the revealed truth, and attains it, in so far as Tradition attains its inner, intrinsic development.[3]

---

2 When the text, as emandated in the fourth Schema, was presented to the Fathers to be voted upon, they could do this, with regard to each chapter as a whole, by *placet, non-placet,* and *placet iuxta modum,* this last voting enabling them to express still some remarks about the text of that chapter.

3 Cf. DOGMATISCHE CONSTITUTIE, pp. 100-102.

Attention is then called in the text to the words of the ancient Fathers of the Church, which, as preserved in their extant writings, bear witness to the living Tradition, to the Christian faith believed and practised in the early centuries, and which have continued to foster it in the succeeding centuries.

The next sentence provoked the strongest agitation among the Fathers of the Council, as we shall soon see in connection with the third paragraph. The conclusion of the second paragraph reads: "Thus God, who spoke of old, uninterruptedly converses with the Bride of his beloved son; and the Holy Spirit, through whom the living voice of the gospel resounds in the Church, and through her in the world, leads unto all truths those who believe, and makes the word of Christ dwell abundantly in them (cf. Col 3:16)."

The third paragraph intends to delineate the mutual relationship between Tradition and Scripture; and we have now come to the main point of controversy among the Fathers. The principal objection the majority of them had against the first Schema, apart from the general ones already mentioned, was precisely the way in which Tradition and Scripture were spoken of as the twofold source of revelation, as if they were two distinct sources, of which the former contains more divinely revealed truths than the latter. Strong diversity of opinion on this point came immediately to the fore among those who had to draw up the second Schema, for no formula to express the relation of Tradition to Scripture could reach the required ⅔ of the vote. A proposal was then made that, in order to arrive at a text which would likely obtain at least such majority, expressions should be avoided that either affirm or deny a wider extension of Tradition with respect to Scripture, as also expressions which would seem to separate Tradition from Scripture, and vice versa. This proposal received the large majority of 29 votes against 8, and 1 absention.[4] And the principle laid down by it was scrupulously adhered to, in spite of much opposition. But only after more discussion and dispute the following text entered into the second Schema:

Sacred Scripture, therefore, and Sacred Tradition are so related between themselves, that the one is not alien to the other. There exists even a close connection and communication between them. For both of them, flowing from the same wellspring, in a certain way merge into a unity and tend toward the same end. Both, therefore, are to be accepted with the same sense of devotion and reverence.

In this text the word 'wellspring' (translation of the latin *scaturigo*) is used instead of the more common word 'source' (translating the latin

4 LA CONSTITUZIONE DOGMATICA, p. 35.
5 *Ibid.*, 496; DOGMATISCHE CONSTITUTIE, p. 62.

fons), which would do very well here as denoting the origin of both Scripture and Tradition. It has purposely been avoided in order that its application to each of them separately may nevertheless not be hampered. (Although the majority of the Fathers did not agree with this usage, it had been customary in the Church). Thus, the debated question remains open, both with regard to its terminology as well as to its substance. The last sentence of the text has been taken from the Council of Trent.[5]

In the third Schema the text was only slightly retouched by suppressing the words: 'are so related . . . to the other', since these say the same as: 'there exists . . . between them'. But their mutual relationship is now further indicated by denoting the precise difference between Scripture and Tradition. What the third Schema said about Scripture encountered no difficulties; its text, however, concerning Tradition, though substantially correct, demanded a clearer formulation. Further, it needed a proper distinction between the apostles (who directly received divine revelation from Christ and through further illumination of the Holy Spirit), and their successors who had but faithfully and integrally, with the help of the Holy Spirit, handed on that revelation. Hence the revised text reads in the fourth Schema:

> For Sacred Scripture is the word of God inasmuch as it is consigned to writing under the inspiration of the Holy Spirit. To the successors of the apostles Sacred Tradition hands on in its full purity God's word, which was entrusted to the apostles by Christ the Lord and the Holy Spirit. Thus, led by the light of the Spirit of truth, these successors can in their preaching preserve the word of God faithfully, explain it and make it more widely known.

From this text we learn that Tradition and Scripture have something in common, which implies a certain identity: they both came from the same wellspring, God, though Scripture has, in this respect, its proper charism of divine inspiration; both alike transmit the same divine revelation; both equally tend toward the same end, man's salvation. And it is because of their common origins, object and purpose that both are to be accepted with the same sense of devotion and reverence. However, by asserting that Tradition and Scripture alike transmit the same divine revelation, the one orally, the other in writing, and are thus as to their object qualitatively the same, the text carefully avoids saying whether or not they are also quantitatively identical.[6] And here we must return to the sentence of the second paragraph, which for the moment we left alone, and which runs as follows: "Through the same Tradition also the sacred writings themselves are known to the Church and unceasingly made active in her."

---

6 *Ibid.*

It was precisely on this sentence of the third Schema that the debate concerning the relation of Tradition to Scripture became concentrated, for it implicitly conveyed, according to many Fathers, that no other revealed truths are known to the Church through Tradition. The text did arrive at some emendation, because several Fathers rightly observed that mention should be made of the full canon of the sacred writings, since the Catholic Church acknowledges more sacred, divinely inspired writings than the Protestants or the Jews, the latter, of course, only with regard to the Old Testament. It should also be made clear that it is on account of an always more profound understanding of the sacred writings, that these are unceasingly made active in the Church.[7] The text, corrected in this twofold sense, was thus presented in the fourth Schema. "Through the same Tradition the Church's full canon is known, and the sacred writings are more profoundly understood and unceasingly made active in her." But the main difficulty remained, and can be very well realized from the two opposite views on the matter, as they were exposed at the Council by an exponent of each of them in the Theological Commission.

The representative of the minority of the Commission pointed out that the common teaching of the Church has been of the opinion that there are more revealed truths known to the Church by Tradition, and by Tradition alone. He pointed out that this view was upheld by Vatican I, confirmed by various encyclicals of the last four Popes, and previously upheld by the Provincial Council of Cologne (1860) and Utrecht (1865), both approved by the Holy See. Moreover, this opinion has been taught in all the catechisms of the last four centuries and defended by the theologians. Finally, it is not only in plain accord with the belief of the faithful, but also with the constant teaching of the Eastern Orthodox Churches. Not to reconfirm this doctrine clearly by Vatican II would cause serious difficulties to reconcile, e.g., the position of Vatican II with the hitherto common teaching of the Church. It would also bring about grave confusion among the faithful as well as the theologians, and encourage a forced exegesis to find at all costs every revealed truth somehow or other in Sacred Scripture. Further, it would show disregard of Pope Paul's demand, expressed in his allocution at the closing of the second period of the Council, when, referring to questions as yet not having been settled and to be still further studied and discussed, he said: "Such e.g. is the question of divine revelation that defends the sacred deposit of faith against errors, abuses and doubts."[8]

On the other hand, the exponent of the majority thus defended the

---

7 Dogmatische Constitutie, p. 92.
8 *Ibid.,* 74-86; La Contituzione Dogmatica, pp. 305-311.

other view. After having observed all that the Church is and possesses, has been affected and permeated by the living Tradition, he textually subjoins:

This applies first of all to Sacred Scripture itself, as indissolubly connected with the Church. Not only does it derive its force and activity from Tradition, but from the same Tradition it also receives an irrefutable testimony concerning its full existence and nature. By this latter assertion the particular importance of Tradition is borne out, in so far as Tradition at least in one point, as to its objective contents, exceeds Scripture, viz. in the testimony Tradition renders with regard to the full canon and the inspiration of the sacred books. And here we touch in this matter the limit beyond which, as it seems to us, we may not go. There are, indeed, Fathers who would prefer that, apart from Tradition's proper testimony concerning Scripture, the transmission of other revealed truths should be attributed to Tradition alone. But those Fathers may reflect that there are no cogent reasons to make that affirmation. We are here concerned with a question *de facto,* and nothing compels us to apply what has been attributed to Tradition, in respect of truths regarding Scripture, to any other concrete truth. Of no one truth has the teaching authority of the Church up till now declared that it lacks all foundation in Scripture, nor has it ever defined a truth as being contained in Tradition alone. To everyone freedom is thus left to find, either in Scripture or Tradition, the foundation of any given divinely revealed truth. This freedom, based on the way of acting of the teaching authority, is also in our Schema likewise preserved.[9]

Having carefully considered the various reactions of the Council with regard to this most debated question, and realizing that the vast majority of the Fathers agreed with the latter standpoint, the Theological Commission decided not to change the text that was proposed or to add anything to it. When the whole chapter was then voted upon at the Council, it obtained 1874 *placet,* 9 *non-placet,* 9 *voids,* but also 354 *placet iuxta modum,* a number higher than at the voting of any other chapter.[10] It soon appeared that most of those 354 *modi* were again concerned with that main point of controversy. They demanded that it should be made clear in the text, in some way or other, that not every revealed truth can be known or demonstrated from Scripture alone.

After much deliberation[11] those charged by the Theological Commission to classify the *modi* and to give their opinion which should be accepted, were inclined to insert, just before the conclusion of the third

---

9 *Ibid.,* 61; 495.
10 La Costituzione Dogmatica, p. 54.
11 From here on till the end of what is said about the third paragraph, my information is mostly taken from Caprile. The numbers of the various votings are from La Costituzione Dogmatica, p. 59f.

paragraph, this sentence: "Consequently not every Catholic doctrine can directly be proved from Sacred Scripture," thus modifying their opinion:

> It is proposed to admit the aforesaid addition on which all agree, and in which the more delicate questions are avoided. For everything can indirectly be demonstrated from Scripture, inasmuch as Scripture clearly teaches the existence of the teaching authority and of the indefectability of the Church.

But the Theological Commission did not approve this proposal. Its minority refused it, because one could then conclude that Tradition was not necessary to prove any revealed truth at all; whereas the majority, attacking the given modification, argued that every truth, defined by the authoritative and indefectable Church, would thus have to be taken as revealed, even if in no way it could be traced back in Scripture. So it was decided with 15 votes against 10, not to add anything at all.

On account of the uneasiness created by this decision, the Theological Commission returned to the matter a few days later, and put this question to the vote, whether, after all, an addition should not be made. The result was: 13 in favor, 11 against. This addition was then proposed: "The Sacred Scriptures relate the Christian mystery as a whole, without all revealed truths being expressly enunciated in them"; and this was accepted with 14 votes against 10. But when later on some Father observed that this formula favoured the opinion that all revealed truths would thus be implicitly contained in Scripture, and he, moreover, took the opportunity of promoting the theory of the twofold source of revelation, the accepted addition was voted down: 18 against 6, with the modification: "Since our Commission does not want to deviate in any way at all from the accepted and by now well known position, it is of the opinion that the text should be left unchanged."

In the meantime the Pope, having been carefully and continually informed about the situation, had already sent a letter in his name, expressing his desire that account should be taken of Tradition as constitutive, viz, whether Tradition itself, of its own, constitutes truths of faith. He referred to this text of St. Augustine: 'There are many things which the universal Church holds, and which are, therefore, as prescribed by the apostles, rightly believed, though they are not found in writing'. But now, after the Theological Commission's decision not to alter the text, the Pope, urged by many Fathers and after a colloquium with the Cardinals Moderators of the Council, sent another letter. With regard to the so strongly debated point, he asked the Commission to reconsider, with benevolence, but freely, whether it would not be opportune to perfect the text concerning Tradition, not by altering the text itself, but by adding one of the seven formulae, forwarded to the Pope by different Fathers and attached to the letter, which apparently met with the approval of highly qualified representatives of even the so-called majority. Further, he demanded that Cardinal Bea, chairman of the Secretariate for Christian Unity should be present at the discussion of the Pope's request concerning the addition.

When, on the following day the Theological Commission assembled for that purpose, Cardinal Bea pleaded for the admission of one of those seven formulae. Passing to vote upon it, the first ballot did not come to $\frac{2}{3}$ of the votes for any of them. At the second ballot the third formula obtained 19 of the 28 votes, exactly the required majority, and was thus accepted. It is the one in the actual text of the third paragraph (just before its conclusion) and reads: "Consequently, it is not from Sacred Scripture alone that the Church draws her certainty about everything which has been revealed."

In explaining this addition at the Council, the exponent of the Theological Commission pointed out that it was inserted in that particular place of the text to give some elucidation of the preceding words concerning Tradition (handing on God's word faithfully) as well as a further justification of the subsequent text, e.g., that Tradition and Scripture are to be accepted and venerated with the same sense of devotion and reverence. Moreover, the Catholic teaching confirmed by the constant *praxis* of the Church that she draws her certainty about revealed truths only from Scripture as connected with Tradition, is guaranteed; hence, where Scripture alone does not suffice to obtain that certainty, Tradition can offer the decisive demonstration. Finally, since in the whole second chapter Tradition is nowhere presented as a quantitative supplement of Scripture, nor Scripture as the codification of Tradition, it is evident that, by the addition, the tenor of the text remains unaltered as to its substance, and has merely become clearer in its expression.[12]

Still a few words are in order about the fourth and last paragraph of our second chapter, which did not give rise to particular difficulties. We recall what has been said above concerning the inner, intrinsic development of Tradition. Relative to the function of the whole church, including both the faithful and teaching authority, it is now pointed out that this Tradition together with Scripture, as one sacred deposit of the word of God, has been committed "to the entire holy people united with their shepherds." Further, it states precisely "in holding to, practising and professing the heritage of faith, there results on the part of the faithful and the bishops a remarkable common effort." This is a very important statement, clearly reaffirming the essential role of the faithful in the transmission of divine revelation.

---

12 DOGMATISCHE CONSTITUTIE, pp. 102-104.

Particular to the living teaching office in the Church is "the task of authentically interpreting the word of God, whether written or handed down." But the Council, as such then representing that teaching office, has made it quite clear that it stands not above divine revelation, but is merely there to serve it, "teaching only what has been handed on, listening to it devoutly, guarding it scrupulously, and explaining it faithfully by divine commission and with the help of the Holy Spirit; it draws from this one deposit of faith everything which it presents for belief as divinely revealed."

And the conclusion of this fourth paragraph and of the whole second chapter reads: "It is clear, therefore, that Sacred Tradition, Sacred Scripture and the teaching authority of the Church, in accord with God's most wise design, are so linked and joined together that the one cannot stand without the others, and that all together and each in its own way under the action of the one Holy Spirit contribute effectively to the salvation of souls."

In order to understand better the opposite views concerning the relation of Tradition to Scripture, which manifested themselves so strongly and tenaciously during the composition of this chapter on the transmission of divine revelation, from the very beginning right up to the end, a few words are as yet to be added to explain that opposition.

One of the main points of the Reformation was, and has been ever since among Protestants, that divine revelation is only contained in Sacred Scripture. Hence all teaching of the Church not to be found in Sacred Scripture was rejected as not belonging to divine revelation. Against this contention the Council of Trent upheld and defended that divine revelation, "as the source of all saving truth and moral discipline," is contained in Sacred Scripture "and in non-written traditions, which the apostles had received from Christ himself or through the dictation of the Holy Spirit, and as such handed on have come to us." And the Council declared "that, therefore, both Sacred Scripture and those traditions concerning faith and morals, as coming directly from Christ or through the dictation of the Holy Spirit, and by continuous succession preserved in the Catholic Church, are to be accepted with the same sense of devotion and reverence." [13]

We notice in this text, as has been mentioned earlier, that the word 'source' is used here to denote divine revelation as the common object of Sacred Scripture and those traditions. Trent did not present them as two distinct sources or the twofold source of revelation, and the question, whether those traditions contain more of revelation than Scripture, is not touched upon at all. As a matter of fact, the text speaks of traditions, in the

---

13 Denzinger-Schonmetzer, ENCHIRIDION SYMBOLORUM, n. 1501.

plural, for the Council had in mind various points of Catholic doctrine denied by the Reformers: not only the practice of indulgences which occasioned Luther's revolt, but also the primacy of the Pope, the ecclesiastical hierarchy, infant baptism, that there are seven sacraments, and so on.

When in the course of time even more points of Catholic doctrine were denied by Protestants as not being supported by Sacred Scripture and, therefore, not being divinely revealed, it became more and more customary to defend and demonstrate them from what had been orally transmitted from apostolic times on. For the plural 'traditions' the singular 'Tradition' came into use, as a counterpart of 'Scripture' even to the extent that there grew a danger of over-valuing Tradition at the expense of Scripture, and of opposing to the *Sola Scriptura* of the Protestants a more or less *Sola Traditio* theory on the part of the Catholic Church. Not that Scripture was not always acknowledged in the Church as containing divine revelation, but one felt more at ease by relying on Tradition, where every truth of faith could be found, which might not be immediately demonstrated from Scripture, e.g. the more recent dogmas of Papal Infallibility, of the Immaculate Conception and of the bodily assumption into heaven of Our Lady, also of her perpetual virginity. This way of defending Catholic doctrine against the Protestants gave rise to the custom of speaking of Tradition and Scripture as two distinct sources, or the twofold source of divine revelation, a custom more or less sanctioned by the First Vatican Council which commonly used this terminology in its dicussions. It was taken over by theologians and other writers of treatises on the matter.

The formulation of the relationship between Tradition and Scripture presented by Vatican II reflects a very strong reaction against the over-emphasis on Tradition, although Tradition itself is firmly maintained. God is the only and unique source of all divine revelation, transmitted as well by Tradition as by Sacred Scripture, but in such a way that these can not be looked upon as two distinct, separate means of handing on that revelation independent of one another. Both having the same origin, object, and purpose, they must be intimately related to each other, must form some unity. The transmission of divine revelation started with Tradition as oral preaching, most of which, however, was soon consigned to writing in the sacred books of the New Testament. These, together with the sacred writings of the Old Testament, contain without any doubt the principal part of divine revelation. The latter can be learned and understood far more readily and easily from those written documents, composed under a very special inspiration of the Holy Spirit, than from what had but been transmitted orally, albeit also with the help of the Holy Spirit. It is first of all Sacred Scripture which has been preserved, transmitted, explained, meditated upon in the Church by Tradition. Consequently, Tradition itself became ever more impregnated by Scripture. To distinguish what precisely Tradition has of its own, what through the permeation of Scripture, is extremely difficult. It would be the task of the teaching authority of the Church. Now it is very significant that she never made such a distinction, whenever she authentically presented a truth as object of faith. She always solemnly declared that such a truth belonged to divine revelation, supporting her declaration by arguments from Scripture as well as from Tradition; but she never asserted of any truth that it is only to be found in Tradition, or lacks any foundation in Scripture. This was her *praxis* even at the time she defined the last dogmas, when there was that tendency to over-emphasize Tradition to the prejudice of Scripture.

It was on account of all these considerations that the majority of the Council insisted on the intimate union of Tradition and Scripture in the transmission of divine revelation, and remained reluctant to admit that Tradition contains something which is not to be found in Scripture as well, precisely because this cannot be proved.

The addition inserted at the very last moment was, undoubtedly, accepted out of reverence for the Pope; but also because the tenor of the whole text was not changed by it, while satisfying both parties. By affirming "it is not from Sacred Scripture alone that the Church draws her certainty about everything which has been revealed," in other words, every Catholic doctrine can not be 'proved' from Scripture alone, it is not excluded that some doctrine may be 'contained' in Tradition alone. On the other hand, where Scripture alone does not suffice to give certitude about a certain revealed truth, Tradition will have to come in to supply what in this regard is somewhat obscure in Scripture. Sacred Scripture, however, remains the principal means to demonstrate the revealed truths; and that this is the idea and purport of the whole Dogmatic Constitution is confirmed by the fact that, in the following chapters, there is only question of Sacred Scripture.

The so fiercely disputed point, i.e., whether Tradition is more extensive with regard to revealed truths, has thus been left open. Consequently, not only is one free to have his own opinion about it, but also the question itself, not yet mature to be decided definitely, should be studied further.

Bernhard W. Anderson

HUMAN DOMINION OVER NATURE

Some time ago an article appeared in the *New York Times* under the arresting title, "Think Rhinoceros, Or All is Lost."[1] The author's initial question, "Who needs a rhinoceros?" most readers could quickly answer in the negative. This animal, surely one of the homeliest in God's creation, does not claim our attention outside of a zoo. But within a couple of sentences the author was calling into question our whole way of life which has found some support in the Bible. "Unless you take your Adam and Eve straight," he wrote, "you cannot believe that man came into a lonely world. Nor without those species that preceded them would mankind ever have happened. Earth has always been for sharing." He went on to observe that most species of plants and animals were well established before man assumed his tyrannical role of "tearing down, robbing, and polluting the earth." He suggested that human destiny on this planet is ominously threatened by the fate of the whooping crane or the snow leopard and "the passing of the last rhinoceros." Even the ant came in for praise, to the detriment of human beings. The article concluded with praise for Thoreau, who declared that "in wildness is the salvation of the world."

It would be unjust to dismiss the "rhinoceros essay" as merely an expression of a romantic back-to-nature movement *à la* Thoreau, the famous naturalist. In the time when the United States celebrates the bicentennial of its nationhood one of the major crises to be faced is ecological, that is, the crisis resulting from enterprising initiative which conquers the wilderness and thereby subjects nature to human control. This crisis is manifest in debates about strip mining, food and world population, the use of energy resources, disposal of waste, and so on. As we well know, hard-headed, scientific realists, who are unaffected by the romanticism of Thoreau, have emphasized the gravity of the crisis, even in eschatological terms. Time is running out, we hear from members of the Club of Rome and others. Now is the time for repentance, that is, a change of lifestyle. One can almost hear with new accent the words of an ancient prophet: "An end! The end has come upon the four corners of the land. Now the end is upon you . . ." (Ez 7:1ff).

From the time the Pilgrims landed on the soil of the New World and began to push back the wilderness, Christianity has had a great influence in shaping our way of life. Indeed, some would go so far as to maintain

BERNHARD W. ANDERSON is Professor of Old Testament Theology, Princeton Theological Seminary, Princeton, New Jersey.

1 Daniel L. McKinley, *New York Times,* Sunday, July 18, 1971.

that the present crisis is traceable to Christian sponsorship of the view of human dominion over nature expressed in the passage about the *imago Dei* (Gn 1:26-28). This position is taken, for instance, in a well-known and much discussed essay by Lynn White, Jr.[2] He maintains that Christianity in the Latin West bears "a huge burden of guilt" for the ecological crisis; for our lifestyle in Western civilization has been profoundly shaped by a biblical theology that establishes a sharp dichotomy between man (history) and his environment (nature). In sharp contrast to paganism and most Asian religions, Christianity "not only established a dualism of man and nature but also insisted that it is God's will that man exploit nature for his proper ends." He concludes by nominating St. Francis of Assisi, "the greatest spiritual revolutionary in Western history," as the patron saint of the ecological cause, for in vain "he tried to substitute the idea of the equality of all creatures, including man, for the idea of man's limitless rule of creation." Christianity's culpability was also discussed at a theological conference held in Claremont, California (1970), again with reference to the doctrine of the image of God. The *New York Times* of May 1, 1970 carried an article with the bold headline: "Christianity Linked to Pollution. Scholars Cite Call in Bible for Man to Dominate Life."

This indictment of Christianity makes good headlines, even though the case may not stand up under examination. It is undoubtedly true, however, that Christianity in the West has to some degree accommodated to the new economic climate that superseded medieval life. Strikingly, Karl Marx could speak a word of appreciation for capitalism which, in its own way, is "permanently revolutionary," for it has produced "a stage of society compared with which all earlier stages appear to be morely *local progress* and idolatry of nature." His further comments in the GRUNDRISSE well describe the modern enterprising spirit:

> Nature becomes for the first time simply an object for mankind, purely a matter of utility; it ceases to be recognized as a power in its own right; and the theoretical knowledge of its independent laws appears only as a strategem designed to subdue it to human requirements, whether as the object of consumption or as the means of production.[3]

It is understandable that Christians, in the new age dominated by technology and the profit motive, would turn to biblical texts to find a warrant for the new way of life which has reached its highest peak of achievements in the New World. If Christianity has both shaped, and been shaped by,

---

2 Lynn White, Jr., "The Historical Roots of Our Ecologic Crisis," *Science* Vol. 155 (1967), pp. 1203-07; reprinted in THE ENVIRONMENTAL HANDBOOK, ed. by Garrett de Bell (New York: Ballentine Books, 1970), pp. 12-26.

3 Quoted by Spencer Pollard in his review of Marx's GRUNDRISSE, *Saturday Review*, Aug. 7, 1971, p. 27.

the revolutionary spirit of the modern age, it is time to seek a new understanding of the biblical texts in their appropriate biblical contexts, and to learn anew what it means for people to be the image of God. In what follows we shall address ourselves to the question of the role of Man (humanity) in God's creation, with special attention to the related passages Genesis 1:26-28 and Psalm 8:5-8.

I

In an important essay that appeared in the mid-sixties as a forerunner of our current ecological concern, the late Gerhard von Rad issued a call for a more balanced theological understanding of Man in relation to his natural environment. He emphasized that ancient Israel had "a phenomenal sense of history;" for "it was above all in the realm of political history that the Hebrew of Old Testament times become aware of the sovereignty of God." But he went on to say that "we are nowadays in a serious danger of looking at the theological problems of the Old Testament far too much from the one-sided standpoint of an historically conditioned theology" and ignoring or neglecting "the greater part of what the Old Testament has to say about what we call Nature."[4]

We approach the task of a "theology of nature" in a post-Cartesian period, which means that inevitably we bring to biblical interpretation distinctions that did not exist sharply in Israel's experience. The vocabulary of the Old Testament does not contain words that are equivalent to our terms "history" and "nature." What we distinguish as two separate realms constituted for Israel a single realm of Yahweh's sovereignty, as can be seen from the Exodus story where both "natural events" (the driving back of the Reed Sea, manna in the wilderness, etc.) and "historical events" (the liberation from Egyptian bondage, victory over the Amalekites, etc.) are regarded equally as signs of Yahweh's activity. The same easy shift from what we would call nature to history is found in some of Israel's psalms which praise Yahweh as Creator. This is evident, for instance, in Psalm 33 which belongs to the genre of the hymn. The psalmist's hymnic praise is motivated by Yahweh's power as creator of heaven and earth:

By the word of Yahweh the heavens were made,
 and all their host by the breath of his mouth.
He gathered the waters of the sea as in a bottle,
 he put the deeps in storehouses.
Let all the earth fear Yahweh,
 let all the inhabitants of the world stand in awe of him!
For he spoke, and it came to be,
 he commanded, and it stood forth.   — Ps 33:6-9 (RSV)

---

4 Gerhard von Rad, "Some Aspects of the Old Testament World-View," in THE PROBLEM OF THE HEXATEUCH AND OTHER ESSAYS, trans. by E. W. Trueman Dicken (New York: McGraw Hill, 1966), pp. 144ff. The essay appeared in German in 1964.

The psalmist immediately considers how the Creator's soverignty is manifest in the realm of historical affairs: He is the one who "fashions" the hearts of men, who brings the counsels of the nations to nought, and whose "eye" is upon all people. Here the movement of praise proceeds smoothly, without any distinction, from the Creator's sovereignty over heaven and earth to his sovereignty over human affairs, both constituting the unified area of his control.

In recent years scholars have called into question one of the favorite themes of biblical theology of the past, namely, that Yahweh was known and confessed as the God of history and that history was the primary mode of his revelation.[5] Extending this criticism beyond the Old Testament, a Scandinavian scholar, Bertil Albrektson, has challenged the prevalent view that the religions of neighboring peoples were simply "nature religions." From Mesopotamian sources he adduces evidence that testimonies to divine activity in history were not peculiar to ancient Israel. In the end, however, Albrektson has to admit that "the idea of divine acts in history" in Israel on the one hand and in Mesopotamia on the other "may well have occupied a rather different place in the different pattern of beliefs."[6] That is true. The sporadic evidence adduced stands in contrast to the fundamental role of historical remembrance in the Israelite cult (Dt 26:5-9) and, as von Rad observes, to Israel's "stubborn need to push forward to the perception of far-reaching historical continuities," as in the historical works of the Old Testament.[7] Nevertheless, Albrektson's study is a healthy reaction to the one-sided emphasis upon history in Old Testament theology. At times this has been carried to the extreme of saying that Israel's "conception of the world is so little influenced by religion that it was rather an obstacle than an aid to faith;"[8] or some theologians, influenced by Bultmann, have existentialized faith to the point that "nature" is left out of account.

I do not see how we can escape our situation today which demands that we make a distinction between history and nature, or a Cartesian distinction between mind and matter (subject and object), even though such distinctions are alien to the Old Testament. My colleague, George

---

5 See James Barr, "Revelation through History in the Old Testament and Modern Theology," *Interpretation*, Vol. XVII (1963), pp. 193-205; Brevard S. Childs, BIBLI-

6 Bertil Albrektson, HISTORY AND THE GODS: AN ESSAY ON THE IDEA OF HISTORICAL EVENTS AS DIVINE MANIFESTATIONS IN THE ANCIENT NEAR EAST AND IN ISRAEL (Lund: C.W.K. Gleerup, 1967). Quotation from p. 115.

7 Gerhard von Rad, WEISHEIT IN ISRAEL, (Neukirchen-Vluyn: Neukirchen Verlag, pp. 366ff., especially footnote 3. ET, WISDOM IN ISRAEL, trans. by James D. Martin (Nashville: Abingdon Press, 1972), pp. 289ff.

8 Edmund Jacob, THEOLOGY OF THE OLD TESTAMENT (New York: Harper, 1958), p. 146. He quotes favorably the verdict of Victor Monod (DIEU DANS L'UNIVERS, 1933, p. 16) that "the material universe is only the temporary and removable setting of the divine-human drama. It does not possess permanent worth" (p. 149).

Hendry, who emphasizes this point, has proposed that "a better answer to Descartes would be, not to attempt to rescind the bifurcation of reality which he introduced, but rather to inquire whether, by placing the particular problem with which he was concerned in a larger framework, the two perspectives could be combined in a stereoscopic vision, to which the doctrine of creation might appear in a new light."[9] Granted that, in the last analysis, such a "stereoscopic vision" is possible for God alone, the question is whether some intimations of it may be provided by Israel's experience of divine reality.

One of the best discussions of this subject, which has apparently been overlooked in recent biblical theology, is H. Wheeler Robinson's chapter on "The Hebrew Conception of Nature" in his posthumous INSPIRATION AND REVELATION IN THE OLD TESTAMENT.[10] It is noteworthy that immediately after his initial statement about the unity of God's creation he slips into the distinction between nature and history and gives theological primacy to the latter. "Yahweh's ultimate relation to things," he writes, "is a derivative from his primary relation to men" (p. 2). This epistemological starting-point cannot be ignored if indeed, as the Old Testament witnesses throughout, Yahweh reveals himself as personal will in relationship to his people, rather than in natural processes (Baalism). The Old Testament, as we well know, speaks of Yahweh in bold anthropomorphisms and intolerantly avoids the theriomorphisms found in surrounding culture. Moreover, the primary motifs for expressing the faith of Israel, such as the promise to the fathers, Exodus and covenant (treaty), and the Kingdom of God, are derived from social, political experience. Once this starting-point is granted, however, it is important to hear Robinson's further elaboration:

> History supplied a revelation of God which Nature, notwithstanding all its rich content and variety, could never afford. Yet the conception of the God who works in history is inseparably linked to His manifestation in natural phenomena. He is what Nature, as well as history, reveals himself to be, and Nature is His peculiar language. (p. 4)

This "peculiar language," which is used in the anthem of praise sung by the heavens (Ps 19:1-3), proclaims the "glory" (*kabod*) of the Creator, or as Paul puts it, "his invisible attributes, that is to say his everlasting power and deity, have been visible, ever since the world began, to the eye of reason, in the things he has made" (Rom 1:20 NEB). Here it is impossible to deal with the various connotations of "nature's language" as

---

9 George S. Hendry, "Eclipse of Creation," *Theology Today* XXVIII (1972), pp. 406-25. Quotation from p. 423.
10 This work, published in 1946 (Oxford), constituted the prolegomenon to Robinson's projected Old Testament Theology.

perceived by Israel's interpreters: torah writers, psalmists, prophets, and sages. Robinson refers to several aspects of Israel's theology of nature: the esthetic appreciation of natural phenomena as reflected, for instance, in the Song of Songs; the awesome awareness of the many mysteries in nature which will not disclose its secret to man's inquiring search (the Book of Job); the awareness of the marvelous order of nature in which every aspect of God's earthly creation has its own *min* ("species, classification;" Gn 1:11) and in which the whole is governed by regularity (Gn 8:22; 9:13ff.; cf. Jer 5:24); and the view that material objects are "alive," animated, as though having a psychical life of their own — a view that is strange to the modern notion of nature as dead and mechanical. "Nature is alive through and through," he says, "and therefore the more capable of sympathy with man, and of direct response to the rule of its Creator and Upholder, on whom it directly depends" (p. 16). This does not imply, as we shall see, "a democracy of all God's creatures," as Lynn White seems to advocate in the name of St. Francis of Assisi. Clearly, however, there is a kinship between Man and Nature. Indeed, "earth has always been for sharing," to think once again of the threatened rhinoceros.

II

There is one limit, however, beyond which Israel's theology of nature cannot go. While heaven and earth reveal the "glory" of deity, Israel refused to suggest that the creation is a direct self-revelation of Yahweh, as though it were an emanation of his being or as though he were a power immanent within it. As Creator, he transcends the whole creation. This means, in the first place, that the creation language of the Bible "unquestionably connotes origination."[11] The initial word *re'shit,* especially when Gn 1:1 is read (as it should be) as an independent sentence, points to "the absolute beginning of the world."[12] In the second place, the world is absolutely dependent upon the Creator. This dimension of God's creative work is admirably expressed in Ps 104:27-30, where the verbs in the Hebrew imperfect indicate continuous action (*creatio continua*) :

These all look to thee
    to give them their food in due season.
When thou givest to them, they gather it up;
    when thou openest thy hand, they are filled with good things.
When thou hidest thy face, they are dismayed;
    when thou takest away their breath, they die and return to their dust.
When thou sendest forth thy spirit they are created,
    and thou renewest the face of the ground.

11 George S. Hendry, p. 420.
12 Walther Eichrodt, "In the Beginning," ISRAEL'S PROPHETIC HERITAGE, ed. by Bernhard W. Anderson and Walter Harrelson (New York: Harper, 1962), pp. 1-10. See also Claus Westermann, GENESIS, Biblischer Kommentar (Neukirchen-Vluyn: Neukirchen Verlag, 1966), pp. 130ff.

Were it not for the sustaining and upholding power of the Creator, the creation would lapse into chaos. The regularities of nature — "seedtime and harvest, cold and heat, summer and winter, day and night" (Gn 8-22) — are not based upon laws of a self-existent cosmos; rather, they are signs of the faithfulness and dependability of the Creator who, according to the priestly theologian, has made an "everlasting covenant" with "every living creature of all flesh that is upon the earth" (Gn 9:16).

Israel was not unique in the formulation of myths that expressed these two aspects of creation. There were various ancient myths that told about origination, that is, the creation of individual Man or the creation of the world as a whole; and there were myths that expressed the dependence of the world upon the God who insured the regularity of the seasons and the annual renewal of fertility. Undoubtedly these myths, mediated to Israel through Canaanite culture or through the cosmopolitan atmosphere of the Davidic-Solomonic court, belong to the prehistory of Israel's creation-faith.[13] Recognizing that Israel borrowed mythical material and shared humanity's elemental experiences, the question arises as to the point at which Israel's world-view differed from her neighbors.

Gerhard von Rad, in his essay referred to previously, locates the point of difference in Israel's strict prohibition of images, that is, "any likeness of anything that is in heaven above, or that is in the earth beneath, or that is in the water under the earth" (Ex 20:4) — in other words, in the whole realm of creation, pictorially conceived. Ancient religions, he points out, gave a central place to cult-images, for in some sense the deity was present in the image; the image was a means of contact between God and human life, a source of blessing and saving power.

> Without the gods, and without concrete representations of them, man would be lost in the world! Yet the mystery of godhead bursts out all around him. From it he may gain a blessing and bring order and purpose into his life; apart from it he could not exist. In the sphere of human life there is an infinite variety of points at which divinity shines through, and every point in man's world is at least potentially a point of divine intrusion, an expression of deity, and to this extent a means of communication between God and man. It is this understanding of the situation which makes possible the extraordinary tolerance which idol-cults extend to one another.[14]

From the Mosaic period on, however, Israel was intolerant of images. This aniconic faith received its supreme expression in the prophecy of Second Isaiah. Proclaiming the unfathomable wisdom and inexhaustible power of Yahweh, the Creator, the prophet asks:

---

13 This prehistory receives great emphasis in Claus Westermann's GENESIS-KOMMENTAR. See especially pp. 26-65.
14 Von Rad, "Some Aspects of the Old Testament World-View," p. 147.

> To whom then will you liken God,
>   or what likeness [*demut*] compare with him?   — Is 40:18

After satirizing the foolish manufacture of idols, once again the question is asked:

> To whom then will you compare me,
>   that I should be like him? says the Holy One.
> Lift up your eyes on high and see:
>   who created these?
> He who brings out their host by number,
>   calling them all by name;
> by the greatness of his might,
>   and because he is strong in power
>   not one is missing.   — Is 40:25-26

According to the prophet, Yahweh is the transcendent God: the Creator who originated the universe and whose soverign power undergirds the whole historical drama from beginning to end. The world is under the sole control of the God who "declared the end [*ah*ᵃ*rit*] from the beginning [*re'shit*]" (Is 46:10).

In the light of this, what is the meaning of the affirmation that Mankind is the image (*selem*) or likeness (*demut*) of God? We must now turn to Gn 1:26-28 and the related passage in Ps 8:5-8. In the history of interpretation these texts have received emphasis out of all proportion to the weight given them in the Old Testament itself, where they stand virtually alone.

III

Some kind of relationship exists between these two passages, which is not surprising since both reflect the liturgical usage of the Jerusalem cult. It is difficult to say whether Psalm 8 is older and possibly influenced the formulation of Gn 1:26-28, or whether the latter existed first, perhaps in the form of a cultic legend used in the Jerusalem temple, and as such provided the inspiration for the psalmist's composition. Probability favors the first alternative.

Psalm 8 is a hymn which begins and ends with an exclamation of praise to Yahweh whose "name" is majestic throughout all the earth. The hymnic invocation at the beginning is expanded by an elaboration, the purpose of which is to portray Yahweh's majesty in the heavenly realm. Unfortunately, the meaning of the hymnic expansion (vss. 1a, 2) is not clear in the Hebrew original. Apparently the psalmist draws upon mythical language, perhaps Canaanite in origin, to portray Yahweh's sovereignty in the cosmic sphere.[15] In any case, the subsequent theme of the coronation of

---

15 At least three matters seem to stand out: a) Yahweh's splendor is "above" (*'al*) the heavens; b) Yahweh has established a "bulwark" (*'oz*) in the heavenly sphere; and c) from this citadel, situated above the heavenly vault, Yahweh subdues his foes.

Man is placed in the context of Yahweh's transcendent sovereignty. The main part of the hymn begins in vs. 3 with *ki* ("when", "for") and provides the motive for earthly praise, corresponding to the praise that resounds in the cosmic temple (cf. Is 6:1-4!). When looking up at the starry vault, the work of Yahweh's "fingers," and the heavenly bodies which Yahweh has set in their ordered place, the psalmist marvels that the Creator is mindful of his comparatively small and transient creature, "Man" (cf. Jb 7:17-18). The question, however, does not stand by itself but provides the lead into the contrasting statement that follows: Such an insignificant and transient creature, yet one who is so richly endowed with glory and honor! Hence the hymn continues with a transition which in Hebrew is marked by an "adversative waw," to be translated as "but, yet, nevertheless:"

Yet you have made him to fall short slightly from divine beings,[16]
and with glory and honor you have crowned him.
You have caused him to rule over the works of your hands,
everything you have put under his feet:
    small and large cattle — all of them,
    also the beasts of the field,
    birds of the heaven and fish of the sea —
    whatever courses through the ocean paths.   — Ps 8:5-8

The hymn concludes with a refrain which echoes the opening exclamation of praise.

The creation account in Gn 1:1-2:4a once may have served a liturgical purpose.[17] In its present form, however, it is detached from a cultic setting and stands in the so-called Priestly Work, which starts from the creation of the world and from this universal scope narrows down genealogically to Israel, reaching its climax in the establishment of the tabernacle and the constitution of the people as a worshipping community. This chapter is not hymnic praise, as Psalm 8 is, but theological reflection upon the cosmic implications of Israel's knowledge of God mediated through her historical traditions and confessed in worship. The climax of Gn 1 is the creation of Man (*'adam*-"human being") an event which, in terms

---

Dahood maintains that the psalmist poetically employs mythical language, as in Ps 89:11-12, to portray Yahweh's cosmic majesty. He compares the Canaanite myth of Baal who vanquishes his adversary *Yamm* (Sea) and afterwards builds a heavenly palace. See Mitchel Dahood, THE PSALMS, Anchor Bible (Garden City, N.Y.: Doubleday, 1966), *ad loc.*

16 In this translation I assume that *'elohim* refers not to God directly but to the divine beings (Septuagint: *angeloi*) of the heavenly court, so NAB, NEB translates "a god."

17 Paul Humbert maintains that the priestly creation story was a festival legend for the seven-day Feast of Tabernacles with which the New Year began, on the analogy of the Babylonian *Enuma elish* which was the myth-libretto for the *akitu* or Babylonian New Year Festival. See "La relation de Genèse 1 et du Psaume 104 avec la liturgie de Nouvel-An israelite," OPUSCULES D'UN HEBRAISANT (Neuchâtel: Université de Neuchâtel, 1958), pp. 166-74.

of the present seven-day scheme, occurs on the same day as the creation of other living creatures according to their species: cattle, beasts of the earth, and creeping things. It is in this context that the solemn announcement is made, apparently in the Heavenly Council, of God's resolution to create Man "as our image, after our likeness" (vs. 26). The preposition here translated "as" (*be*) refers to Man's function; hence God's decision is to give Man dominion over fish, birds, cattle, wild animals, and land reptiles.[18]

The affinities between these two passages, Ps 8:5-8 and Gn 1:26-28, are very close. 1) Both passages apparently presuppose the view of the Heavenly Council (the "sons of God" or *'elohim*-beings) within which, as in the Babylonian *Enuma elish,* the decision to create Man is announced. 2) In both passages Man is brought into close proximity to the status of *'elohim.* In the priestly account it is stated that Man is created as the image of *'elohim;* the psalmist uses a circumlocution: Man is made slightly inferior to *'elohim.* 3) Finally, in both passages Man's high position in God's creation carries with it the power to exercise dominion over the animals. The question is: what does the motif of the *imago Dei* say or imply concerning Man's dominion over his natural environment?

There is, however, one major difference. The clearest evidence of the independence of Psalm 8 is the motif of the coronation of Man: "with glory and honor you have crowned him." Here there is no suggestion that Man's dominion is based upon a divine blessing that empowers him to multiply and subdue the earth, as in the priestly story (Gn 1:28). Rather, Man's dominion over the earth is the consequence of Yahweh's elevating him to royal position. It could be argued that the verb "crown" is intended here in a general sense, as in Ps 103:4 where it is said that Yahweh crowns a person with steadfast love and mercy. But the language of Psalm 8 suggests royal investiture. Man is crowned with "glory and honor", terms that are used of an earthly king (Ps 45:4f.; 110:3). Yahweh has "caused him to rule" (*mashal*), a verb that is also used of a reigning king (Is 19:4; Mi 5:2). And Yahweh has put everything "under his feet," like booty (cf. Ps 2:8). H. J. Kraus appropriately remarks in this connection: "The Creator and Lord of the world, Yahweh, hands over to Man the world, as

---

18 The prepositions *be* and *ke* can be reversed, as in 5:3, which makes precise interpretation difficult. Too much emphasis should not be placed on the translation of *be* as "in," for the preposition is used with various meanings in the Old Testament. It can be used to express "the quality or manner in which an entity shows itself" (Kohler-Baumgartner, p. 102), and probably it should be so construed in this case, that is, "as our image." So Gerhard von Rad, GENESIS, Old Testament Library (Westminster, 1961), p. 56. Notice that the parallel preposition in Gn 1:26-27 (*ke*) has the same use in Is 40:23: "(he) makes judges of the earth as nothing."

The words "over all the earth" in vs. 26 (RSV) represent a defective text which is to be restored according to the Syriac and the animal sequence in vss. 24, 25, 28: "over all wild animals on earth" (see NEB and NAB).

to a king whom he has installed."[19] There can hardly be any doubt that the language of royal theology is used in Psalm 8, much more openly than in the parallel passage in Genesis 1. According to the psalmist, Man is invested with a royal splendor that not only raises him above the animals but draws him into the sphere of God's kingly rule. The "glory and honor" which belong to the Creator (Ps 29:1; 104:1) are reflected to a degree in Man's majestic position on earth. The name of Yahweh is glorious on earth *through* Man who is crowned as his viceroy.

IV

Who is this "man" that is described in such exalted terms? Is he everyman? Or a particular man who represents the divine rule on earth? Since so many of the psalms are colored by the royal theology prevalent in the Jerusalem court, it is possible that there is some influence from ancient mythical views which portrayed the king as "the son of God" or "the creation of God." In Ez 28:11-19, for instance, the king of Tyre is portrayed as "royal First Man." According to the myth, there once lived in Eden, the Garden of God located on the sacred mountain, a glorious being who, from the day of his creation, was "the signet of perfection, full of wisdom and perfect in beauty." The Primordial Man is described as a royal figure who wore a pectoral studded with precious stones. The *Urkönig* walked freely in the Garden of God which was adorned with flashing gems ("stones of fire"). But his wisdom and beauty went to his head and the Creator expelled him from the sacred mountain and hurled him to the earth. In Ezekiel's interpretation, the mythical tragedy is a portrayal of the fall of Tyre.[20] It may well be that this myth lies behind Job 15:7-8:

Are you the first man that was born?
Or were you brought forth before the hills?
Have you listened in the council of God?
And do you limit wisdom to yourself?

Scandinavian scholars have adduced these passages to support the view that the statements of Psalm 8 about the coronation of Man originally referred to the king or, more properly, the First King (*Urkönig*), who, as God's creation, was invested with royal splendor. Aage Bentzen is a major advocate of this position. He maintains that this psalm belongs in a circle of psalms that presuppose a cultic drama celebrated at the New Year Festival when worshippers reactualized the divine battle against powers of chaos (Sea, Rahab, Leviathan). In Psalm 8, he says, "the poet views the

---

19 H. J. Kraus, PSALMEN I, Biblischer Kommentar (1960), p. 70.
20 See H. G. May, "The King in the Garden of Eden," ISRAEL'S PROPHETIC HERITAGE, ed. by Bernhard W. Anderson and Walter Harrelson (1962), pp. 166-76; also John L. McKenzie, MYTHS AND REALITIES (Milwaukee: Bruce, 1963), pp. 154-56, 175-81.

heaven as a bulwark established by the Lord against all enemies; this work is greater than all of Yahweh's works, even greater than the creation of the First Man to be king of the world."[21] This view is seconded by Helmer Ringgren who insists that the words of Ps 8:4-8 refer to the king who acted in a representative capacity for the people.[22]

There is much to be said for the corporate or representative conception of "man," especially when the psalm is considered in the context of Jerusalem theology which was heavily influenced by ancient Near Eastern views of king and temple. The royal interpretation of Psalm 8 could be supported by appeal to Ps 80:17, where the poetic parallelism makes the meaning clear:

Let thy hand be upon the man of thy right hand,
    the son of man (*ben 'adam*) whom thou hast made strong
    for thyself!

Here the psalmist refers to the king who is seated "at the right hand" of God (Ps 110:1) and who is "made strong" through his election or adoption as God's Son (Ps 2:7). Further, the ascription or dedication of Psalm 8 to David, according to the superscription, may indicate that this was one of the psalms to be used in the cult. In any event, David was regarded as "a leading and archetypal figure in Israel," as Christoph Barth points out, one "in whom their own existence as the people of God had found an expression that was valid for all time."[23] Finally, it is noteworthy that elsewhere the dominion of the king is said to include rule over animals as well as over man, for instance in Jer 27:4-6:

Thus says Yahweh of hosts, the God of Israel: . . .

It is I who by my great power and my outstretched arm have made the earth, with the men and animals that are on the earth, and I give it to whomever it seems right to me. Now I have given all these lands into the hand of Nebuchadnezzar, the king of Babylon, my servant, and I have given him also the beasts of the field to serve him.

However, the fact that in Psalm 8 "royal" dominion is over animals, birds, and fish, not over *men* and animals, should warn us against a messianic interpretation of the psalm. The royal man of Psalm 8 is *not* em-

---

21 Aage Bentzen, MESSIAS, MOSES REDIVIVUS, MENSCHENSOHN (Zürich: Zwingli-Verlag, 1948), p. 12. See pp. 38-41 where he discusses Ez 28:12-19.

22 Helmer Ringgren, THE MESSIAH IN THE OLD TESTAMENT (London: SCM, 1956), p. 20: "At first sight these words seem to refer to man in general, or to Adam; but there is reason to believe that they were originally said about the king. Since the creative acts of God and man's dominion over creation were actualized in the annual Festival, it is conceivable that the proclamation of that dominion (Gn 1:28, 29) was repeated and addressed to the king who, so to speak, played the role of Adam as the representative of mankind."

23 Christoph Barth, INTRODUCTION TO THE PSALMS (New York: Scribner, 1966), p. 65. Barth calls attention to the fact that "in the prayers of an individual the king is always more or less closely associated with him, while in the prayers of the king the individual Israelite is included at the same time." p. 26).

powered to overcome his enemies, as elsewhere in royal psalms (Ps 2:7-9), but rather to have dominion over the everyday aspects of the world, which include hunting and fishing, pasturing of flocks, use of meat for food, and so forth. The most natural reading of "man" || "son of man" is that the parallel terms refer to mortal man, everyman (as in Nm 23:19; Jb 25:6; 35:8; Is 51:12; 56:2 etc.), who despite his transcience and limitation is elevated to a position of honor and glory in God's creation. If the king used this language in the cult, it must have had the meaning of the king's prayer in Ps 144:3-4 (ET) where the parallel terms *'adam*||*ben 'enosh* refer not to his royal status but to his identification with transient humanity:

> O Yahweh, what is man that thou dost regard him,
> or the son of man that thou dost think of him?
> Man is like a breath,
> eyes, he may see it is by the wonderful providence of God that
> his days are like a passing shadow.

To be sure, royal terminology is employed in Psalm 8; and perhaps the myth of kingly First Man is in the background. But the psalm represents an early stage in the "democratization" of the royal theology of the ancient Near East. It is appropriate to refer to John Calvin's illuminating commentary on Psalm 8, where the democratization of Man's royal rule is interpreted as dominion over the ordinary aspects of the everyday world:

> For there is no man so dull and slow-witted, but if he will open his eyes, he may see it is by the wonderful providence of God that horses and oxen yield their service to men; that sheep bear wool to clothe them with; and that all kinds of cattle yield even their flesh to feed them. The more visible the proof of this dominion is, the more it becomes us to be touched with the sense of God's grace, as often as we either eat meat, or enjoy other comforts.[24]

Nevertheless, the messianic interpretation of the psalm in the New Testament (Heb 2:5-18), which was influenced by the Septuagint translation, picked up overtones that were present in the psalm from the first.[25]

V

In view of the close affinities between Ps 8:5-8 and Gn 1:26-28, we would expect to find some evidence of the language of royal theology in the priestly creation story too. This expectation, however, is not amply rewarded. To be sure, in the Genesis passage human dominion over the earth is described by verbs which may be used in the context of royal theology. This is true of the verb used in 1:26, *rada* ("tread," "rule"), which is used of the king in Ps 110:2 ("rule in the midst of your foes!")

---

24 John Calvin, COMMENTARY ON THE PSALMS, Vol. 1, revised translation by T. H. L. Parker (London: James Clarke, 1965), p. 95.
25 See the illuminating article by Brevard S. Childs, "Psalm 8 in the Context of the Christian Canon," *Interpretation* XXIII (1969), pp. 20-31.

or Ps 72:8 ("May he have dominion from sea to sea"). It is striking that, with the exception of this scant linguistic evidence, the motif of the coronation of Man, which figures prominently in Psalm 8, is absent from Genesis 1.

Nevertheless, some Scandinavian scholars insist that the mythical First Man or *Urkönig* is the subject of the Genesis passage. Aage Bentzen writes:

> The first man in Gen. 1:26-28 is portrayed as the first king of the world. We read here in the creation account — the evangelium of the New Year's Day Festival — about God's blessing in connection with the enthronement of the first royal pair of the world: Man is to "rule" (*mšl* [sic], vs. 26) over all living beings of the earth, to bring the earth under his subjection.[26]

Comparing the first pair with the Babylonian king who was regarded as "the image of God," he concludes that the "royal" pair were divine (*göttlich*). In support of this view, he adduces the curious passage in Ps 45:7 where, according to the received text, the king is addressed as *'elohim*. The latter mode of address, however, which belongs to extravagant court style, is the only instance of its kind in the Old Testament. There is no clear evidence that Israel adopted the whole conception of "sacral kingship."[27]

The question of royal theology in the priestly creation story requires a consideration of the statement that Man is created as "the image of Elohim." In recent years biblical theologians have challenged the spiritualizing interpretations that have been influential in the Christian tradition, according to which the image is Man's spiritual capacity: reason, will, freedom, conscience, moral consciousness, immortal soul, self-transcendence, etc. Without denying that the image points to Man's relationship to God, attention has been called to the corporeal aspect of *ṣelem* which is softened somewhat in the parallel term *demut* (pattern, likeness). Köhler, for instance, asserts that the image means that Man, in distinction from the animals, has an upright form that enables him to have dominion over his environment. "With the additional words 'in our form, to look like us'," he says, "[Man] is raised above the beasts and made to approach nearer to God."[28] It is doubtful, however, that the intention of the text is to stress Man's external, physical form in such a one-sided fashion. Theologians have rightly insisted that the separation between the bodily and the

---

26 Aage Bentzen, p. 12. Actually the verb *mashal* is not used here; rather, we find other verbs of dominion (*rada, kabash*).

27 This matter is discussed judiciously by Martin Noth, "God, King, and Nation in the Old Testament," THE LAWS IN THE PENTATEUCH AND OTHER ESSAYS (Philadelphia: Fortress, 1967), pp. 145-78.

28 Ludwig Köhler, OLD TESTAMENT THEOLOGY (Philadelphia: Westminster, 1957), p. 147.

spiritual is alien to the Old Testament and that, therefore, the image refers to the whole person. The image is not something *in* Man, but is Man himself. Gerhard von Rad, stressing the corporality of the image, maintains that the language indicates Man's *function* in the totality of his bodily, historical being. In a famous passage he writes:

> Just as powerful earthly kings, to indicate their claim to dominion, erect an image of themselves in the provinces of their empire where they do not personally appear, so man is placed upon earth in God's image, as God's sovereign emblem. He is really only God's representative, summoned to maintain and enforce God's claim to dominion over the earth.[29]

This is an illuminating interpretation, but unfortunately it finds no clear support in the Old Testament. The various usages of *ṣelem* show only that the term is used for something concrete like a statue (Nm 33:52; 2 Kgs 11:18; Am 5:26; Ez 7:20), a copy (1 Sm 6:5,11; Ez 16:17 [*ṣalme zakar*, "images of men" — idols]), or a drawing of men sketched on a wall (Ez 23:14). One thinks especially of the *ṣelem* set up by Nebuchadnezzar, before which all people were to bow down or to be cast into a fiery furnace (Dn 3). These instances show that in the ancient world a sharp distinction was not drawn between an original and its copy, that is, a copy was regarded as something more than a mere resemblance. The idea of "representation" deserves more exploration. Following the lead of Bentzen but without necessarily adopting his conclusion, we might well inquire whether extra-biblical sources throw any light on the meaning of *imago Dei*.

Von Rad's thesis concerning the functional or representative character of the image finds considerable support from recent studies of Mesopotamian and Egyptian texts. Scholars have drawn attention to various Akkadian texts in which "image" (*ṣalmu*) is used of the king. In the context of the *Königs-ideologie* of the ancient Near East, the term is said to describe the relationship of the king to the deity and specifically his function as the god's representative in his royal office. It is argued, however, that the dominant ancestry of the Genesis *ṣelem* is the court style of ancient Egypt where, beginning especially with the 18th Dynasty, Pharaoh was called "the likeness of Re," "image of Re," "living likeness on earth," etc. Strikingly, the usage often appears in creation contexts. The word of Amon Re to Pharaoh Amenophis III is especially pertinent to our inquiry:

> "You are my beloved Son, produced from my members, my image which I have established on the earth. I have made you to rule the earth in peace."

H. Wildberger and W.H. Schmidt, who quote and discuss the above texts

---

29 Gerhard von Rad, GENESIS, Old Testament Library (Philadelphia: Westminster, 1961). p. 58.

and others, have concluded independently that Gn 1:26 stands on the whole much closer to Egypt than to Mesopotamia, although the Genesis passage has been "democratized" by being referred to mankind or *'adam*.[30]

We may concede that ancient mythical views lie behind Gn 1:26-28, just as they lie remotely behind the opening portrayal of chaos (Gn 1:2). Using mythical language, the priestly writer affirms that Man stands in close relationship to God (the Heavenly Council) and is the agent of the divine rule on earth. The myth, however, has been changed in reinterpretation. The writer stresses the transcendent majesty of God and thereby establishes a sharp differentiation between Creator and creature. Any lingering doubt about the writer's democratization of the image is dispelled when we turn to Gn 5:3 and find the same writer using the terms "image" and "likeness" to describe the relationship between Adam and his son Seth. We read:

> When Adam had lived a hundred and thirty years, he became the father of a son in his own likeness (*demut*), after his image (*selem*), and named him Seth.

Here the metaphor used in regard to Man's relationship to God is applied to the relationship between father and son in society. Just as Man is God's representative and thus the sign of his rule on earth, so the son is the representative of his father, one in whom, in some sense, the father appears.[31]

The democratization of the motif is clear in the priestly description of human dominion: "Then God said: 'Let us make Man as our image, after our likeness, and let *them* have dominion. . . .'" What is involved here is not a single man, the Adam of the Book of Generations (Gn 5:1a), but rather a collective whole, that is, mankind or humanity. Accordingly, the jussive verb in vs. 26 ("let them have dominion") is in the plural, as are the imperatives of the blessing in vs. 28 ("be fruitful, multiply, fill the earth, tread down, dominate"). Furthermore, this corporate meaning is evident in the shift of pronouns from "him" to "them" in the sentence which reports the execution of God's resolution (vs. 27):

> So God created man as his own image,
>   as the image of God he created *him;*
>   male and female he created *them.*

Dominion is given to mankind as a whole and therefore to *man and woman.* Here the priestly view departs from royal theology found in

---

30 See H. Wildberger, "Das Abbild Gottes," *Theologische Zeitschrift* 21 (1965), pp. 245-59, 481-501 (especially pp. 484ff.) and W. H. Schmidt, DE SCHÖPFUNGSGES-CHICHTE DER PRIESTERSCHRIFT (Neukirchen-Vluyn: Neukirchen Verlag, 1964), pp. 136-42. This view is discussed and rejected by Claus Westermann in his GENESIS-KOMMENTAR (pp. 209-213), but his negative arguments are not convincing to me.
31 Cf. Werner H. Schmidt, p. 144.

Egypt, for it is not said that Pharaoh *and* his wife represent together the image of God. In this respect Psalm 8 stands much closer to royal theology; for despite its democratization of the dominion-motif, "man" is spoken of in the singular and no reference is made to male and female.

VI

In summary, Psalm 8 and the related passage in Genesis 1 are evidences of the new situation which prevailed in Israel when, with the rise of David, Israel accepted the alien institutions of temple and king and came under the influence of the royal theology of the ancient Near East. Yet in both cases, though in different degrees, the mythical views were transformed when brought into the context of Israel's faith which from the very first emphasized the incomparability of Yahweh and prohibited any image or likeness of him. In Psalm 8 the royal theology is, at least, implicit. The coronation of Man is seen in the context of Yahweh's heavenly rule in his exalted palace from which he comes to rout his foes — the powers of chaos who manifest their uncanny influence in the threats of disorder. If our interpretation is right, the royal theology has already been democratized, so that the "man" of the psalm is not the king, but everyman. Man is Yahweh's viceroy on earth, having a status only slightly inferior to divine beings. His dominion is the way that Yahweh's name becomes glorious on earth. The siutation is different in Gn 1:26-28. Here the democratization of royal theology has been carried to its conclusion, leaving only vestigial remains, especially the motif of the image of God which entitles Man to have dominion over the earth. Man (*'adam*) is the collective whole of humanity, differentiated according to male and female. Perhaps the priestly writer could use the motif of the "image" boldly, without fear of its pagan meaning, because his theological presentation is based on the holiness and transcendence of God and the sharp distinction between Creator and creature. The psalmist, on the other hand, may have been more reticent about using this motif directly in a context clearly influenced by royal theology and therefore he resorted to a paraphrase. Both biblical passages represent different responses to the mythical view of kingship.

Israel's interpreters have made one fundamental exception to the iconoclasm inherent in the Mosaic faith and eloquently expressed by Second Isaiah: it is *Man* who is crowned with honor and glory reflecting the splendor of God; it is *Man* who is created as the image of God. Though an ephemeral creature, in comparison to the stars, he is the one whom God has elevated to be his representative on earth, the one with whom God enters into personal relationship, and the one in whom the praise of the whole creation can become vocal. "There is only *one* legitimate image through whom God manifests himself in the world," writes Wildberger, "and that is Man. It is of the most far-reaching significance that Israel, who so passionately rejected all image-worship so as not to fall into idolatry, and who evidently would not accord the title *selem 'elohim* even to the king, proclaimed, in the boldest reinterpretation of the image-theology of the environment, that Man is the form in which God himself is present."[32] This is what prompts the hymnic praise of the psalmist. It is not just that the Creator pays attention to his transient human creature. Far more than that: the Creator has displayed his grace by elevating Man to a supreme place in his creation, crowning him as a king and putting the earth at his disposal.

I conclude, then, that it is essentially correct to say that the Judeo-Christian heritage stresses human dominion over the earth rather than a primitive or romantic attitude toward nature. If the *imago Dei* has contributed to our ecological crisis, by becoming a warrant for conceptions of the modern period such as those springing intellectually from the Enlightenment or economically from free-wheeling capitalism, then it is time to understand what the biblical language intends to say. It is clear from the context of Genesis 1 that God's elevation of Man does not entitle us to exercise power in an unlimited and autonomous manner by exploiting and subjugating nature. True, the verbs used of human dominion in Gn 1: 26-28 may have a violent meaning in other contexts.[33] But violence does not appear in this context where, according to the priestly story, human dominion is to be exercised in a situation of paradisiac peace and harmony in which there was to be *no killing*. Not only were animals and Man created together on the sixth day of creation, indicating their interdependence, but together they "share the same table" upon which the Creator provides their common food, plants and fruits (Gn 1: 29-30). Even when this rule was relaxed in the priestly narrative at the time of the Flood, with the result that permission was given not only to eat the green plants but *"everything"* (Gn 9:3), there was a clear recognition of the sacredness of life (blood), both animal and human. Under strict limitations, animals may be slaughtered for food; but the prohibition against one killing a fellow human being is as apodictic as at the time of creation. Furthermore, this same writer declares that the Noachic covenant is an "everlasting covenant," predicated unconditionally upon God's sovereignty and embracing not only mankind but the birds, cattle, wild animals, "and every living creature of all flesh" (Gn 9:8-17).

Thus Man's special status, as the image of God, is a call to respon-

---

32 Wildberger, pp. 49ff.; cf. Werner Schmidt, p. 144.
33 The verb *rada* can mean to "tread, trample" as in the treading of the winepress (Jl 3: 13); the other verb, *kabash*, can refer to acts of forcible subjection such as rape (Jer 34:15; Est 7:8).

sibility, not only in relation to fellow men but in relation to nature. Human dominion is not to be exercised wantonly, but wisely and benevolently so that it may be, in some degree, the sign of God's rule over his creation. Some of Israel's laws place restrictions upon the careless harming and spoiling of nature, for instance the law prohibiting the taking of a mother bird (Dt 22:6), or the command not to muzzle an ox while it treads the grain (Dt 25:4). Modern military leaders who have carried out the defoliation of trees as an act of warfare could well ponder the implications of the law in Dt 20:19-20:

> When you besiege a city for a long time, making war against it in order to take it, you shall not destroy its trees by wielding an axe against them; for you may eat of them, but you shall not cut them down. Are the trees in the field men that they should be besieged by you?

The Yahwist's story in Genesis 2 emphasizes that Man is to be a caretaker of God's garden, that is, he "works" and "protects" it (Gn 2:15). This custodianship involves working upon and changing what is given as well as the conservation of natural resources.

It would be going too far to say that, according to Israel's creation theology, the world is created only for the sake of mankind. The priestly creation story reaches a climax with the announcement that God saw *everything* that he made and gave the approving verdict, "very good" (Gn 1: 31). It presents a picture in which every creature, including Man, is assigned its proper place in God's creative order and, by performing the assigned function, serves tand glorifies the Creator. Psalm 104, which is closely related to Genesis 1, announces that in wisdom Yahweh made *all* of his creatures (vs. 24) and declares that Yahweh "rejoices" in his manifold works (vs. 31).

It would be wrong to suppose that we can simply turn to the Bible to find a solution to the ecological dilemma. However, the biblical motif of human dominion over nature, when understood in the full context of Israel's creation theology, calls into question present practices of exploitation and summons people to a new responsibility. The priestly creation story suggests that Man, *if* he will, may perform his proper role in the order and harmony of the creation to the glory of the Creator. It is precisely that qualification, "if he will," which introduces the contingent element, necessitating the supplementary story of Paradise Lost (Gn 3) in the priestly edition of the Pentateuch and, later on, the story of the catastrophe of the Flood owing to human "violence" that had corrupted the earth. (Gn 6:11-13).

Eugene B. Borowitz

WHAT KNOWLEDGE DOES JUDAISM THINK IT POSSESSES

Many discussions in contemporary philosophy of religion have dealt with the questions: to what extent can it be said that religion gives knowledge (in the technical sense of that term)? What does religion give us if not knowledge? Most such discussions have centered around the application of these questions to Christianity both as the dominant religion in our culture and as the religion which has had the longest and most creative interchange with Greek philosophy. As a Jew I have frequently been led to ask myself how the various points made in these discussions about religion as a general human activity apply to Judaism as a particular variety of religious experience and thought. This paper outlines an introduction to the question of what knowledge Judaism feels it possesses.

I have permitted myself to range through the entire span of Jewish history and literature rather than confine myself to the Bible or a similar restricted sphere. I have done this, bringing in the great imprecision that must result from so broad a scope for two reasons. First, I felt it would be more helpful to me personally to try to find a general trend or pattern for Judaism as a whole. Second, because the textual and methodological problems involved in raising a question of this kind in relation to one part of Judaism remain so great that the risks of the holistic approach seem, by its possible insights, worth taking.

Permit me a word of explanation. Both historically and contemporaneously, such questions have rarely been asked in Judaism. The Jewish tradition grew and took its characteristic form in biblical and rabbinic times *before* having had intimate contact with various forms of discursive thinking. With the brief exception of Philo, preserved, significantly, by the Church and unknown to the Synagogue until modern times, Jewish philosophical reflection does not begin until the 10th century and continues through its peak in Maimonides in the 12th century to a decline by the 15th century. By this time, as we shall see, the basic Jewish decision with regard to knowledge had already been fixed. Philosophy does not resume until the 19th century and there is good question as to whether it has ever been of more than peripheral concern to Judaism as a whole.[1]

EUGENE B. BOROWITZ, Reform Rabbi, is Professor of Jewish Thought at Hebrew Union College — Jewish Institute of Religion, New York City.

---

1 So Husik, A HISTORY OF MEDIEVAL JEWISH PHILOSOPHY. in his introduction pp. xvff., points out that even in Jewish philosophy it was the Bible and Talmud which were basic to Judaism and the Aristotelianism of the middle ages were an addition to this previously independent base. Thus too in tracing the decline of Jewish philosophy, (and note the almost poignant passage of conclusion p. 432), he does not hesitate to

When one compares this with the place of philosophy in the thinking of the leaders and shapers of the church from Irenaeus on, one begins to sense the vast difference involved.[2]

One of the most characteristic results of philosophic activity is the increase of self-awareness. That which might once have been taken as real and true is now subjected to analysis and test and thus there arise intellectual systems to weigh experience and determine whether it is meaningful. Such philosophic self-consciousness is largely missing from Judaism of the classical periods, the biblical and the rabbinic. They move rather in the naivete of their immediate experience. Not that we do not find evidences of reflection there, but they are fragments, remnants, not questions self-consciously raised, considered and pursued. Hence, when we today apply such a question as that of the sense of knowledge to such non-reflective material, we find ourselves with the need to work from one level of discourse to another and face great difficulties in being faithful to the classic text.[3]

Equally as unfortunate is the small amount of contemporary attention which has been devoted to such problems in Judaism except for the literary analysis of some major ideas or documents. Thus there is little or nothing available directly on this theme of Judaism's sense of religious knowledge in the post-Kantian, post-positivist sense in which the question is raised.[4]

The Bible itself makes little effort to answer our question. It moves almost entirely on the level of myth, history or inspired utterance. None of these feels the need to justify itself more than to say that they were dictated by God, spoken by God, or the judgments involved were simply the judgments of God Himself. The Bible knows that YHWH is God,

point out that in the face of persecution "philosophy and rationalism began to be regarded askance, particularly as experience showed that scientific training was not favorable to Jewish steadfastness and loyalty" (p. 429 and see the context). Philosophy never became central in any way.

2 When Gilson speaks of "Christian Philosophy" he means a philosophy suited to and integrated with Christianity. Husik means by "Jewish Philosophy" the philosophizing carried on by some Jews to link their faith with what reason taught them about truth. The difference is great.

3 Urban, LANGUAGE AND REALITY, p. 575ff., stresses the point that theological language can never be free from the poetry which is its basic and unconditional religious root but admits that the passage from the mystic roots to the theological level is a difficult and slippery one, 595 ff. See too the general explanation of the problem in Langer, PHILOSOPHY IN A NEW KEY, pp. 163-165. And if this is true in general of translations from mythic forms to philosophic concepts where there are centuries of effort behind one, how much the more difficult is such an enterprise in Judaism where the effort of philosophic translation has been sporadic and discontinuous.

4 The article on "Jewish Symbolism" by Israel Abrahams in the Hastings ENCYCLOPEDIA OF RELIGION AND ETHICS deals in a very modest way with the meaning of some Jewish ceremonials. This is typical of much more contemporary writing on Jewish religion which can explain it only in terms of its practices. Abraham Heschel's article "Symbolism and Jewish Faith", which also misses the real problem will be discussed below.

that He has acted in certain ways in the past and can be expected to do certain things in the future; that He has chosen Israel for His service and expects certain conduct from them. The Bible in its literal sense seems to know a great deal. But such knowledge is given to us in mythic or poetic form. This is obviously true in terms of the early stories in Genesis, of the great acts of the heroes and of the speeches of the prophets. Even the more historical passages are seen in mythic form.[5] The mythic form is a way of knowing, but the myth itself cannot be called knowledge of a clear and verifiable sort. Hence, we may gain much from biblical myth, history and poetry, but we cannot say they give us knowledge.[6]

When we deal with biblical law, however, we enter an area where the formulations are precise, unemotive and intended for literal obedience. Where the non-legal material is always emotional and imaginative, the legal material is, as with all laws, coldly and most prosaically stated. Indeed the Bible itself feels that the laws of God are knowable and available, not esoteric or mysterious.[7] It is of more than casual significance that the prophets are rather specific and precise about the sins of the people and what they ought rather to be doing and imprecise and poetic when speaking about God or other such matters of theory.[8]

This dual attitude toward matters of law as against those of theory, particularly as given in the Torah, the basic book of Judaism, became a fixed part of later Jewish religious discourse.

For the sake of a more rounded view, it should be pointed out that there are certain arguments or logical movements which various authors seek to carry out in the Bible. Thus in Deuteronomy we have an argument for the existence of God from the wonders done for the Jews in leaving Egypt.[9] In Isaiah we have a *reductio ad absurdum* of idolatry and an affirmation of the uniqueness and existence of God on the basis of demonstrated prophecy.[10] Here experience rises above the immediate almost to

5 This idea of history as revelation is expounded most clearly by Richard Niebuhr in THE MEANING OF REVELATION. His view of history as revelation in the significant events which illumine the rest of our lives is true to what the Bible does. See particularly p. 93 ff.
6 On myth as a form of apprehending reality, see the clear and vigorous statement of Cassirer in LANGUAGE AND MYTH pp. 32-33 and 57-58 which is supplemented in AN ESSAY ON MAN pp. 100-110. On religious language as "numinous poetry" and for a discussion of Santayana's "Religion and Poetry" see Urban, p. 578 ff.
7 Dt 30:11-20 is the *locus classicus* where all the other fragmentary statements about the law are summarized, almost systematized, in an unusually discursive way.
8 Isaiah 6 may be taken as typical with a comparison to Isaiah 1 for a more concrete emphasis. It is not surprising that later prophecy gives way to visions and finally to apocalyptic — but this element never enters the realm of law.
9 Deuteronomy 4 is the first statement and the argument occurs frequently in the book. Particularly if we see this as the work of a writer many centuries after Moses' time we see it not as an existential plea but a form of religious argument.
10 Isaiah 44:6-20 is a splendid example of the satire against idols and see 43:1-13 for the argument from fulfilled prophecy.

the realm of reflection. Yet it is clear to the modern reflective temper that such argument is always limited to its experiential and emotional base. It can be meaningful and convincing only to him who has previously had a similar experience. It is not knowledge of a philosophically demonstrable sort.

One thing further should be pointed out about Biblical Judaism. It does insist it has some negative knowledge about God and this even reaches the level of law. Its most pervading theme is that God is not an idol, cannot be made into one or one made of Him, under any circumstances.[11] This negative notion of our knowledge of God is one which we shall see plays a continuing role in Jewish religious thought and it is important to note that already at the beginning of Judaism this was a significant motif.

When we enter the rabbinic period we are already in a different intellectual world. The rabbis have the Bible before them, not just the Torah, the basic document, but the prophetic and other writings as well. They must clarify and explain which verses are to be taken literally, which figuratively, which are dominant, which subsumed. The rabbis are reflective in their own way and almost from the very beginnings of the period, as we can trace it, a distinct and technical difference is drawn between two areas of Jewish religious discourse, the *halacha* and the *aggada,* and each of these has its own rules and authority.[12] Here, implicitly, a distinction between two forms of religious knowledge is introduced and the analysis of these forms makes clear what may be considered known or not.

The *halacha* is the realm of law, literally of "the going, the way".[13] It has authority and force.[14] The Jew who will not abide by it may be punished by the Jewish court by fines, stripes, excommunication or, in times when this was within its power, death. The *halacha* is therefore fixed, objective and precise. It must be in order to be meaningful. Indeed, making the *halacha* more precise, more specific in terms of the new situations which continually arise is what fills the pages of most of the traditional works on the *halacha*.[15]

---

11 The fight against idolatry as the central motif of Biblical Judaism has been championed convincingly by Ezekiel Kaufman in his HISTORY OF THE JEWISH FAITH. It is the opening sentence of the eight volume work, and while the first chapter of vol. 1 deals with it intensively, it is continued throughout the whole.

12 The origin of this distinction and its authority, is completely lost to us, most unfortunately. It can only be described as an organic development. See Waxman, HISTORY OF JEWISH LITERATURE, vol. 1, pp. 50-54.

13 For the derivation and meaning of the term, see the articles "Halakah" and "Halakot" in the JEWISH ENCYCLOPEDIA, vol. 6, p. 163 b. A better and more inclusive exposition of the term and its place in Judaism is given in the article. "Halachah" in the UNIVERSAL JEWISH ENCYCLOPEDIA,, vol. 5, pp. 172-175, particularly sections 1 and 3.

14 A good definition, including a discussion of the way in which something becomes *halacha* is to be found in Strack, INTRODUCTION TO TALMUD, pp. 6-7.

15 The character of the *Halacha* as contrasted with the *Aggada* is brought out most clearly in Bialik's essay "The Halacha and the Aggada" but to the detriment of the

This latter point should indicate that the fixity of the *halacha* is somewhat relative and not absolute in Judaism. That is, the *halacha* was not set once in such a way that there could never be any development or change. It was rather given in a form which contains within it a principle of growth and development. In times of crisis even direct commands of the Torah may be abrogated, and under normal circumstances the rulings of a competent scholar are considered as equivalent in authority to Sinaitic revelation. At a given moment in history two teachers may disagree as to the *halacha* and the followers of each are considered as fulfilling their religious duty.[16]

Yet insofar as there is binding authority in Judaism it is here, in the realm of the *halacha*. Obviously then Judaism feels it has real knowledge here. What then does the *halacha* contain?

It does not contain statements of belief or outlines of theological principles. The one exception to this known to me, the necessity of believing that resurrection is taught in the Torah, was obviously a matter of inter-party strife and hence a political expedient.[17]

The *halacha* deals almost exclusively with the conduct of the Jew. This covers such ritual affairs as holidays and observances and ethical considerations such as involved in civil law and social obligations. Such distinctions are, of course, unknown to it, but all actions from awakening until sleep, from birth to death are part of "the way".

But the *halacha* does contain some regulations which come close to manifest statements of theoretical principle. So for example the laws concerning idols and idolatry are given in great detail. A considerable corpus exists with regard to the treatment of God's name, the tetragrammaton. This may never be mentioned according to rabbinic law, and elaborate precautions must be taken both to treat it with respect and to avoid accidentally vocalizing something like it.[18] While this is in large measure a magical consideration, it is another example of the negative ingredient in Jewish religious knowledge: man may not presume to equality with God and thus call Him by His name, yet man can know what God's name is. (To pursue the matter; yet we know only the consonants, for the correct knowledge of the vowels has been lost.)

So too the *halacha* regulates the times, the order and the contents of the prayers. But the latter is not done in terms of this phrase or that idea as

---

Halacha. For an opposite statement, clarifying the value of the fixity of the *Halacha,* see Louis Ginzberg, ON JEWISH LAW AND LORE, the esssay "The Significance of the Halachah" particularly pages 77-79.

16 Montefiore and Loewe, A RABBINIC ANTHOLOGY, p. 163, and A. Cohen EVERYMAN'S TALMUD, p. 157 for the references in English.

17 Finkelstein THE PHARISEES, vol. 1, pp. 157-158.

18 JEWISH ENCYCLOPEDIA, art. "Names of God", vol. 9, pp. 160-165.

at a Church Council in formulating a creed. Rather, the already traditional prayers are given their proper place in the service and differing versions are each assigned an appropriate place. Occasionally we hear of the composition of special prayers for the service but not of debates as to whether this idea or that was a necesary component of Jewish prayer.[19]

The *halacha* thus gives us no manifest information about Jewish religious ideas. It has occasionally been suggested that one might trace the theological assumptions of the *halacha* and thus derive the required Jewish belief implicit in the practice of Judaism, but the difficulties in the way have made the task impossible.[20] Indeed when one considers the many minds and circumstances which combined to make up the *halacha*, it is unlikely that any integrated, systematic view of Judaism would be found underlying the *halacha* as a whole. This in its turn is evidence that Judaism would seem to indicate that it knows really, only what God would have us do, not what He is, or the like. Ideas are left for the realm of the *aggada*.[21]

The *aggada* by contrast is flexible, open and unfixed. One may find the most contradictory statements within it and there is no penalty attached to differences in this realm. In post-Talmudic times one often hears the dictum "one does not debate aggadic interpretations." Here the imagination is given free reign and anthropomorphisms and anthropopathisms abound.

Jewish religious ideas come within the realm of *aggada*, which is to say that the classic rabbinic statements of Jewish belief are aggadic, not halachic statements.[22] If one examines almost any work on Judaism's beliefs he will note that the passages cited from the rabbis are almost never from legal, that is binding, material but are aggadic.

This should not be taken to mean that there are no limits at all to aggadic interpretation. In early rabbinic times we hear condemnation of

19 Idelsohn, Jewish Liturgy, pp. 22-33.
20 Ginzberg's "Pioneer Study", note 15, despite his unique competence in this area is not convincing, showing rather the subjectivity of such an enterprise rather than producing firm and authoritative results.
21 On the *aggada* in general, see Strack, p. 7; the article *"Haggalah"* in the Jewish Encyclopedia, vol. 6, p. 141a; the article *"Haggadah,"* longer and more helpful, in the Universal Jewish Encyclopedia, vol. 5, pp. 155-156.
22 Montefiore and Loewe, p. 131; B. Heller, Authority in Judaism, p. 326; and the lecture of Leo Baeck "Jewish Theology Today" reported in *Commentary Magazine* (June 1950, vol. 9, no. 6), pp. 571-2.
23 I know of no systematic treatement of this theme and have had to dredge these from my recollection of previous studies of aggadic texts.
24 So Baeck maintains that the kind of codification of the *halacha* is impossible in the realm of the *aggada*, i.e., a creed may not be made, p. 572b.
25 S. Schechter, Some Aspects of Rabbinic Theology, pp. 17 and 20, and note that this follows a most careful statement of the difficulties. This introduction too could have been cited as a fine statement of the mobility of the *aggada*.
26 *Judaism*, vol. 1, p. vii.

those who "show themselves interpreting the Torah", a phrase of much debated meaning. It seems clear there were no fixed limits for the *aggada* but rather that when aggadic interpretations proceeded to a point where it was felt they passed beyond the border of Judaism, they were condemned. Over a period of time there came to be certain specific areas which are not permitted, such as the doctrine of the "two powers", but we cannot find any general principles limiting the scope of the *aggada*.[23]

This may explain from the intellectual side why Judaism has never had a creed or dogmas in the Christian sense of the term. Ideas are in the area where free expression is permitted.[24] The implications of this for Jewish religious knowledge are clear: Classic Judaism did not think it possessed knowledge of a metaphysical sort.

Does this mean that Judaism had no beliefs, that there are no ideas basic to the Jewish religion? Not at all. We are assured by the most competent students of rabbinic Judaism that the unity of its ideational structure outweighs its divergences.[25] Moore can even speak of the "definitive form" of Judaism.[26] But where Christianity has been based on an idea of God which involved elaboration of concepts of sin and atonement, Judaism has been based on the dedication of a people to the service of God.[27] Ideas are crucial to the former, but actions have this role in the latter. Jewish theology must be understood in its own terms, not in those of another faith whose primary notion here is alien to it. In Judaism theology is a flexible area though there are certain major tendencies to be found within its development.

The division of Jewish religious discourse into *halacha* and *aggada* has continued unchanged through all of Jewish history until modern times. Even the philosophical activity of the middle ages did not alter this two-part language of faith coming as it did so many centuries after Judaism had fixed these basic categories of its intellectual activity. The philosophy itself was a form of *aggada* as the varying size and emphases of the "creeds" formulated by the philosophers show.[28] None of them ever became official, and though Maimonides' thirteen principles were often included in the prayerbook, their repetition was only desirable, not required.[29]

The philosophers did indeed think that we could know a great deal religiously with certainty. They all provided proofs for the existence of God and His unity. Many of them felt they had demonstrated free will and explained providence. In all of this there is some considerable variation with no authority available to render a decision and no tradition requiring such a decision to produce one where none existed.

---

27. *Ibid.*, vol. 1, pp. 219-234.
28 Husik, p. 1 and see the article "Articles of Faith" in the JEWISH ENCYCLOPEDIA, vol. 1, p. 148-152.
29 Hertz, THE AUTHORIZED DAILY PRAYER BOOK, p. 249.

Yet even here, the high point of Jewish religious knowledge, an outstanding feature of all the major thinkers is their emphasis that our knowledge of God is most true when it is negative. Two of the major figures even deny the value of philosophic speculation, Crescas from an internal point of view[30] and Halevi from that of living religion.[31] Yet even the professed rationalists follow Bahya's course in emphasizing the negative attributes of God.[32]. The doctrine of negative attributes reaches its heights precisely in the most rational of all Jewish thinkers, Maimonides, who flatly states that the negative attributes are the only true ones.[33] It is hard not to see here the direct extension of the prohibitions of idolatry and pronouncing the name of God. Judaism does not claim knowledge about God as it does about His law for man. It is probably true that Maimonides' great legal code. *The Strong Hand* was of more significance to Judaism than his philosophic *Guide for the Perplexed.* It should be no surprise after this that the Guide itself has as its climax and conclusion a section on the meaning and validity of the law.[34]

It is of interest to compare with this, even briefly, the position of the foremost contemporary systematic interpreters of Judaism. Mordecai Kaplan does not hesitate to discuss the nature of God, even going so far as to define Him and to insist that it is by means of such definition that Jewish religious belief can be revived.[35] This implies an enormous reliance upon the competence of human reason and langauge, though we do not find in Kaplan's major work any detailed treatment of this theme. The definition of God in itself is a radical deviation from historical Judaism though Kaplan obviously feels the peril of our time requires this bold step.[36]

By contrast Martin Buber is keenly aware of what we do not know about God. Though we meet Him as person, we may not even say He is personal, but only that He meets us in the way we meet other persons. We know that He is, but that is all we really know. Having known Him we feel the need to live on the basis of this meeting and give this urge concrete form, primarily moral, possibly ritual — but we do not know His

---

30 Husik, 389-391. He was, however, one who insisted on some positive attributes, but just those which would make a living religious relation between man and God possible.

31 *Ibid.,* pp. 154-155.

32 *Ibid.,* pp. 86, 94-95.

33 *Ibid.,* pp. 264-266.

34 *Ibid.,* pp. 294-302.

35 "The Meaning of God in Modern Jewish Religion", pp. vi and vii, 9-29, 330-368.

36 This type of argument makes it hard to believe that this idea of God is anything more than an instrument of national survival. In other words, the criterion for a proper definition of God seems to be that which will best help the Jewish nation survive. Either this is the most far-reaching kind of knowledge or else it is a rather elaborately phrased effort at human manipulation.

will as content; religious forms are only our creation based on our encounter.[37]

The more fully traditional view is maintained by Abraham Heschel. What we know best and clearest is what God wants of us. Heschel rejects all symbolic, anti-traditional notions of the commandments and insists that they are what God wants of us. Any other understanding of Judaism he considers a mockery.[38] Indeed, though he begins his philosophy of religion with the radical amazement through which he finds God, it seems reasonably clear that it must be because of the voice heard at Sinai, the basis of his philosophy of Judaism, that his radical amazement leads him to God rather than elsewhere.[39]

Yet, the decline of the traditional form of Jewish practice would indicate that most Jews no longer agree that what Judaism knows best is what God actually wants of us, at least as Judaism has previously understood this. For today's Jew, as for today's Christian, doubt is an integral element of faith and hence knowledge, in the technical sense, is not what religion affords him. Since providing such knowledge has not been an essential feature of Jewish religion in pre-modern times perhaps the flexible Jewish attitude toward religious ideas may prove particularly adaptable to the contemporary situation. As to knowledge of "The Law", the Reform movement differs from Conservative and Orthodox Judaism on the question of the *halacha,* rather than on matters of *aggada.* For Orthodoxy, the *halacha* is nearly absolute and while capable of change, not quickly subject to social change or style. The Conservative Jews believe Judaism cannot be maintained without the maintenance of the *halacha* though they insist it is natively flexible enough to meet the current changed Jewish social situation. The Reform Jews take the more radical position, that one may claim binding authority only for matters of moral conduct and basic relation to God (prayer, study and the like) but that all ceremonial and ritual must be recognized as human creations, though many are still of worth and beauty.[40] Even in dispute the center of Jewish concern remains Jewish action. Jews are not today as certain as they once were of what God wants them to do. But they know they do not have enough certainty about religious doctrines to make them the center of their debates. They care about deeds and must think they know something of what God wants them to do, otherwise they would not care so much about different ways of living one's Jewish faith.

---

37 Maurice Friedman, MARTIN BUBER, pp. 70-76.
38 Heschel's vigorous poetic polemic is clearly enunciated in his essay "Symbolism and Jewish Faith", pp. 53-79 in RELIGIOUS SYMBOLISM, ed. F. Ernest Johnson, as well as in his MAN'S QUEST FOR GOD, chapters 3 and 4 which were first addresses to rabbinic bodies.
39 MAN IS NOT ALONE, pp. 241-4. This is precisely the theme of GOD IN SEARCH OF MAN, his philosophy (sic) of Judaism.
40 Samuel Cohen, commenting on the paper of B. Heller, pp. 381-383.

Raymond S. Brown, S.S.

THE IMPACT ON CATECHETICS OF OUR NEW APPROACHES TO THE BIBLE AND TO THEOLOGY

In this essay I wish, first, to explain why there is a type of crisis in theology today, and, second, to discuss how this affects the teaching of Catholic doctrine. Of course, I do not pretend to have a *complete* insight into either the theological crisis or its effect on doctrinal teaching, nor do I pretend that I can give totally satisfactory solutions. I shall be quite satisfied if I can add to our mutual understanding of theological development and doctrinal teaching, for I think that one of the greatest dangers facing the Catholic Church in America today is a polarization arising from a lack of understanding.

I. THE CRISIS IN THEOLOGY

Let me begin with the crisis implicit in current Catholic theological development. Theology is an attempt to give expression to our faith in God and our understanding of how he has worked in the world. In the course of Christian history theology has developed, not smoothly but in spurts. Too often, in describing theological development, we have used the imagery of a mainstream flowing smoothly down the ages, fed by gentle rains and small tributaries. But if one wishes to use the river imagery, a much truer historical picture would be that of a stream, at times placid and even sluggish, but at other times violently agitated by floodwaters, as swollen tributaries pour into it their soil-laden currents, changing its color and even the direction of its flow. By the tributaries I mean the great contributions to Christian theology at various periods of history when new bodies of knowledge were made part of our religious heritage. One may think of the upheaval in Christian theology in the fourth to the sixth centuries as the tributary of Greco-Roman knowledge, especially Platonic philosophy, gave new color and direction to teachings that had their headwaters in a Semitic world. Or again, the upheaval that occurred in the high Middle Ages when Aristotelian thought, which came by the route of Arabian commentators and Christian thinkers, like Thomas Aquinas, poured into the Christian mainstream and once more changed the hue and direction. Or even the 16th century when both the Reformation and the Renaissance had their turbulent effect on Catholic theology.

And in every period of major theological change there has been resistance to the new ideas and the new knowledge that were being put to the service of Christianity. We must not forget how bitterly oppoosed in

RAYMOND S. BROWN, S.S., is Auburn Profesor of Biblical Studies at Union Theological Seminary, New York City.

their own times were the inaugurators of Catholic theological progress, even if latter centuries justified them. Jerome's magnificent attempt to bring the Church to the "Hebraic truth" of the Old Testament was fought by Augustine on the ground that the *Greek* translation of the Scriptures had been used in the past. Positions taken by Thomas Aquinas were regarded as dangerous innovations and departures from tradition by influential contemporaries of his day. Propositions held by Thomas along with others were condemned after his death by the bishop of Paris.

This understanding of the irregular, spasmodic growth of theology in the past, with its accompanying hostile divisiveness, may enable us to grasp a little better the period of tremendous theological change in which we are living — a period when another tributary, that of knowledge flowing from recently developed sciences, pours its waters into the Christian mainstream of thought. Only those unaware of great theological changes in the past will be astounded by theological changes in the present. And it is no surprise that the present theological changes are once more producing divisive results in the Catholic community. On the one side (and inevitably) there will be a naive enthusiasm as if the new scientific knowledge and methods had all the answers - an enthusiasm that mistakes the tributary for the mainstream. On the other side, and more dangerously, there is the equally inevitable rigid opposition to the new knowledge. Once more the simplistic arguments against change will be brought forward. To admit that there can be theological change is to say that the Church of the past was wrong. How can we learn new things about Jesus Christ 2,000 years after he lived? Such arguments stem from the failure to recognize the *human* component in all past (as well as present) phrasings of God's revelation. God and Jesus have always been understood through the prism of human minds limited in what they can grasp by the interpretive skills of their times. A God described in Semitic categories was understood differently from a God described in Platonic categories. Yet neither the Semitic nor the Platonic insight was exhaustive, nor did they totally agree. And today a God looked at through a world view aware of developments in the physical and social sciences will be understood differently from a God reflected upon by a medieval mind dominated by Aristotelian categories.

If one gives proper emphasis to the different human components in man's seeking to know God down through the ages, then it does not make sense to ask why the past did not formulate theology the way we do, when we have at our disposal a body of knowledge that was not available to the past. The fairest way of judging Christian theological endeavors of the past is on the basis of whether or not they used the knowledge at their disposal. And we Christians of today are liable to be judged harshly by the future if we do not use the new knowledge at our disposal in reflecting upon God. Those voices of the extreme right that want us to turn our back on all modern theological development would have the effect of reducing the Church to a small sect frightened by the times in which it lives and seeking refuge in the past. The larger Christian vision is that, if there is new knowledge, we can use it to understand God anew, because knowledge that is true can always be put to the service of truth.

Changed Attitude on Biblical Criticism

I have spoken in broad terms of new knowledge, stemming from a scientific mode of thought, that has been influencing contemporary theological insights. Let me illustrate this for you from the theological field I know best: Catholic biblical studies in the 20th century.

Physical, historical, and linguistic methods, known to us only in approximately the last 100 years, have produced a scientifically critical study of the Bible, a study that has revolutionized views held in the past about the authorship, origin, and dating of the biblical books, about how they were composed, and about what their authors meant. In the first 40 years of this century (1900 to 1940 approximately) the Roman Catholic Church very clearly and officially took a stance against such biblical criticism. The Modernist heretics at the beginning of the century employed biblical criticism, and the official Roman condemnations of Modernism made little distinction between the possible intrinsic validity of biblical criticism and the theological misuse of it by the Modernists. Between 1905 and 1915 the Pontifical Biblical Commission in Rome issued a series of conservative decisions on the composition and authorship of the Bible. Although phrased with nuance, these decisions ran against the trends of contemporary Old and New Testament investigation. Yet Catholic scholars were obliged to assent to these decisions and to teach them.

After 40 years of rigorous opposition, the Catholic Church in the 1940's under the pontificate of Pope Pius XII made an undeniable about-face in attitude toward biblical criticism. The encyclical *Divino Afflante Spiritu* (1943) instructed Catholic scholars to use the methods of a scientific approach to the Bible that had hitherto been forbidden to them. Within about ten years teachers trained in biblical criticism began to move into Catholic classrooms in seminaries and colleges, so that the mid-1950's really marked the watershed. By that time the pursuit of the scientific method had led Catholic exegetes to abandon almost all the positions on biblical authorship and composition taken by Rome at the beginning of the century. No longer did they hold that Moses was the substantial author of the Pentateuch, that the first chapters of Genesis were really historical, that Isaiah was one book, that Matthew was the first Gospel written by an eyewitness, that Luke and Acts were written in the 60's, that Paul wrote Hebrews, etc. This dramatic change of position was tacitly acknowledged in 1955 by the secretary of the Pontifical Biblical Commission who stated that now Catholic scholars had *"complete freedom"* with regard to those decrees of 1905-1915 except where they touched on faith or morals (and very few of them did).

Obviously this turn-about was not without opposition and anguish. Inevitably, clergy and religious who had been trained according to the earlier anti-critical positions were appalled at hearing a new generation of Catholics now teaching the very ideas they had been taught to consider as wrong and even heretical. But, in general, the change sparked a renewed interest in the Bible, indeed the greatest flowering of biblical study and writing that the Roman Catholic Church had ever seen. And so, wisely, the Church did not reverse the direction taken by Pius XII, despite the objections of those who were opposed to it. Rather, his ideas on the Bible became part of the final schema on Revelation (*Dei Verbum*) of Vatican II.

In fact, the Church pushed on beyond the positions of Pius XII. The 1964 Pontifical Biblical Commission's *Instruction on the Historical Truth of the Gospels* dealt frankly with the delicate question of how accurately the Gospels report the words and deeds of Jesus. Much to the delight of Catholic biblical critics, the commission made clear to Catholics that the Gospels were *not* literal, chronological accounts of the words and deeds of Jesus but are the product of a development through years of preaching, selection, synthesizing and explication. And, as a further sign of the Church's commitment to biblical criticism, in 1972 Pope Paul VI restructured the Pontifical Biblical Commission so that scholars, instead of being merely consultors, now constituted the commission itself. Those scholars whom he named were, in several instances, men who had suffered in the long battle to get biblical criticism accepted (David Stanley and Stanislaus Lyonnet); and the new secretary of the commission, Bishop Descamps of Louvain, was a pioneer among Catholics in applying critical analysis to the resurrection narratives of the Gospels. All those appointed were men dedicated to the scientific approach to the Bible that is perfectly consonant with the best in Catholicism — men who would never have us go back to the fearful spirit that governed the dark days at the beginning of this century.

Pluralism In Church History

In the history I have given you, I have told you how for the first 40 years of the century the Roman Catholic Church rejected biblical criticism and then how in the next 30 years it came to accept much of that criticism. That brings us up to the 1970's and the last third of the century. I venture to predict that this period into which we are now entering will be taken up with the impact of biblical criticism on the Roman Catholic understanding of doctrine. But before I show why this is likely to come about, let me give a reminder that in talking about our growth in biblical knowledge, I have chosen only one example of the new knowledge that has been put at the service of theology in our times. Many other examples might be cited. If there has been a development of our scientific knowledge of the history of biblical times, the same may be said of our knowledge of the history of Christianity. An older pattern of uniform development with occasional heretical deviations is no longer tenable, and we have come to recognize that pluralism existed since the earliest days. As we reread today the records of Church disputes, and of the councils called to repudiate errors, we realize how the theology books of the last centuries have over-simplified the doctrinal conclusions based on such records. If we turn to moral or ethical theology, the availability of scientific psychology, sociology, and anthropology has challenged our generalizations about human behavior and its motives and the patterns of "natural law."

We may think too of the impact of ecumenism. Once more, for the first part of this century, the Roman Catholic Church was very apprehensive of world and regional ecumenical movements. Then suddenly, with Vatican II we embraced ecumenism with fervor. Dialogue group after dialogue group has been re-examining some of the most divisive questions of Christian theology and developing stances acceptable to both sides. Before 1965 it was virtually forbidden for Catholic students of theology to read the books of Protestant theologians and commentators without obtaining special permission or assurance that they were "safe." Now, I would guess, students in Catholic theology courses read as many non-Catholic works as Catholic ones. Obviously this broad reading, along with the presence of Protestant teachers in many Catholic institutions, brings new knowledge into the Catholic perspective.

And so in many fields besides the biblical, the knowledge explosion of our times is offering raw material for contemporary theological reflection. Yet, in a certain way this abundance of riches comes at a time when Catholic theology is not totally prepared to receive it. The years from 1700 to 1950 will probably be judged as a less productive period of Catholic thought, and indeed as a time when many attitudes were created that cause us difficulty today. Frightened by the upheavals of the Reformation, Catholic thinkers, of necessity, became apologetic in outlook — "apologetic" in the sense of defending past positions against the innovations of the reformers. Authority was more and more centralized in Rome in order to prevent further Protestant inroads; and often Catholic theological positions were established by Roman condemnations of dangerous ideas, with theologians left only to supply arguments for what was already decided. Frequently leadership and direction in Catholic theology came from papal encyclicals and pronouncements and the decrees of the Roman Congregations. One may object to this picture by citing the names of a Newman or a Scheeben or the Catholic Tübingen school, but the sparsity of such names in a period of 250 years is itself an attestation that theological thought was coming from the top down and not from the bottom up. The net result of all this is that we have become unaccustomed to theological innovation and tend to look on it askance, as if it were a usurpation to have theologians thinking for themselves.

However, if this general attitude that theology should "follow the leader" is an obstacle to the impace of the contemporary knowledge explosion on Catholic theology, there are other factors which will heighten the impact. If I may return to the biblical field, biblical criticism can have an enormous effect on theology precisely because the Second Vatican Council raised biblical exegesis from the status of second-class citizenship to which it has been reduced among Catholics by an over-reaction to the Protestant claim for its autonomy. The Council (*Dei Verbum* ii 9) stated that "sacred tradition and sacred scripture are to be accepted and venerated with the same sense of devotion and reverence." The living teaching office of the Church "is not above the word of God but serves it" and must listen to the word devoutly as part of the process of interpreting it (ii 10). The model, then, is not one of autonomy, either of tradition over scriptural interpretation (the popular Catholic model of post-reformation times) or of scriptual interpretation over Church tradition (a popular understanding of the Protestant position); the model is one of mutual influence. And this mutual influence will inevitably involve tension when one serves to modify the other in promoting the Church's grasp of God's truth.

Doctrine and Its Formulation

The possibility that biblical and other knowledge may modify tradition is heightened by another insight that has become respectable in Catholic circles in the aftermath of Vatican II. In the speech with which he opened the Council (Oct. 11, 1962), Pope John XXIII made one of the most important magisterial admissions of modern times: "The substance of the ancient doctrine of the deposit of faith is one thing, and the way in which it is presented is another." In other words the Pope opened the possibility of distinguishing between a revealed doctrine and the way in which it has been formulated. The key to biblical criticism was the recognition that, while the Scriptures are the word of God, they do not escape the limitations of history. Rather the Scriptures reflect the limited views current in specific periods of human history, and this historical context must be taken into account in interpreting the weight and import of their inspired message. And now the Pope's statement led many theologians to the conclusion that the doctrinal statements of the Church were under a similar historical limitation. While doctrinal formulations of the past capture an aspect of revealed truth, they do not exhaust it; they represent the limited insight of one period of Church history which can be *modified* in another period of Church history as Christians approach the truth from a different direction or with new tools of investigation.

Notice that I said "modified," for the majority of Catholic theologians maintain that past insights are not wiped out by subsequent developments. For them, a truly Christian sense of tradition limits the possibilities of change. In other words, when theologians like Avery Dulles speak of "this historical relativity of all doctrinal statements" (THE SURVIVAL OF DOGMA, p. 173), they are not rejecting the infallibility of past dogmas but are seeking to sharpen our understanding of the range of infallibility against an over-simplified concept that removes doctrinal statements from all limitations of space and time. Very often the "modification" that modern theological speculation makes possible is in bringing the Church to distinguish between those elements of previous formulations which are permanently helpful and those elements which are so time-conditioned that they can best be dispensed with. By way of example, the physical sciences, which have traced patterns of human evolution, and biblical criticism, which has given a better understanding of the type of literature represented by the early chapters of Genesis, have helped Catholics to see that in the ancient doctrine of God's creation of man it is *no longer necessary* to maintain that man's body was directly created by God from the earth, or that woman's body was directly created from man's. In times past such a direct creation of the body would have been considered part of the doctrine; today we continue to maintain the doctrine of creation without trying to rule out the possibility of evolution.

In this whole process wherein modern knowledge *contributes* toward reformulation or modification of ancient doctrine, the key word is "contribute." No theologians, no matter how impressive their evidence, can formulate Catholic doctrines. They can only make a contribution that must be assessed in the wider context of the Church's life guided by the Spirit. They can put their evidence at the service of the official magisterium which often by a tolerance of new theological views acknowledges the impact of the opinions of theologians. Thus, in the instance I cited, it would be foolish for us to expect that Catholic Church authorities will pronounce that man's body has evolved from a lower animal form — that is a question of science — but the fact that Catholic theologians are allowed to teach the possibility of evolution represents a change in the Catholic position.

The cooperation between theologians and the official magisterium of pope and bishops remains absolutely essential in a time of polarization toward extremes. I have pointed out that there is no major tendency among Catholic theologians to reject in any casual manner the doctrines of the past, but only to recognize their limitations; similarly there is no major tendency to usurp the authority of the magisterium and to pretend that theologians can formulate doctrine. On the other hand the positive attitude of the magisterium toward modern biblical studies and modern theology has been very beneficial precisely in preventing an exaggerated swing to the left.

The Ultra-Conservative Press

The continued support of the magisterium is all the more necessary now that a danger both to theology and magisterium has arisen on the right. With increasing frequency ultra-conservative or fundamentalist Catholics are usurping the authority of the magisterium by trying to condemn as heretical all theological speculation that shows any sign of nuance with regard to past doctrine. They do not respect the positions of the popes or the bishops who have permitted modern biblical and theological advances; rather these Catholic fundamentalists denounce as heretical the freer Catholic positions that have emerged from Vatican II. It is no accident that in the past six months several prominent American cardinals have had to denounce the irresponsibility of the arch-conservative sector of the Catholic press with its very negative attitude toward modern developments in the Church. And, we may note, in theological questions journalistic abuse is often the only road open to such Catholic fundamentalists, for their opinions have little or no scholarly respectability, and so Catholic colleges and universities and reputable Catholic scholarly periodicals will give them no voice. Despite the annoyance caused by their arch-conservatives, our great assurance for the future is that the real organs of Catholic theological education are solidly in the hands of those who accept modern insights.

Nevertheless, in the face of this tendency of right-wing vigilantes to pretend to be able to speak for Catholicism when they attack every new idea, it is important that the bishops support the legitimacy and the rights of responsible Catholic theological investigaion, so that it will be clear in the minds of the Catholic people that there is nothing unCatholic about studying the theological problems that have arisen in our time. We must dispel once and for all the fundamentalist supposition that a theologian is more loyal to the Church if he does not recognize that a difficult problem exists. The trust between theologians and bishops that arose at Vatican II led to great progress in the Church; and theologians must take care on their part not to let that trust be eroded. They must make it apparent to the bishops that there is no danger to the Church from responsible modern theological reflection, no matter how sensitive the areas it probes. The real danger is from those ultra-liberals who scorn serious theology and from those ultra-conservatives who see in every investigation a threat to faith.

II.   THE EFFECT ON THE TEACHING OF CATHOLIC DOCTRINE

Thus far I have been attempting to explain why we are in a time of theological change so acute that it may be called a crisis. We have become conscious that all human formulations of truth are limited, and in the light of vast new bodies of knowledge we are attempting to rethink past understandings of divine truth to see if enriching new insights and modifications are possible. But in such a time of change, how do we communicate Catholic doctrine to new generations of Christians? Because theologians are rethinking aspects of past doctrines, are teachers of doctrine to become tongue-tied as if there were nothing certain that they could pass on? — as if everything doctrinal were "up-for-grabs"? Personally I can think of no greater disaster for Catholicism.

But before I face directly the problem of communication of doctrine in a time of theological change, let me comment on a rather simplistic way of attempting to solve the problem. I refer to a misunderstanding of the distinction between "faith" and "theology." We cannot answer our problem fully by stating that in catechetics teachers are communicating Catholic faith independently of theological disputation. When "faith" is used in such a statement, what is generally meant is the content of belief — the formulations of faith, the dogmas, the doctrines. But such a sharp distinction between the formulations of our faith and theological discussions may give the erroneous impression that such formulations were not the product of theology, as man reflected upon his God, but rather came down ready-made from heaven. This is simply not so. *Every formulation that we accept as part of the contents of our faith is the product of theological reflection.*

While God has revealed himself in creation and in history (particularly in the history of Israel and in the life of Jesus and his Church), he has not directly revealed a body of formulas. The vocalizing of revelation, the development of the formulas that capture for each age necessary insights into revelation, is achieved by God's guiding *men* in their understanding and reflection to a grasp of truth. God has also guided his Church to recognize formulas that are more adequate than others to express divine truth (and, in addition, to reject some formulas as inadequate or false). Consequently, the distinction between (the formulas of) "faith" and "theology" is really a distinction between *theological formulas that the Church has made her own* by declaring that they reflect divine truth and *theological formulas to which the Church has made no formal commitment*. By emphasizing the fact that theological reflection is involved in both (the formulas of) "faith" and "theology," we see that it is too simple to say: Teach the faith and forget about theology. This is especially true today since modern theological discussion is not focused on marginal questions but on a contemporary reunderstanding of the *fundamental* teachings of Christianity.

Catechetics and Formulations of Faith

If teachers cannot facilely ignore theological discussion when they are communicating the formulas of faith, how then do we avoid having catechetics reduced to uncertainties? It is here that our understanding of the *validity* of past formulations plays a role. Precisely because past formulations reflect a *valid* if limited grasp of divine truth, we can use those formulations, provided that we are aware of both their validity and their limitations. As a good, practical example of this, let us turn our attention to the January 1973 publication by the American bishops of the *Basic Teachings for Catholic Religious Education*.

First of all, the bishops have taken an admirable step in insuring that our catechetics should communicate content as well as attitude. It may be true that in the past we were too content-oriented in catechetics, too interested in formulas rather than in formation of Christian character. But it is also true that there has been recently a danger of over-reaction in the other direction, as if the learning of formulas and prayers were not part of Christian education. In a catechetical period that is laudably interested in formation, the bishops have insured that the ancient content of our faith is not forgotten.

Second, the bishops have expressed their *Basic Teachings* in a way that shows a sensitivity about both the validity and the limitations of past conceptions of doctrine. They cover the necessary span of Christian teaching: The Triune God; his creation; Jesus, his Son, true God and true man; the incarnation and resurrection; the sacraments and the Church; man and his freedom; his sin, original and personal, and his morality; and finally the Virgin Mary, the Mother of God and the model of the Church — in short, all that we Christians should consider the authentic teachings of the faith. Yet, as far as I can see, the bishops have taken care *not* to include in the formulations of these ancient doctrines phrasings that would hinder the legitimate discussions of modern theology.

Let me give some examples. The bishops have spoken of God's creation of the world, but there is not a word against evolution and no indication that the Genesis account of creation must be taken literally. The bishops speak about the humanity of Jesus, mentioning the only difference that Scripture and the Council of Chalcedon make between his humanity and ours: he is like us in everything *except sin*. The bishops wisely stress that he is "the perfect man," which means that he has all the perfections that men have — but they never attribute to his humanity perfections that do not belong to men, for instance, omniscience. Thus, there is nothing in the bishops' document contrary to modern biblical and theological speculation which takes the limitations of Jesus' knowledge very seriously. Again, the bishops state that "by God's design the Church is a society with leaders, i.e., with a hierarchy," but they do not get into the disputed theological question of whether the hierarchy stems from the historical Jesus or whether it was developed under the guidance of the Spirit.

Catechetics and the Will of the Arch-Conservative Press

I could give many more examples showing the subtlety of the bishops' document and their care not to cause conflict with genuine theological interests. I emphasize this because in our polarized Church liberals may have a tendency to dismiss carelessly the bishops' *Basic Teachings* as old-fashioned and too content-oriented. This is to play into the hands of arch-conservatives who will be only too happy to monopolize this document and interpret it as a condemnation of modern theology. Indeed, the very week that the bishops approved the document, there appeared in the Catholic right-wing press the claim that the bishops had contradicted new theology at almost every point.

I have said above that the arch-conservative section of the Catholic press has usurped the authority of the Church's magisterium to judge what is orthodox in theology — these propagandists think they can condemn theologians as heretical. But more seriously they are trying to usurp the bishops' authority to determine what can be taught as Catholic doctrine to the youth. They do not hesitate to denounce catechisms approved by the bishops with an incredible demand to return to the Baltimore Catechism. Often they seek to set up their own catechetical schools to seal off the youth from any contact with ideas more enlightened than their own and thus to divide this group of Catholic youth from their confreres who attend the regular catechetical instruction. And now they will have the arrogance to impose on the bishops' *Basic Teachings* their own interpretations that go beyond what the bishops have said and to use these interpretations to frustrate the freedom the bishops have allowed. These voices from the extreme right are alienated and unhappy voices in the Roman Catholic Church today — that is a tragedy that I wish with all my heart could have been avoided. But it will be a greater tragedy if through a manipulation of catechetics which tries to turn the clock back on genuine Catholic theological progress, they succeed in creating a future generation of youth that will be even less at home in the Catholic movements of this century than their parents are.

An effective way for teachers of Catholic doctrine to combat this divisive tendency is to follow the lead the bishops have given us. Teachers should present in catechetics the fundamentals the bishops have underscored in their document, and yet at the same time pedagogically prepare the students for a future encounter with theological discussions about aspects of doctrine that the bishops have left open. For instance, we should teach the students the doctrine of original sin, and we should point out that this doctrine has been phrased in terms of the Adam and Eve story of Genesis (a story with which students should be made familiar). But we should stress that the Genesis story is only a vehicle for the doctrine of original sin and not the substance of the teaching. Moreover, in loyalty to modern biblical scholarship, we should point out that the Genesis story is not an exact historical account of the origins of man. Thereby we prepare students for the possibility that, under the impact of theological reflection, the Church may not always phrase the doctrine of original sin in terms of a sin committed by Adam and Eve as sole parents of the human race.

The kind of teaching I am suggesting requires a double effort: an effort to examine with precision the basic doctrines of our faith, such as those listed by the bishops; and an effort to keep abreast of modern theological discussion, so that the limitations of past understandings of those doctrines are not imposed on the students as if they had to be believed. The bishops have made clear their desire that teachers should not impose on students modern theological reflections as if they were doctrine, but that does not mean that teachers should not prepare the students for the effects of modern theological discussions. Nor does it mean that teachers can impose on students discredited or dubious theological reflections of the past simply because it causes less disturbance to parents. In the long run, a failure to prepare the students for modern insights into the limitations of our past understandings of truth equips a student poorly to face the world in which he or she will live. It is a dangerous invitation to a loss of faith through confusion.

Let us have the courage, then, to present our doctrines with an appreciation of their greatness; yet at the same time to prepare our students to survive in an age of theological change. It is a challenge, but a challenge that stems from a period of great Christian vitality. After several rather barren centuries in the history of Catholic theological thought, we have come alive again theologically. Let those who are afraid of the changes of our times condemn them; *our* task is to capitalize on the opportunity of our time to preach with joy the Good News of our faith in what God has done, not only what he has done in the past, but what he is doing today as well.

A respect for the past and an openness to the present is what I am urging. The recognition and communication of the valid insights in past doctrinal formulations *build values*. An openness to present insights and to what God has enabled us to see anew about his revelation in our times *gives meaning*. To neglect either the heritage of the past or the contribution of the present is a failure in *religious education*.

THE DIVINE WARRIOR AND THE WAR OF YAHWEH IN NAHUM

A few years ago, F. C. Fensham wrote:
One of the most astonishing facts of Old Testament research is the almost total neglect of the Book of Nahum. In the past decade or so only a few papers on Nahum were published. If this lack of interest can be detected somewhere, I think it is our task to go and search for it.[1]

I read this statement only after publishing my own NAHUM IN THE LIGHT OF NORTHWEST SEMITIC (*Biblica et Orientalia* 26; Rome: Biblical Institute Press, 1973), a work which is essentially a philological study. Fensham's words are a source of encouragement therefore to further research on Nahum. The following essay is a result of reflection on the works of three scholars in particular. Recently, P. D. Miller has published a significant contribution entitled *The Divine Warrior in Early Israel* (Harvard Semitic Monographs 5; Cambridge, Mass., Harvard University Press, 1973) a work which, as he acknowledges (p. 4), is an outgrowth of work done by his teacher, F. M. Cross, the second scholar to whose works we shall pay special attention.[2] The third scholar to be singled out is F. C. Fensham, who has written an important article on the Day of Yahweh,[3] and another on Nahum which has been referred to already at the beginning of this paper (see footnote 1).

A Hymn of Theophany: Na 1:2-8

The oracles of Nahum are introduced by a hymn of theophany which comprises 1:2-8 (possibly 1:2-9 or 10).[4]

2   A jealous and avenging God is Yahweh,
      avenging is Yahweh and a Lord of wrath.[5]
   Avenging is Yahweh on his foes,

KEVIN J. CATHCART is Professor of Semitic Languages, University College, Dublin, Ireland.

1 "Legal activities of the Lord according to Nahum," in BIBLICAL ESSAYS 1969: PROCEEDINGS OF THE TWELFTH MEETING OF DIE OU TESTAMENTIESE WERKGEMEENSKAP IN SUID-AFRIKA (Potchefstroom: Pro Rege-Pers Beperk, 1969), p. 13.

2 CANAANITE MYTH AND HEBREW EPIC: ESSAYS IN THE HISTORY OF THE RELIGION OF ISRAEL (Cambridge, Mass.: Harvard University Press, 1973). Abbreviated CANAANITE MYTH below.

3 "A Possible Origin of the Concept of the Day of the Lord," in BIBLICAL ESSAYS (1966) (see n. 1 above), pp. 90.97.

4 Cf. O. Eissfeldt, THE OLD TESTAMENT: AN INTRODUCTION (Oxford: Basil Blackwell, 1965), p. 414; G. Fohrer, INTRODUCTION TO THE OLD TESTAMENT (New York: Abingdon Press, 1968), p. 449.

5 Philological commentary on this version of Nahum 1:2-8 will be found in the writer's NAHUM IN THE LIGHT OF NORTHWEST SEMITIC, pp. 36-59, and notes will be given only when the translation differs from the one found in that work.

and he rages against his enemies.

3   Yahweh is slow to anger but great in power,
        and Yahweh will certainly not acquit (the guilty).
    In the whirlwind and in the storm is his way,
        and the clouds are the dust of his feet.

4   He rebukes the sea and dries it up,
        and all the rivers he parches.
    Bashan and Carmel wither,
        and the bloom of Lebanon withers.

5   The mountains shake before him,
        and the hills melt away.
    The earth is laid waste before him,
        the world and all who dwell in it.

6   Before his indignation who can stand,
        and who can rise in the heat of his anger?
    His wrath pours out like fire,
        and the rocks are broken up before him.

7   Yahweh is good, indeed[6] a fortress on the Day of distress,
    He cares for[7] those taking refuge in him when the flood
                                    sweeps over.

8   He will destroy his assailants,
        and his foes will pursue into Darkness.

As I have asserted elsewhere,[8] the language of this theophany of Yahweh is borrowed to a large extent from the Canaanite descriptions of the theophany of the storm god Ba'al. Reading the texts from Ugarit, one sees that Ba'al "thunders in the storm cloud" (UT 51:V:70),[9] and in UT 76:II:33, he is the god "Haddu, lord of the stormcloud" (*hd d'nn;* note Na 1:3, *w'nn 'bq rglyw,* "and the clouds are the dust of his feet"). On one occasion Ba'al is told: "Take your clouds, your wind, your rain-cloud, your rain" (UT, 67:V:6-7) and in the Assyrian recension of Atrahasis, the Babylonian story of the flood, Adad is described as riding on the winds: "Adad rode on the four winds, [his] asses."[10] Of particular importance is the theophany in UT, 51:VII:29-35, "Ba'al gives forth his holy voice, Ba'al repeats the utterance of his lips, His holy voice [shatters] the earth.

---

6 Taking the *lamed* as asseverative as suggested to me privately by Dr. Duane Christensen.

7 Note Ugaritic *il dyd'nn,* "The god friendly to him," which supports our comments in NAHUM IN THE LIGHT OF NORTHWEST SEMITIC, pp. 55-56, and consult B. Margulis, "A New Ugaritic Farce (RŠ 24.258)," UGARIT-FORSCHUNGEN 2 (1970), pp. 132, 134.

8 NAHUM IN THE LIGHT OF NORTHWEST SEMITIC, pp. 41, 47, 52.

9 UT — C. H. Gordon, UGARITIC TEXTBOOK (Analecta Orientalia 38; Rome: Pontifical Biblical Institute, 1965).

10 Cf. W.G. Lambert and A.R. Millard, ATRA-HASIS: THE BABYLONIAN STORY OF THE FLOOD (Oxford: Clarendon Press, 1969), p. 123.

At his roar the mountains quake, Afar [   ] before Sea, The highplaces of the earth shake,"[11] and in one of the Tell El-Amarna texts we read: "who gives his voice from heaven like Haddu, and all the mountains shake at his voice."[12] When Ba'al had fought the dragon Lotan and destroyed him, "The heavens withered and drooped, Like the loops of your garment" (UT, 67:I:4-5).[13]

Further discussion of the theophany in UT, 51:VII:29-35 is rewarding. Ba'al is finally in his palace, for by conquering his enemy Sea (*ym*), he now establishes his kingship. After the final battle with Sea, Ba'al marched triumphantly to his palace, capturing cities and towns on the way, and having arrived in his palace, uttered his "holy voice". The actual battle between Ba'al and Sea is described in UT, 68. Several times Sea is called Prince Sea and Judge River. Precisely this parallelism of *ym* || *nbr* is found in Na 1:4. The Theophany in Nahum portrays Yahweh the Divine Warrior who has conquered Sea and drawn reaction from the cosmos. The first seven lines of UT, 51:VII, are broken, but, as Miller[14] points out, they probably contain an account of the final battle with Sea. After an analysis of UT, 51:VII, and Biblical parallels like Psalm 29 and Psalm 18, Miller concludes that the "picture of Yahweh as storm god, warrior, and king bears striking resemblance to that of Ba'al in the same roles in Canaanite mythology."[15] Indeed it is a major thrust of Miller's work to show that just as the gods in Canaanite mythology fought wars to assert their positions in the divine world, and "to save or punish peoples of the earth,"[16] so also in Early Israel the "primal acts of deliverance and the process of forming a people or nation was centered in these wars of Yahweh when a commander of the armies of heaven and earth, he fought for Israel."[17] Of particular interest is Miller's point that the idea of Yahweh as warrior and leader of the heavenly army ("the hosts") coming to Israel's aid is not confined to older sources, but is found, for example, in the later prophetic books, and in apocalyptic literature.

When dealing with the earlier poetry, Miller shows that in poems like Ex 15; Dt 33:2-5, 26-29; Jgs 5 and Ps 68, we have basic elements of theophany, establishment of kingship, and settlement of Israel in the

---

11 Translation of F. M. Cross, CANAANITE MYTH, p. 149.
12 Cf. J.A. Knudtzon (ed.), DIE EL-AMARNA TAFELN (Leipzig: Heinrichs, 1915), text 147: 14-15.
13 Cross, CANAANITE MYTH, p. 150.
14 THE DIVINE WARRIOR, p. 33.
15 *Ibid.*, p. 37. Pertinent too is Miller's observation (p. 28) that in the Ugaritic myths Ba'al parallels Marduk as a god seeking kingship. From a history of religions point of view, Yahweh, Ba'al and Marduk are of the same "phenomenological type." Our own remarks (NAHUM, pp. 40 and 46) comparing Yahweh in Na 1:2-3 and Marduk in *ludlul bēl nēmeqi* I, 3-10, may be more pertinent than we first thought.
16 *Ibid.*, p. 64.
17 *Ibid.*

promised land or deliverance of Yahweh's people.[18] For Yahweh's actions, including his battle with chaos, are for the deliverance of his people. When Miller comes to examine later prophetic writings (e.g. Is 13:1ff.; Jl 4:9ff.; Is 40:26 and 45:12; and Zech 14), he stresses the appearance of the Divine warrior theme and the wars of Yahweh imagery especially in connection with the Day of Yahweh.

The theophany in Nahum is not discussed by Miller. This is not a criticism, for he says that he is concerned only with those passages which focus on the "march of Yahweh and his armies."[19] Although Cross has little to say about Nahum, he is of the opinion, nevertheless, that Nahum 1 ("the war oracles in Nahum 1") is from the sixth century and from the same background as Is 24:19-23; 26:21; 34:4, 8-10; 35:1-10; 42:13-15; 50:2f.; 59:16-19; 63:19b-64:2; and 66:15f. — all these passages, according to Cross, are proto-apocalyptic along with, for example, Zech 14:5b-9.[20] The precise dating of Nahum will not concern us here. We wish rather to emphasize that if one recognizes in Na 1 the motif of the Divine Warrior, then the book of Nahum as a whole can be seen in a new light.

The sacking of Nineveh and the overthrow of the Assyrians were historical acts of war by the Babylonians, but they were also acts of war by Yahweh. The "scatterer" ($mpyṣ$) [21] who attacks Nineveh (Na 2:2) is the "jealous and avenging God ($'l qnw' wnqm$) of Na 1:2,[22] the "Lord of wrath" ($b'l ḥmh$), who rages against his enemies. He is a mighty warrior ($gdl kḥ$). The storm god who overcomes Sea (Na 1:3-4) to establish his dominion, is the same Yahweh who "establishes political-historical order."[23] It is Yahweh the king who decides the fate of the king of Assyria (Na 1:14). When the victorious Ba'al has been enthroned in his palace "Neither king nor no-king, shall establish the earth as a dominion."[24] This is noteworthy. Of Yahweh's kingship, Miller writes: "Unlike the basic tenet of most Near Eastern mythology, his kingship was established not primarily by the mythological battle of the gods, but by the historical victories of Yahweh and his earthly and heavenly armies over

---

18 *Ibid.*, p. 86.
19 *Ibid.*, p. 135.
20 Canaanite Myth, p. 170.   On p. 135, he dates Na 1:4 "from the end of the seventh century B.C. (at the earliest)."
21 With *mpyṣ*, "the Scatterer," compare *ypṣw* in Nm 10:35, "Arise, Yahweh, let your enemies be scattered (*wypṣw*)," part of an archaic formula according to Cross, Canaanite Myth, p. 100.
22 With *'l nqm* and *nqm yhwh*, one must now compare the Phoenician personal name, *nqm'l*, and the Ugaritic personal name *nqmd*. For full discussion and references, see now, F. L. Benz, Personal Names in the Phoenician and Punic Inscriptions (Studia Pohl 8; Rome: Biblical Institute Press, 1972), p. 363. Most interesting too is Miller's translation (The Divine Warrior, p. 41) of Ugaritic *gmr hd*, an epithet of Ba'al, by "Annihilator Hadad" or "Avenger Hadad."
23 Cross, Canaanite Myth, p. 58.
24 Miller, The Divine Warrior, p. 36.

the enemies of Israel."[25] The warriors (the *gbwry kḥ* of Ps 103:20) of Yahweh are fighting with the earthly *gbry ḥyl,* "the mighty warriors" of the Babylonians (Na 2:4), to conquer the enemies of Israel. Because Yahweh loves Israel, "he cares for those seeking refuge in him" (Na 1:7),[26] and he will deliver them (Na 1:13).

The Messenger of Yahweh

Worthy of special attention is the appearance of the Divine Messenger (*mbśr*) in Na 2:1. P. Miller in studying the "Divine Assembly,"[27] both in Syria-Palestine and in Israel, notes the particular role of the "messengers" of the god or gods. In Israel the "messenger" could be a prophet.[28] Certainly the messenger proclaimed the will and message of the deity. The message from Yahweh, as noted by Miller,[29] was often a judicial verdict. The message of the *mbśr* in Nahum is delivered in imperatives, typical of message formulae in Ugaritic also.[30]

2:1   Celebrate your feasts, O Judah!
   Fulfill your vows.

and, addressing Nineveh,

2:2   Guard your fortifications, watch the road;
   Strengthen your loins,
   Summon all your strength.

In short, the messenger is announcing that Yahweh is about to fight a great battle and win a great victory, and deliver his people. The deliverance of Israel and restoration of Israel's fortunes is stressed.[31] Cf. Na 2:3.

The Language of 1:10; 2:4-14; 3:1-18

Chapter 2 and 3 of the book of Nahum are concerned with the fall of Assyria and the sacking of Nineveh, and in language which is frequently like language used in those passages speaking of the Day of Yahweh. The following examples will illustrate:

Na 1:10   *'klw kqš ybš ml'*
   They will be consumed like very dry chaff.

Jl 2:5   *kqwl lhb 'š 'klh qš*
   Like the crackling flame of fire consuming the chaff.

Ob :18   they shall burn them and consume them.

---

25 *Ibid.,* p. 83.
26 On the possible covenantal significance of *yd'* in Na 1:7, and also of *ṭwb,* cf. Fensham, BIBLICAL ESSAYS 1969, p. 18. For interesting comments on the "friends" of Yahweh in Judges 5:31, cf. Miller, THE DIVINE WARRIOR, p. 101.
27 *Ibid.,* pp. 12-23; 66-74.
28 Cf. Cross, CANAANITE MYTH, p. 229: "The war oracle was pronounced by the prophet as courier of the Divine Warrior, Yahweh of Hosts."
29 *Ibid.,* p. 68.
30 *Ibid.,* p. 71.
31 For discussion of the *mbśr* in Is 52:7-12, cf. Cross, CANAANITE MYTH, p. 108; and of the *mbśrwt* in Ps 68:12, cf. Miller, THE DIVINE WARRIOR, p. 108.

> *whyh byt y'qb' š*
> *wbyt ywsp lhbh*
> *wbyt 'św lqš*
> *wdlqw bhm w'klwm*
> The house of Jacob shall be a fire
> and the house of Joseph a flame,
> and the house of Esau chaff;
> they shall burn them and consume them.

Mal 3:19 *ky hnh hywm b' b'r . . . wkl 'šh rš'h qš*
> For behold, the day comes, burning . . . and all
> evildoers will be chaff.

Na 2:5 *bhwṣwt ytḥwllw hrkb*
> *yštqšqwn brḥbwt*
> *mr'yhn klpydm*
> *mr'yhn klpydm*
> *kbrqym yrwṣṣw*
> Through the streets wildly race the horses,
> they rush to and fro in the squares;
> their appearance like torches,
> like lightning they flash by.

Am 5:6   *rḥbwt//ḥwṣwt*
Jer 46:9 *whthllw hrkb*
> and charge wildly, steeds.

Jl 2:9   *b'yr yšqw*
> *bhwmh yrṣwn*
> They rush through the city,
> they run along the wall.

Na 2:9 *wnynwh kbrkt mym*
> *mymy hy' whmh nsym*
> *'mdw 'mdw*
> *w'yn mpnh*
> Nineveh is like a pool of water,
> its waters running away;
> Stop! Stop!
> but no one turns back.

Jer 46:5   *nws* (**MT***wmnws*) *nsw*
> *wl' hpnw*
> They flee in haste,
> they do not look back.

Jer. 46:21 *ky gm hmh hpnw*
> *nsw yḥdyw*
> *l' 'mdw*

They too turned
and fled together,
not one stood his ground.

Na 2:10   *bzw ksp bzw zhb*
      w'yn qṣh ltkwnh
      Plunder the silver, plunder the gold,
      for there is no end to the treasure.

Is 2:7   *wtml' 'rṣw ksp wzhb*
Is 2:7   *w'yn qṣh l'ṣrtyw*
      Its land is filled with silver and gold
      and there is no end to its treasures.

Na 2:11   *wlb nms wpq brkym*
      wḥlḥlh bkl mtnym
      wpny klm qbṣw p'rwr
      Melting hearts and trembling knees;
      And there is anguish in all loins,
      and the faces of all gather paleness.

Is 13:7-8   *'l kn ydym trpnh*
      wkl lbb 'nwš yms
      Therefore all hands will be feeble
      and everyman's heart will melt.
      kywldh yḥlwn
      They will be in anguish (or: they will writhe)
      like a woman in travail.

Jl 2:6   *mpnyw yḥylw*
Jl 2:6   *kl pnym qbṣw p'rwr*
      Before them peoples are in anguish
      all faces grow pale.

Na 3:2   *wqwl r'š 'wpn . . .*
      wmrkbh mrqdh
      And the sound of the rumbling wheel . . .
      and jolting chariot.

Jl 2:5   *kqwl mrkbwt 'l r'šy hhrym yrqdwn*
      With the noise of chariots, they leap on the
      tops of the mountains.

Na 3:10   *gm 'llyh yrṭšw*
      Her little ones were dashed to pieces . . .

Is 13:16   *w'llyhm yrṭšw*
      Their little ones will be dashed in pieces.

Na 3:10   *w'l nkbdyh ydw gwrl*
     And they cast lots for her nobles.
Jl 4:2   *w'l 'my ydw gwrl*
     And have cast lots for my people.
Ob :11   *w'l yrwšlm ydw gwrl*
     And cast lots for Jerusalem.

One could give several more examples. In our opinion it is significant that one can find language in any of the Day of Yahweh passages which has a counterpart in Nahum. It is true that a common "war-language" is to be expected, but, nevertheless, it is remarkable that a number of phrases are not found outside Nahum and the Day of Yahweh texts. This can be taken as an indication that Yahweh, the vindicating God, whose herald has brought a message of victory and judgement, by this war against the Assyrians, is carrying out his task on the Day of Judgment, the Day of Yahweh. Most modern scholars have accepted G. von Rad's association of the Day of Yahweh with the Israelite tradition of the Holy War. Von Rad's position has been questioned by F. C. Fensham:

> If von Rad is correct that the Day of the Lord is best to be explained from the setting of the Holy War, why should in the majority of cases the destructive effect of the day be prophesied against Israel? Is it not true that the idea existed that a holy war was usually waged against the enemies of Israel, a war in which the holy and purified soldiers of Israel participated as the soldiers of the Lord?[32]

While agreeing with von Rad that the concept of the Day of Yahweh originally had nothing to do with eschatology but was a "traditional prophetic expectation that the enemies of Israel would be defeated in the end by Yahweh,"[33] Fensham accepts that in those passages where the Day of Yahweh is associated with war, then von Rad is justified in connecting the Day with the holy war. He believes, however, that there are ideas left which cannot be connected with war, e.g. the idea of the coming of the Lord of wrath, the effects on nature — the changing of the sun, moon and stars, dark clouds, darkness etc. But it seems to me that Miller's study of the theophanies and of the Divine Warrior solves the problems raised by Fensham.

    Whether the Day of Yahweh was a day directed against foreign enemies (e.g. Edom or Babylon), or whether it was against an unfaithful Israel, in all cases it is a day on which Yahweh punishes the guilty. For Yahweh is not only warrior, but also judge.[34] Most interesting therefore is the observation of Fensham that when the enemies of Israel are being

---

32 BIBLICAL ESSAYS 1966, p. 91.
33 *Ibid.*, p. 90.
34 Cf. Miller, THE DIVINE WARRIOR, p. 139.

punished, it is a day of blessing and victory for Israel. He states that this "develops as a result of the covenant, because according to military-clauses in ancient treaties, we know that the main partner promises protection against enemies."[35] In the light of what Fensham says, the war waged by Yahweh in Nahum, is a war to protect Israel and to free her from the yoke of Nineveh. Fensham understands much of the Day of Yahweh language, e.g. that connected with darkness, as having a "curse-background".[36] Thus in his opinion, curses directed against Israel are treaty-curses, brought against Israel for breach of the covenant, but curses against the enemies of Israel, who do not have a covenant with Yahweh or Israel, are typical of the common curses brought against any enemy. Fensham writes:

> The idea of the curse is that at some time it must come into operation. In the case of foreign enemies the natural result of such an operation would be a battle in which the various effects of certain curses could be exacted. It is thus obvious that in all the cases where the Day of the Lord is mentioned in connection with foreign foes a battle is envisaged. In such a case the idea of a holy war predominates.[37]

If Fensham is right, then our understanding of a war of Yahweh against the Assyrians in Nahum and its link with the Day of Yahweh stands up. On the face of it, Fensham's remarks would seem to throw into question our earlier study of treaty-curses in Nahum.[38] However, Fensham has suggested more recently that Nahum regarded the covenant as binding not only on the Israelites but on mankind generally.[39]

Conclusion

In Nahum, *'l nqm,* "the avenging God," is the one who carries out the curses as punishment of the Assyrians, to save Israel. As the Divine Warrior he wages a war against these Assyrians; as king he topples the king of Nineveh from his throne and asserts his kingship, for "it is the establishment of Yahweh's eternal rule and sovereignty that is the ultimate goal of Yahweh's wars."[40]

---

35 BIBLICAL ESSAYS 1966, p. 92.
36 *Ibid.,* p. 94.
37 *Ibid.,* p. 95.
38 K. J. Cathcart, "Treaty-Curses and the Book of Nahum," *Catholic Biblical Quarterly* 35 (1973), pp. 179-187.
39 BIBLICAL ESSAYS 1969, p. 14.
40 Miller, THE DIVINE WARRIOR, p. 174.

Carroll Stuhlmueller, C.P.

REALITY OF PRESENCE AND PRAISE IN THE PSALMS

I   Song: Prayer at the Heart of Reality

The Book of Psalms can be called, in a quick thumbnail description, *The Bible in Miniature*. Better still, a strong case can be made for the psalms as the *heart* of the Bible. This figure of speech, comparing the Bible to the human body and the psalms to the heart, might enable us to clarify some ideas about the Bible and, in particular, to sharpen our vision for reading the psalms more appreciatively.

A. The Psalms, the Heart

The Bible may be likened to the human body, which through the changing years of its growth, maturity and retirement is consciously aware of remaining the same identical person. Life thus becomes a blend of consistency and continuity, the two ingredients of all responsible, adult behavior. Every seven years, we are told, the entire material composite of the human body is renewed and replaced. The body, moreover, never remains exactly as it was, because the body is always in the process of harmonizing its parts to reflect the age, health, needs and environment of its "owner." It compensates, if possible, for the loss of impairment of one faculty by the increased activity of another. If the body belongs to a family migrating to a hotter or colder climate, or to a higher or lower altitude, a further adaptation is set in progress, evolving at times over long generations. In the midst, however, of all these changes there is consistency with continuity in the identity of the person or the family.

The Bible, like the human body, maintains its own consistency within the ongoing continuity of Israel's history. Israel steadily found her identity in the faith-conviction that she was God's chosen people, redeemed by Him in the ongoing contiuity of Israel's history. Israel steadily found heridentity in the faithconviction that was God's chosen people, redeemed by Him from slavery and assured the Lord's continual, protective presence. In his love she found the courage to seek the future with hope (Dt 7; 32-33; Hos 11; Is 44:1-8; Rom 9:1-5). Strength flowed into the system, not by a satisfying contemplation of past achievements, but rather by courageous expectation for the future. Deutero-Isaiah sang out his faith: "Those who wait upon the Lord renew their strength" (Is 40:31). Because of this abiding self-consciousness inspired by faith, Israel was continuously advancing out of the past and into the future. Her vision of the golden age

CARROLL STUHLMUELLER, C.P., is Professor of Old Testament at Catholic Theological Union, Chicago, Illinois.

lay not in a shadowy bygone age, but always ahead in the un-known future. Because of her strong reliance upon God, Israel could face the problems of change and continuous adaptation which a future orientation always demands of a people.

The Bible reflects this consistency within change, for it tells of Israel's being transformed from a semi-nomadic style of life to an agricultural and even urban existence. Government underwent change, at times abrupt and revolutionary — as when David established a royal dynasty in place of the more democratic form of Judges. The same David and his son Solomon were responsible for a radical transformation in liturgical practice, in building a temple as a fixed abode for the Ark of the Covenant, which up till then roamed with the wanderings of the people. All the while, the historical-religious traditions which found their way into the Bible were living within these changes and, like the human body, absorbing their effects.

Of all the organs of the human body, the *heart* is, perhaps, the most sensitive to change, delicately registering the fluctuations of life, sometimes before the mind is conscious of anything different. The heart beats faster or more slowly, or even skips a beat, depending upon excitement, or drowsiness, or shock, or overwork, or hypertension. The heart of the Bible can be located in the Book of Psalms. Here Israel's faith-interaction with all the changing circumstances of her history was registered. The entire life of Israel flowed into this heart and made it what it was. The Psalms thus became like a mirror to Israel's desert wandering and agricultural pursuits, to the gratifying peace and turbulent wars of her politics, to her prophetic threats and wise men's speculation, to her royal protocol and, most of all, to her worship and liturgical prayers. The psalms, we must remember, reflected *life,* which is never static (unless it has stopped in death) but is continuously evolving. Israel's praise and prayer in the psalms beat with the action and movement of her long history.

The figure of speech, comparing the Bible to the human body and the psalms to its heart, can be developed still further; but here we can be brief, as we developed this idea in an earlier article published in *The Bible Today,* March 1965, and reprinted in THE BIBLE TODAY READER, pages 256-264. The blood, which circulates in and out of the heart and then through the entire body, thus keeping the entire organism alive, is similar to Israel's faith in God's goodness, strength and fidelity. As blood meant life — and life was the property of God alone (Lv 17:11; Gn 9:4) — Israel's blood or life of faith was charged with the very presence of God himself. God, within this life-giving blood, sustained every moment of Israel's existence with purpose, vitality and continuity.

The beat of the heart, energetically circulating this blood into all parts of the body, is comparable to the liturgical ceremonies during which ancient traditions were recited and the psalms chanted.

If this analogy is correct, comparing the psalms to the heart of the Bible, one will appreciatively respond to the psalms to the extent that one knows the Bible in ever greater depth and detail. We add one final observation by way of footnote to this comparison of the Bible and the psalms to the human body and heart. What the psalms were to the Bible, the liturgical books of the Lectionary and Sacramentary are to the Christian life. Those two books are at the heart of a long, evolving history. In their various modifications and reforms, they reflect centuries of popular piety, social environment, theological discussion and world history. *Lex orandi* (the law or way of prayer) is not only the *lex credendi* (the law or norm of faith) but also the *lex vivendi* (the law or reality of life).

B. The Psalms, Prayer Within the Real

The human body can survive only within the real world of earth and fresh air, fire and water, shared within a family and community. Because God is real and, in fact, can be contacted only within the real, his presence is somehow incarnated within the real environment of human life.

One is reminded, in this context, of a passage in Second Isaiah, where God's ways and thoughts are said to be as far above the ways and thoughts of men and women as the heavens are above the earth (Is 55:9-11). Nonetheless, God's ways and thoughts reach us, not suspended like majestic clouds in mid-air, to be admired in wonder from afar, but rather like rain and snow which soak the earth and reach again towards the heaven in such earthly products as bushes, trees and vegetables. The passage reads:

As high as the heavens are above the earth,
    so high are my ways above your ways
    and my thoughts above your thoughts.
For just as from the heavens
    the rain and snow come down
And do not return there
    till they have watered the earth,
    making it fertile and fruitful,
Giving seed to him who sows
    and bread to him who eats,
So shall my word be
    that goes forth from my mouth;
It shall not return to me void,
    but shall do my will,
achieving the end for which I sent it.   (NAB translation)

God's thoughts return to him clothed in the earthly fabric of human language, closely interrelated with the evolving context of human history. The total reality of Israel's life finds its way with a sense of destiny into the Bible and eventually into the heart of the Bible, the psalms.

This quality of *reality* may help to explain why the psalms seem to be such *unreal* prayers or, at least, such uncomfortable prayers for many of us modern men and women. When we pray, we are accustomed to appear before God scrubbed clean and dressed up in our Sunday best. Before we pray, we cover over our rough thoughts and scrub away our impatient words. We arrive polite, reverential, noble, pure, devout, grammatically correct, preferably in the ancient idiom of "thou" and "thee", musically in tune, even majestic and pompous! We normally place ourselves before God, not as we truly are (and as God truly sees us to be), but rather, attired in our make-believe Halloween costumes for Allhallows Day!

Not so the psalms! Of course, majestic paeans like Psalms 96-99 proclaim God's glorious royalty! Wonder and honor are parts of the real — but not the only part and certainly not its ordinary part. Discouragement and threats, anger and curses, monotony and routine, quiet relaxation, also stately philosophical moments — in fact, all of life — pulse within the psalms. Above all else, the psalms are *honest*. If a person feels that God is distant, or even asleep during the storms of life, he or she can shout with the psalmist, "Lord, wake up!" (Ps 44:24) just like the disciples rudely shook their Master, Jesus, out of sleep (Mk 4:38). If a person or community burn with anger, they curse (Pss 69:23-29; 137:9)! If Israel judges that she has received a raw deal from God, she can put her problem plainly before God with Psalm 44.

Another part of the difficulty in understanding the psalms derives from the common problem of making sense out of life. Prayer for the psalmist is not a philosophical or theological disquisition about pain and difficulty! Prayer does not seek to disentangle international issues or personal problems! Frequently in the psalms prayer is nothing more than the realization that God is nearby. Or, to express the same idea a little differently, prayer is the placing of oneself *really* or *realistically* in God's presence. Or, as in Psalm 69, prayer expresses the search for what is already too real and too close to be found. In the agony of loss we sense the ecstacy of union:

You know my reproach, my shame and my ignominy;
    before you are all my foes.
Insult has broken my heart, and I am weak,
    I looked for sympathy, but there was none;
    for comforters, and I found none.
The psalms are prayers within the real.

The psalms are not to be identified simply with surface facts of reality. The psalms plummet to the depth of reality, not so much philosophically as through the insights of faith — the profound conviction that God is truly present — and then sustain and resonate this "vision" prayerfully through human language.

Not all of reality and similarly not all of the human expressions of this reality equally respond to God's redeeming and inspiring presence. In this context one can raise an important question, unfortunately beyond the space limitations of this essay: are there degrees of inspiration within the various passages of the Bible? To take this question one step further, can we ask whether all one hundred and fifty psalms are equally inspired? If not, must we feel obliged to make equal use of all of them? We will return to this question in a moment, but in the meanwhile we want to introduce, at least in passing, another controversial point, the nature of inspiration.

The psalms, and for that matter the entire Bible, voice in a human way the hopes and the ideals, the questions and the problems, the discouragement and even the curses, prompted by God's presence within the real. (Men curse whatever and whoever blocks the realization of divinely motivated hopes.) Inspiration of the Bible, then, is the common faith of all persons, articulated by one person of uncommon insight and ability. An inspired passage becomes part of the Bible when all men and women sooner or later agree that this one person "spoke God" for them and not simply to them. It is the community through its leaders who decides the question of "canonicity" or of what belongs in the Bible. Moreover, if the community can respond to God's inspiring and sanctifying presence in varying degrees, the reflection of this inspiration in the various parts of the Bible will manifest these degrees of inspiration.

This short paragraph is an overly quick and very popular attempt to explain the scholarly pursuit for the "social character of biblical inspiration," an explanation which proceeds beyond — hopefully not against — the more narrow definition of inspiration by Pope Pius XII in *Divino Afflante Spiritu* and of Vatican II in Chapter 2 of DE REVELATIONE. Interestingly enough, Chapter 5 of this same document on the formation of the Gospels equivalently adapts the newer position about the social character of inspiration when delineating the steps in the composition of the gospels.

C. The Psalms and the Totality of the Real

If, as was proposed above, some parts of the Bible (Nm 1; Dt 7:2) and of the psalms (Ps 110:5-6; 137:9) may be less inspired than others, can we, in fact ought we, omit these minimally inspired sections from our

Christian liturgy and ordinary prayer? Are some psalms very inspired and yet too historically conditioned by ancient names and outmoded styles to be suitable for contemporary prayer, especially when this prayer is to draw the worshipers into full participation? These questions are serious, especially in their implications. Let us mention several dangers.

Let us never reject out of ignorance, particularly ignorance of the Bible! Let us never measure the Bible by our standards, but always be ready to ponder anew what we cannot understand or appreciate about the holy Scriptures!

Further, where God seems to be less present — whether in life or in the Bible — we need to pause longer prayerfully and zealously — and not hurry over it or ever skirt around it! Keeping such psalms in our prayers may provide the occasion of instilling a greater response to God's presence in the difficulties of life. If we pray only when it is easy to find God on our own terms, we will be badly prepared to seek his presence on other people's terms or to search for him in his seeming absence. Maintaining all the psalms, at least in the Church's public liturgy of the Eucharist and the Divine Office, may become a powerful incentive to faith in God in the totality of the real. Prayer includes a search beyond the obvious if it is a prayer of faith.

The psalms, moreover, can seem to hinder full liturgical participation for still another reason. Some days we come to the Eucharist, or we begin the Divine Office, happy and thankful in spirit, and we are asked to recite some sorrowful lament or dreadful complaint like:

Save me, O God,
   for the waters threaten my life;
I am sunk in the abysmal swamp. (Ps 69:2)

Just as surely on another day when we happen to be sick or depressed or harassed by problems, the official liturgical prayers call upon us to:

Let the heavens be glad and the earth rejoice;
   let the sea and what fills it resound;
Let the plains be joyful and all that is in them! (Ps 96:11-12)

At times such as these the temptation is abruptly there, impelling us to substitute another liturgical text and to question anew the appropriateness of the psalms for prayer today. Should we not instead, however, question our own narrow-mindedness and face up to the challenge of adapting ourselves to the greater world of reality reflected in the liturgy and the psalms? When we are very joyful, we ought not to forget the poor and the depressed; and when we are suffering pain and feel miserable, we need not cover the entire world with our shroud of mourning. Particularly at the liturgy, we are asked to unite ourselves with a church and a world of vast human dimensions, and like Jesus to open our arms to embrace all men and women. Again, like Jesus on the cross, we might have to submit to nails painfully impaling us in a wide open welcome to the world. The psalms, however, embrace centuries of human experience and so force our prayer out of the prejudicial confines of narrow circles within circles. The psalms can liberate us as they plunge us into the human emotions of all our brothers and sisters of all centuries in Jesus.

"Participation" is the magic word of the liturgy today. The psalms activate powers long dormant within us and, perhaps, totally unsuspected by us, enable us to participate in the totality of the real.

A final footnote by way of a question might be introduced into our discussion at this point. Should we not retain, not just the psalms, but all the liturgically assigned readings from Scripture? We may be forced to think and pray through long stretches of silence, wondering how to harmonize the biblical readings, even among themselves, not to speak of their relation to the feast, the occasion and the mood of the moment. Yet, isn't this search for an ever deeper unity the pressing demand and the glorious discovery of life in community and prayer in Jesus? In the liturgy we are offered an opportunity — call it a challenge for those who persevere — to celebrate a unity far more extensive, and certainly more profound than we ever imagined possible at first.

II   Introducing the Psalms of Praise

One of the easiest types of psalms to be recognized is the *Hymn of Praise*. The literary structure is simple. (a) The *introduction* rings out a summons to "Shout to the Lord all your lands! Worship the Lord gladly! Come into his presence joyfully with a song!" (Ps 100:1-2). Or, the psalm may open abruptly with the entire assembly bursting into song: "Yahweh, our Lord! How magnificent your name across all the earth!" (Ps 8:2). (b) The body or major section of the hymn acclaims the mighty wonders of God across the cosmos (Pss 8; 19; 29; etc.), in Israel's history (Pss 105; 114), at the final eschatological moment (Pss 29; 47; 96-99; etc.), in a time of instruction (Pss 33; 93; 111), and finally in praise of Jerusalem or Zion (Pss 46; 48; etc.). (c) In conclusion the hymn of praise may end repeating the opening refrain (Ps 8:10) or shouting *Hallelu-yah, Praise Yahweh!* (Ps 104; 105), or else orchestrating a grand finale of the major themes (Ps 29:10-11).

There is one psalm whose every line is a hymn of praise, Psalm 136. The wondrous acts of God, whether across the cosmos or through the history of Israel, are announced with Hebrew participles, as though happening now, at the moment of worship. The community responds with an acclamation, repeated twenty-six times in the rhythm of a litany: "His love-bond (in Hebrew, his *ḥesed*) can never end!" Yahweh is announced as:

the one alone making great wonders (v. 4)
the one wisely making the heavens (v. 5)
the one leading forth the Israelites (v. 11).

Even from these few introductory remarks about the hymn of praise, we might be able to venture a definition of this type of psalm and ponder several of its important qualities. *Praise,* we propose, *is a wondrous acclamation of God's redemptive acts as these continuously reoccur among us his people.*

A.   A Wondrous Acclamation

Praise gives nothing to God! Praise is a burst of wonder at what is happening because of God's presence. Praise is the recognition through faith of what is real in its deepest, most personal aspects. What all men can see in nature, the sunrise or the sunset, or in history, the liberation of an oppressed people from slavery, Israel sees with the laser beam of faith. Such a religious perspective enables Israel to experience a still more profound reality. God is acting now because of a love-bond (such is the sense of the Hebrew word *ḥesed* — or with the suffix, *ḥasdo,* in Psalm 136, *his* love-bond) uniting Israel and God as blood-brothers in one "tribe."

Because praise gives nothing to God but simply and joyfully acclaims reality, praise does not demean God nor man. To picture heaven, or for that matter to perform the liturgy as though God would be some despotic, proud potentate who delights sitting upon a glittering throne to receive the fawning adulations of his subjects, is a caricature totally unbiblical.

The ecstasy of praise releases the greatest amount of energy without necessarily producing anything or getting anywhere. In praise faith plummets to the wonder of the real, and the soul is overawed into silence. Praise is the mighty leap of love into a wonder beyond rational control and intellectual explanation! For this reason, in the refrain of Psalm 136,

in Hebrew — *kî*   *le'ôlām   ḥasdo*
in English — Indeed   forever   his love-bond!

the particle *ki* is better translated "Indeed" instead of "because"; or, it can be left untranslated and its meaning communicated by musical accompaniment.

Because the hymn of praise does not give the reason *why* but gloriously acclaims *that* God is mighty in his goodness, this type of psalm may seem to get nowhere. It ends where it begins. At times the conclusion repeats the introduction. For the singer of hymns, reality is wonder beyond analysis. Where science may be satisfied, as determining how the earth was formed, faith never exhausts the wonder of it all:

The wonder of such knowledge [slips] beyond me

    *   *   *

Should I rise on the wings of dawn
    and make my home at the farthest horizon
        of the sea,
Even there your hand rests upon me. (Ps 139:6, 9-10)
        (Ps 139:6, 9-10).

B. A God of Life, Not of Death

The hymn of praise delightfully announces the wonders of life. Death, suffering, sorrow, penance, and all such moments of loss never enter the hymn of praise — at least in so far as these concern God's chosen people. This fact brings up a serious problem. If Israel is God's chosen or elect nation, how do we explain the lot of the non-elect? To put our question bluntly — how can an Egyptian read the Old Testament or a Babylonian sing Psalm 137? This subject of election is too vast to deal with here. This mystery, nonetheless, never disturbed the Israelite, but rather enhanced the inexplicable wonder of the hymn.

Biblically, Yahweh is a God of life, not death. Frequently, the psalms protest the inability of the dead to praise God — not in the hymns, but in the prayers of supplication (Pss 6:6; 30:10; 88:11-12; Is 38:18). Again, as in the case of Israel's election, God's gift of joy to his people raises a serious question from the arena of human life. From the more common attitude and response of men and women, life, joy and the good things of this earth frequently distract from God. Yet, from God's viewpoint, life and joy are the only proper manifestations of his presence. Normally, we seek out the help of a spiritual advisor, not when everything goes well, but rather, when we are beset with difficulties. The request usually heard by a teacher or spiritual advisor, is not "Everything is wonderful, so tell me about God!" but rather "Everything is terrible! Where is God?"

Can it be that our difficulties of sensing God's presence in joy make us consider such psalms as the hymns of praise inappropriate for worship today? In this case, however, the liturgy by maintaining these psalms against our feelings exerts a corrective action and reaches deep into our subconscious, enabling us to recognize the Lord as he is truly and really there, a God of life.

C. The *"Now"* of Biblical Praise

Biblical religion possessed a forward vision. Its golden age was not placed in the bygone long ago, never again to be fully regained; and its religion was not a frantic attempt to grasp and run with what can be salvaged out of the collapsing house of the past. Israel's messianic age always extended from the now into the future. The past was the topic of prayers and recitals because promises came from the past to sustain the present moment as one looked to the future. The past, therefore, was being continually relived. Narratives, hymns and law — in fact, everything which constituted Israel's religious traditions — were re-read and actualized in each new age.

The hymns of praise achieved this actualization of the past in many ways, and all the while the assembly was being drawn ever more actively into a full re-living of Israel's momentous redemptive acts. May we add here that re-living is not simply a repetition but a new experience within an integrally new setting. "Re-living" is here understood as the way in which grandparents live in the lives of their grandchildren.

Some of the means enabling the hymns to actualize the past come to our attention:

(a) The hymns tend to make a great use of participles, a verb form which bypasses any mention of "time," past, present or future, and simply extends the action content of a verb into a continuous happening, as was the case above with 136.

(b) Many liturgical actions accompany the hymn: sing, shout, clap the hands, clang the cymbal, pluck the harp, blast the trumpet, touch the lyre with the rhythmic dance of the bow, yes dance with all the rhythm of the body, march in procession, lift the arms, bow, kneel and prostrate against the ground, offer sacrifice, and assemble around a table for a sacred banquet. See especially Psalms 149 - 150, but also Psalm 68:26-28; 92:4; 95:6; 98:4-6. Accordingly, Israel was responding *now* as she participated at the moment of worship in God's redemptive act.

(c) Another aspect of Hebrew grammar enters our discussion of the contemporaneity of the hymns of praise. Contrary to all Western, Indo-European languages, the Hebrew verb did not primarily express time but the mood of the speaker or writer. Such a person referred first of all to an action complete or incomplete, simple or intense, causing a chain reaction or rebounding back upon the subject. The expression of time was secondary and still remains one of the thorniest problems in Hebrew grammar. It was easy for the past to live now in the interaction and participation of speaker and audience.

(d) Finally, Israel's special name for God, "Yahweh," (normally translated "Lord") can best be explained as the verb "to be" in the continuous, incomplete tense. Whatever the Lord accomplished in Israel's history remained incomplete until *all* Israelites — perhaps even men and women everywhere — would participate in the redemptive action. The past became a promise, sustaining the present in its link to the future. Fr. Albert Gelin thus described the divine name Yahweh: Spoken by Israel,

"Yahweh" was a prayer of faith, "Be there always with us"; and spoken by God himself, "Yahweh" was a promise full of hope, "I am he who is always there with you." That promise and prayer are ours today as we utter the divine name.

This "now" aspect of the hymns of praise was so important that sacred traditions were changed and modernized. For instance, in Psalm 105:33 God still saves his people by the plagues against their enemy, but not as he did in Egypt, destroying flax and barley (Ex 9:31), but rather, by striking down "vines and fig trees," the produce of Palestine! We do not introduce this example for its own sake. Rather, it is a biblical reminder of what can and ought to be done today in Christian worship. Changes ought not to be made in biblical readings abruptly and on the spot. Nonetheless, changes can be made carefully, prayerfully, ahead of time in planning the next day's liturgy.

In Conclusion

This essay has investigated the way by which the Bible reflects life. The reality of life is seen at its depth of meaning in the continuous presence of God's living and powerful kindness. Such divine love establishes a bond deeper and stronger than blood, ever pulsing with power to unite all Israel in every moment of life into one holy people with her God and Savior. The total reality by which God and Israel become one living body produces prayers, laws, ceremonies, recitals — the stuff of life called the Bible. The heart which kept this body alive was the psalms, and the liturgy of Israel was the beat of this heart, joyfully pulsating with life.

Peter F. Ellis, C.SS.R.

PATTERNS AND STRUCTURES OF MARK'S GOSPEL

Scripture scholars in the seventies have many tasks and challenges. The determination of the exact structure of Mark's gospel is but one of them, but it is an important one. The evolution of Markan studies has progressed at an ever accelerating pace from the period of 'simple' Mark (Papias to Wrede) to the period of 'tricky' Mark (Wrede to Marxsen) on to 'subtle' Mark (Marxsen to Minette de Tillesse) and finally in recent years to 'theological' Mark.[1] As in all studies of evolution, however, insights and conclusions have outrun evidence. The next decade of Markan studies promises, as a result, to be a period of continuing investigation into Mark's theology but with ever increasing attention to the search for hard literary evidence to back up the theology. The demise of the Marxsen hypothesis for the *Sitz im Leben* of Mark's Gospel[2] and T.J. Weeden's almost incredible conclusions concerning the Apostles in his TRADITIONS IN CONFLICT[3] point up the need for a more intensive study of the literary aspects of Mark's gospel. As J. Dewey said in a recent article: "Mark was a writer of considerable literary skill if not of elegant Greek; it is only by paying attention to the literary structure he created that we can hope to interpret his gospel correctly."[4]

The need for determining the exact structure of Mark's gospel is one thing, the possibility another. As D.E. Nineham observed back in 1963,

The very fact that such widely differing principles of arrangement have been attributed to St. Mark perhaps suggests that in searching the Gospel for a single and entirely coherent master-plan, corresponding to a set of clearly formulated practical purposes, scholars are looking for something that is not there and attributing to the Evangelist a higher degree of self-conscious purpose than he in fact possessed.[5]

Despite Nineham's and others' pessimism, the search has gone on and

PETER F. ELLIS, C.SS.R., is Professor of Biblical Theology in the Department of Religious Education, Fordham University, Bronx, New York.

---

1 See especially R. Martin, MARK: EVANGELIST AND THEOLOGIAN (Grand Rapids: Zondervan, 1973); J. Quensell, THE MIND OF MARK (Rome: Pontifical Biblical Institute, 1969); P. Meye, JESUS AND THE TWELVE (Grand Rapids: Eerdmans, 1968); T. J. Weeden, TRADITIONS IN CONFLICT (Philadelphia: Fortress, 1971); A. M. Ambrozic, THE HIDDEN KINGDOM: A REDACTION-CRITICAL STUDY OF THE REFERENCES TO THE KINGDOM OF GOD IN MARK'S GOSPEL (Washington: The Catholic Biblical Quarterly—Monograph Series II, 1972); T. A. Burkill, NEW LIGHT ON THE EARLIEST GOSPEL (Ithaca: Cornell Univ. Press, 1972); J. M. Robinson, THE PROBLEM OF HISTORY IN MARK (London: SCM Press, 1957).

2 Cf. Ambrosic, p. 227f.

3 Cf. E. Schweizer, "Neuere Markus-Forschung in USA," *EvangTheol* 33 (June '73) 533-537; Q. Quesnell, *CBQ* 35 (Jan. '73) p. 121.

4 See J. Dewey, "The Literary Structure of the Controversy Stories in Mark 2:1-3:6," *JBL* 92 (Sept. '73) p. 401.

5 Cf. D. E. Nineham, SAINT MARK (Baltimore: Penguin Books, Inc., 1963) p. 29.

with some good results.[6] The work of Lohmeyer, Schweizer, and Perrin among others on the literary aspects of Mark, while not in total agreement, exhibits a surprising unanimity with regard to discernible patterns in the Marcan composition and a substantial agreement in relation to the basic structure of the gospel. Our aim will be to draw together the insights of these and other authors, undergird the insights with new literary evidence, and from the combination of the two suggest what hopefully appears to have been the literary *modus operandi* of Mark when he composed his gospel. We will begin with a full outline of the structure of the gospel and its obvious patterns. We will then look at the literary evidence. We will conclude our investigation with some observations about the Marcan prologue and the place of Mk 8:27-30 in the gospel.

Structure and patterns

PROLOGUE: 1:1-13:
        (1) 1:1-8:   John the Baptist preaches
        (2) 1:9-11:   Jesus is baptized
        (3) 1:12-13: Jesus is tempted by Satan

PART I: 1:14-8:30: The arrival of the kingdom
    SECTION A: 1:14-3:6: Jesus' preaching and the Jews' opposition
        (1) 1:14-15:   Introductory summary
        (2) 1:16-20:   The Apostles
        (3) 1:21-3:6: A narrative complex with two panels,
                        each containing five pericopes:

    FIRST PANEL: a) 1:21-28: A cure at Capharnaum in the
                              synagogue on the sabbath
                              (inclusion with 3:1-6)
                b) 1:29-31: The cure of Simon's mother-in-law
                c) 1:32-34: Cures and exorcisms[7]
                d) 1:35-39: Jesus prays and then preaches
                              throughout Galilee
                e) 1:40-45: Jesus cures a leper[8]

---

6 Cf. E. Trocme, LA FORMATION DE L'EVANGILE SELON MARC (Paris: Presses Universitaires de France, 1963); T. A. Burkill, NEW LIGHT ON THE EARLIEST GOSPEL (Ithaca: Cornell Univ. Press, 1972); H. D. Betz (ed.), CHRISTOLOGY AND A MODERN PILGRIMAGE: A DISCUSSION WITH NORMAN PERRIN (Society of Biblical Literature, 1971). E. Schweizer, THE GOOD NEWS ACCORDING TO MARK (Richmond: John Knox Press, 1970); W. A. Beardslee, LITERARY CRITICISM OF THE NEW TESTAMENT (Philadelphia: Fortress, 1970); N. Perrin, WHAT IS REDACTION CRITICISM? (Philadelphia: Fortress, 1971); E. J. Mally, S.J., "The Gospel of Mark" in the JEROME BIBLICAL COMMENTARY.
7 The presence of the messianic secret formula in 1:34 is indicative along with the "sandwich" style of 1:12-28 of Markan composition.
8 For the explanation of Mark's use of this pericope in this place, cf. J. Dewey, p. 394f.

SECOND PANEL: a) 2:1-12:   Controversy with the scribes re the
power to forgive sins[9]

b) 2:13-17:   Controversy with the Pharisees re
eating with tax collectors and
sinners

c) 2:18-22:   Controversy with the Pharisees re
fasting

d) 2:23-28:   Controversy with the Pharisees re
picking corn on the sabbath

e) 3:1-6:   Controversy with the Pharisees re
cure — in the synagogue on the
sabbath (inclusion with 1:21-28)
Climax (3:6): "The Pharisees
went out and at once began to plot
with the Herodians against him,
discussing how to destroy him."

SECTION B: 3:7-6:6a: Jesus is rejected by his "own"

(1) 3:7-12:   Introductory summary

(2) 3:13-19: The Apostles

(3) 3:20-6:5a: Narrative complex:

a) 3:20-35:   The opposition of the Pharisees
and Jesus' relatives (inclusion
with 6:1-6a)[10]

b) 4:1-35:   The parable discourse on the
kingdom

c) 4:35-41:   The calming of the storm

d) 5:1-20:   The Gerasene demoniac

e) 5:21-43:   The woman with the hemorrhage
and the daughter of Jairus[11]

f) 6:1-6a: Jesus is rejected by his own at
Nazareth (inclusion with
3:20-35).
Climax: "He was amazed at their
lack of faith" (6:6a).

SECTION C: 6:6b-8:30: Who is Jesus?

(1) 6:6b: Introductory summary

(2) 6:7-13:   The Apostles

---

9 Cf. J. Dewey, pp. 394-401 for a brilliant study of the elegant composition of 2:1-3:6.

10 Mark's "sandwich" technique in 3:20-35 makes it difficult to determine whether this
part of the narrative complex should be considered as one unit (3:20-35) or three
3:20-21; 3:22-30; 3:31-35). We prefer to consider it a single unit because of the
"sandwich" technique and the common theme (cf. 5:21-43; 11:12-25).

11 The same can be said for this part of the narrative complex as for 3:20-35 (see n. 10).

(3) 6:14-8:30: Narrative complex introduced and closed by questions concerning Jesus' identity and embracing two balanced panels:

a) 6:14-29: Herod, Jesus' identity, and John the Baptist (inclusion of 8:14-16 with 8:27-30)

FIRST PANEL: 6:30-7:37	SECOND PANEL: 8:1-30
b) 6:30-44: Multiplication of loaves	b') 8:1-9: Multiplication of loaves
c) 6:45-56: Crossing and landing	c') 8:10b: Crossing and landing
d) 7:1-23: Controversy with Pharisees	d') 8:11-13: Controversy with Pharisees
e) 7:24-30: Discussion about "bread"	e') 8:14-21: Discussion about "bread"
f) 7:31-37: Cure of a deaf mute	f') 8:22-26: Cure of a blind man[12]

g) 8:27-30: Jesus' identity: "Who do 'men' say I am?" "Who do 'you' say I am?" (Inclusion with 6:14-16). Climax: "You are the Messiah" (8:29).

PART II: 8:31-10:52: The Suffering Son of Man and Discipleship

SECTION A: 8:31-9:29: Suffering and Discipleship

(1) 8:31: Introductory summary prediction of death and resurrection

(2) 8:32-33: Apostles' obtuseness

(3) 8:34-9:29: Instruction on discipleship:

a) 8:34-9:1: Discipleship calls for taking up the cross

b) 9:2-8: The transfiguration

c) 9:9-13: The question about Elijah

d) 9:14-29: The disciples and the epileptic demoniac

SECTION B: 9:30-10:31: Characteristics and rewards of discipleship

(1) 9:30-31: Introductory summary prediction of death and resurrection

---

12 The cure of the blind man in 8:22-26 is frequently balanced with the cure of Bartimaeus in 10:46-52, but as far as 'balance' is concerned, it is more properly balanced with the cure of the deaf mute in 7:31-37. This is not to deny the strategic placing of 8:22-26 before Peter's confession in 8:27-30 or 10:46-52 after Jesus' instructions on discipleship. It is a matter of two different literary techniques.

(2) 9:32-34:   Apostles' obtuseness
(3) 9:35-10:31: Instruction on discipleship
   a)   9:35-37:   Disciples must serve and be last
                   of all
   b)   9:38-40:   Disciples must be open to others
   c)   9:41:   Reward for charity shown to
                   Jesus' disciples[13]
   d)   9:42-45:   Warning against giving scandal[14]
   e)   10:1-12:   Discipleship and the paradise will
                   of God with regard to marriage
   f)   10:13-16: Jesus and the children
   g)   10:17-22: Poverty and discipleship
   h)   10:23-27: Wealth — an obstacle to salvation
   i)   10:28-31: The rewards for leaving all and
                   following Jesus
SECTION C: 10:32-52: Suffering and Discipleship
   (1)   10:32-34:   Introductory summary prediction
   (2)   10:35-37:   Apostles' obtuseness
   (3)   10:34-52:   Instruction on discipleship
   a)   10:38-40:   Discipleship entails suffering
                    like Jesus
   b)   10:41-45:   Discipleship entails serving, rather
                    than being served by, others
   c)   10:46-52:   Cured, Bartimaeus 'follows' Jesus
                    "along the way" (of suffering
                    discipleship)
PART III: 11:1-16:8: The last seven days and the resurrection
   SECTION A: 11:1-13:37: From the coming of the Messiah to
                            Jerusalem to the coming of the Son of
                            Man in glory.
   (1)   11:1ab: Introductory summary mentioning
                      sites of Jesus' activities for the
                      first three days
   (2)   11:1c-6:   The Apostles
   (3)   11:7-13:37: Narrative complex covering
                      three days:
   a)   11:7-11:   The Messiah enters Jerusalem
                   (inclusion with 13:1-37).

---

13 This isolated saying seems to have been placed here because of the "catch-word" connection of "belong to Christ" (9:41) with "in my name" (9:30).
14 The "catch-word" "little ones" of 9:37 probably accounts for Mark's inclusion here of the two other pericopes dealing with the "little ones" (cf. 9:42 and 10:14).

b) 11:12-25: The withered fig tree and the cleansing of the Temple[15]

c) 11:27-33: Priests and scribes question Jesus' authority

d) 12:1-12: Parable of the wicked husbandmen and the Son

e) 12:13-17: Question concerning tribute to Caesar put by Pharisees and Herodians

f) 12:18-27: Question concerning the resurrection put by the Sadducees

g) 12:28-34: Question concerning the greatest commandment put by scribes

h) 12:35-37: Question concerning the Messiah's relationship to David put by Jesus

i) 12:38-40: Condemnation of the scribes

j) 12:41-44: The widow's mite

k) 13:1-37: The apocalyptic discourse (inclusion with 11:7-11 and perhaps also with 11:12-25)[16]

SECTION B: 14:1-15:47: The passion and death of the Son of Man

(1) 14:1-2: Introductory summary[17]

(2) 14:3-15:47: Narrative complex covering three days:

a) 14:3-9: The anointing beforehand for burial (inclusion with 15:42-47) — first day

b) 14:10-11: Judas plots to betray Jesus

c) 14:12-16: Apostles prepare for the Passover meal — second day

15 Beacuse of the "sandwich" technique and the common theme of the pericopes (the rejection of unrepentent Israel) we have preferred to consider 11:12-25 one unit rather than three (11:12-14; 11:15-19; 11:20-25).

16 The apocalyptic discourse deals not only with the coming of the Son of Man (recalling the coming of Jesus to Jerusalem in 11:7-11), but with destruction of Jerusalem as well (recalling Jesus' rejection of Israel in 11:12-25).

17 The usual format — (1) introductory summary, (2) Apostles, (3) narrative complex — is truncated in sections B and C by the omission of (2). Two explanations are possible. First, the omission of (2) may be explained by the fact that Mark is dealing or at least unnecessarily since his redactional hand is evident throughout the account. Second, Mark wishes to contrast the role of the women with the abysmal role of the Apostles. The women anoint Jesus beforehand (14:3-9), remain on Calvary (15:40-41), and are the first ones at the tomb (16:1-8). The Apostles on the other hand are found sleeping three times in the garden; Judas betrays Jesus (14:43-52); all the Apostles desert Jesus and run away when he is arrested (14:50); and finally Peter betrays him three times (14:53-72).

d) 14:17-21: Judas' betrayal foretold
e) 14:22-25: Institution of the Eucharist
f) 14:26-31: Peter's threefold betrayal foretold
g) 14:32-42: The agony in the garden and the threefold prayer
h) 14:43-52: Jesus arrested in the garden
i) 14:53-72: "Sandwich" account of Peter's threefold denial of Jesus and Jesus' trial before the Sanhedrin
j) 15:1-15: The trial before Pilate — third day
k) 15:16-20: The crowning with thorns
l) 15:21-22: The way of the cross
m) 15:23-41: The crucifixion and death
n) 15:42-47: The burial (inclusion with 14:3-9)

SECTION C: 16:1-8: The resurrection of Jesus
(1) 16:1: Introductory summary
(2) 16:2-8: Narrative:
a) 16:2: On the way to the tomb
b) 16:2-7: At the tomb
c) 16:8: Leaving the tomb

Justification for the above outline is based upon a number of obvious patterns used by Mark in the presentation of his material, upon his use of some summaries as introductory summaries, upon his constant use of inclusions to frame his narrative sections, and upon his pronounced liking for triads and triadic arrangement.

With regard to Mark's patterned style of presentation, it has been apparent to many for a long time that the material in 8:31-10:52 is distributed according to a set pattern. The pattern has three parts: (1) a summary prediction by Jesus of what will happen to him in Jerusalem, (2) an obtuse reaction to and misunderstanding of Jesus' words by his Apostles, and finally (3) an instruction by Jesus on discipleship. The triadic pattern is repeated three times, providing the following parallels:

Introductory summary prediction	8:31	9:31	10:33-34
Apostles' obtuseness	8:32-33	9:32	10:35-41
Instruction	8:34-9:30	9:33-10:32	10:42-52

As far as I know there is substantial agreement among scholars about this triadic arrangement of similar materials. The only real problem lies in determining where the whole section begins — whether in 8:31, as we have it in our outline, or in 8:27, which is favored by most authors. We will deal with the problem after we have looked at Mark's use of introductory summaries and inclusions.

In recent years, a number of scholars have noticed that Mark uses the same triadic arrangement of materials in the first part of his gospel (ch 1:14-8:26 or 8:30)[18] that he uses in part II. An analysis shows that part I contains a triad of parallel triads, thus:

Introductory summary	1:14-15	3:7-12	6:6b
Apostles	1:16-20	3:13-19	6:7-13
Narrative complex	1:21-3:6	3:20-6:6a	6:14-8:30

We have extrapolated from the similar arrangement of parallel triads in part I (1:14-8:30) and part II (8:31-10:52) to a triad of parallel triads in part III (11:1-16:8), thus:

Introductory summary	11:1ab	14:1-2	16:1
Apostles	11:1c-6		
Narrative complex	11:7-13:37	14:3-15:47	16:2-8

As we shall show later, there is some literary evidence, beyond the extrapolation from the similar triadic arrangements of parts I and II, for the triadic arrangement of part III (11:1-16:8).

Our three part structure, therefore, is based very much upon the recurrence in each part of the gospel of the triadic pattern three times repeated. As a comparison of the different structures arrived at by Schweizer, Perrin, Mally and others shows, however, agreement about the existence of these parallel triads has not led to agreement about the overall structure of the gospel. The main reason for this lack of agreement it seems to me, has been a failure to recognize the full significance of Mark's summaries at the beginning of each of these sections as *introductory* summaries combined with a failure to grasp the importance of Mark's use of inclusions and climaxes in part I and a failure to extrapolate from the parallel triads in parts I and II to the possibility of a similar arrangement of parallel triads in part III of the gospel (11:1-16:8).

Let us deal first with the significance of Mark's summaries at the beginning of each of these sections as introductory summaries. As is well known Mark uses summaries regularly throughout his gospel. If the summaries we have postulated as introductory summaries are to be considered as strict indications of new beginnings of distinct sections of the overall structure, it will be necessary to show that they are not simply summaries used to advance the action, as many of Mark's summaries are, nor simply summaries used as transitions, as N. Perrin[19] holds, but true introductory summaries which preview what is to follow in the gospel as a whole or at least in the immediate section of the gospel to which each summary be-

---

18 Cf. E. Schweizer, THE GOOD NEWS ACCORDING TO MARK; E. J. Mally; N. Perrin in H. Dieter Betz (ed.), pp. 6ff.

19 Cf. H. Dieter Betz, p. 6 and see Perrin's note 5 p. 70 concerning the purpose of these summaries.

longs. The summaries at issue are the following: 1:14-15; 3:7-12; 6:6b; 8:31; 9:30-31; 10:32-34; 11:1ab; 14:1-2; and 16:1(?).

The evidence is not equally strong in each case but it is sufficiently strong in six out of nine cases (all but 1:14-15; 11:1ab; and 16:1) to suggest that even in these less obvious cases Mark's summaries are truly introductory summaries. The easiest way to establish the introductory character of these summaries is to show that each of them truly looks forward to the material in the section that follows. A comparison between what is referred to in the summaries and what is treated in the subsequent narratives shows this to be true of the following summaries:

Summary: 3:7-12	*Narrative: 3:13-6:6a*
3:7-8: Jesus withdrew with his disciples TO THE LAKESIDE, and GREAT CROWDS . . . followed him . . . great numbers who had heard of all he was doing came to him . . .	4:1: Again he began to teach by the LAKESIDE, but such a HUGE CROWD gathered round him . . .
3:9: And he asked his disciples to have a BOAT ready for him because of the crowd, to keep him from being crushed.	4:1b: . . . that he got into a BOAT on the lake and sat there.
3:10: For he had cured so many that all who were afflicted in any way were CROWDING FORWARD TO TOUCH HIM	5:27: . . . (The woman with the haemmorhage) heard about Jesus, and she came up behind him through the crowd and TOUCHED his cloak . . . His disciples said to him: 'you see how the CROWD IS PRESSING ROUND you and yet you say, "WHO TOUCHED ME?"'
3:11: And the unclean spirits whenever they saw him, would fall down before him and SHOUT, 'YOU ARE THE SON OF GOD'. But he WARNED THEM STRONGLY NOT TO MAKE HIM KNOWN.	5:7: . . . (The Gerasene demoniac) SHOUTED at the top of his voice, 'what do you want with me, Jesus, SON of the most High God?'
	5:43: . . . and HE ORDERED THEM STRICTLY NOT TO LET ANYONE KNOW about (the raising of Jairus' daughter) . . .

Summary: 6:6b
6:6b: He made a TOUR around the VILLAGES, TEACHING.

Narrative: 6:7-8:30
In 6:7-8:30, Jesus travels back and forth across the lake to Gennesareth (6:53ff), and to the territory of Tyre (7:24ff), through the Decapolis (7:31), to the region of Dalmanutha (8:10), to Bathsaida (8:22), and finally to the villages around Caeserea Philippi (8:27).

The introductory passion prediction summaries in 8:31; 9:30-31; and 10:32-34 summarize the events to be recounted in 14:1-16:8, but while the events take place later, the instructions in 8:34-9:29; 9:35-10:31; and 10:41-52 are all given in view of the suffering foretold in the summaries and are intimately related to the summaries.

Summary: 11:1ab
When they were approaching JERUSALEM, in sight of BETHPHAGE and BETHANY, close by the MOUNT OF OLIVES . . .

Narrative: 11:7-13:37
JERUSALEM is the locale of the passion narrative as a whole: the introductory events (11:7-13:37), the passion (14-15), and the resurrection (16:1-8).
11:11b-12: . . . he went out to BETHANY with the twelve. Next day as they were leaving BETHANY (cf. also 14:3-9).
13:3: . . . and while he was sitting facing the Temple, on the MOUNT OF OLIVES . . .

Summary: 14:1-2
14:1a: It was TWO DAYS BEFORE THE PASSOVER AND THE FEAST OF UNLEAVENED BREAD,[20]

Narrative: 14-15
14:12: On the first day of UNLEAVENED BREAD . . .
14:17: When EVENING came . . .
15:1: First thing in the MORNING . . . 15:25: It was the THIRD HOUR . . . 15:33: When the SIXTH HOUR came there was darkness over the whole land until the NINTH HOUR.

---

20 The two days, reckoning backwards, are the 3rd day, the day of the passion, death, and burial; the second day, the day of the preparation for and eating of the supper (14:12ff). The events of 14:3-11 would belong to the day before the supper.

14:1b: . . . and the CHIEF PRIESTS and the scribes were LOOKING FOR A WAY TO ARREST JESUS BY SOME TRICK and have him PUT TO DEATH.

14:10-12: Judas . . . approached the CHIEF PRIESTS with an offer TO HAND JESUS OVER TO THEM. They were delighted . . . and he looked FOR A WAY of betraying him . . .

14:2: For they said, "It must not be during the festivities, or there will be a disturbance among the people

14:44: now the traitor HAD ARRANGED A SIGNAL with them. 'The one I kiss,' he said, 'he is the man.' (Jesus is arrested at night far from the crowd and the festivities.)

The remaining introductory summaries (1:14-15 and 16:1) present problems, but not as 'introductory'. The introductory summary in 1:14-15 is clearly introductory as it summarizes both the message Jesus preached ("The Kingdom has come" etc.) and the place he preached it (Galilee). It summarizes, however, not just what Jesus does in part I, section A (1:14-3:6) but in the whole of Part I (1:14-8:30). Thus while it differs from the other introductory summaries which look more properly to the narrative or instructional complexes which immediately follow, it is nevertheless truly introductory and must be considered an integral part of the triadic pattern of 1:14-3:6 (i.e., (1) Introductory summary, (2) Apostles, (3) Narrative complex) rather than the concluding pericope of what precedes. In passaing, we should observe that this evidence for attaching 1:14-15 to what follows rather than to what precedes, is in full agreement with the ever increasing number of authors who consider Mark's introductory theological construct as terminating at 1:13 rather than at 1:15.

What Mark's introductory summaries do for establishing the beginnings of parts and sections, his inclusions do for establishing the ends. In each section of part I Mark closes the ring on his narrative complex by means of inclusions. The section A narrative (1:21-3:6) opens with the cure of a demoniac on the sabbath in the synagogue at Capharnaum (1:21-28) and closes with the cure of the man with the withered hand on the sabbath in the synagogue at Capharnaum (cp. 2:1).[21]

The section B narrative (3:20-6:6) opens with a story about Jesus and his relatives and implies their opposition to him (3:20-21, 31-35).

---

21 The utilization of a minor inclusion in "sandwich" style (see 1:22 and 27), which is characteristic of Mark's composition, testifies to the Markan redaction of 1:21-28 and suggests Mark's intention of using this opening pericope to serve as an inclusion with the closing pericope (3:1-6) of section A.

It closes with the story of the rejection of Jesus by his towns-people at Nazareth (6:16).

The section C narrative (6:14-8:30) has the most interesting inclusion of all. It begins with the reports Herod hears concerning the identity of Jesus (6:14-16). It ends with Jesus asking his Apostles what reports they had heard about his identity from others (8:27-28) and who they, the Apostles, say Jesus is (8:29). The inclusion is interesting because it shows Mark redactionally creating a pericope (6:14-16) in order to form an inclusion-conclusion with 8:27-30.[22]

The inclusions in sections A (1:21-28 with 3:1-6) and B (3:20-21, 31-35 with 6:1-6) appear almost artless and accidental. There is nothing either artless or accidental about the inclusion in section C (6:14-16 with 8:27-29). The inclusion in section C confirms our thesis that Mark consciously arranged his material to create inclusions and to thereby draw definite boundaries or frames around each of these three narrative sections of part I.

In part II (8:31-10:52) there are no clear inclusions.[23] In part III (11:1-16:8) two inclusions help define the limits of sections A (11:1-13:37) and B (14:1-15:47). In section A, the narrative begins with the story of Jesus coming as Messiah to judge Jerusalem and the Temple (11:7-10) and ends with the coming of Jesus as the Son of Man to judge the world (13:5-37). In section B, the narrative begins with the anointing of Jesus for burial (14:3-9) and ends with the account of his actual burial (15:42-47).

In order to establish the structure of Mark's gospel as indicated in our outline, we have concentrated on three literary elements: first the consistent use of the same triadic pattern in each part of the gospel — (1) introductory summary (2) the Apostles (3) a narrative or instructional complex; second, Mark's use of summaries at the beginning of each part and section of his gospel as introductory summaries; and third, Mark's use of inclusions to set the bounds or frame his narrative complexes.

There is one more factor that can now safely be mentioned — Mark's propensity for triads and triadic arrangement. The use of the "numbers racket" in the interpretation of biblical authors is suspect and should be used with caution.[24] We have left it to the end, therefore, and use it only as a possibly but not certainly confirmatory indication that we have been on the right track.

---

22 For Mark's redactional work, cf. E. Schweitzer, THE GOOD NEWS ACCORDING TO MARK, p. 132 f.
23 But see N. Perrin in H. Dieter Betz (ed.), p. 30.
24 A. Farrer's, ST. MATTHEW AND ST. MARK (Westminster: Dacre Press, 2nd ed., 1966) is a good example of how authors can become obsessed by numbers and exaggerate their significance beyond tolerable acceptance.

Mark's liking for triads has not gone unnoticed.[25] There are many examples. In Gethsemane Jesus prays three times, and the Apostles are three times exhorted to watch (14:33, 35, 37). It is foretold that Peter will deny Jesus three times (14:29-31) and three times dutifully recounted how Peter fulfilled the prediction (14:53-54, 66-72). The duration of the crucifixion is indicated by a triad of references to the third, sixth, and ninth hours (15:25, 33-34). Three groups (the passersby, the chief priests and the scribes, and those who were crucified with him) mock Jesus on the cross (15:29-32). Three women watch as Jesus is buried (15:40), and three go to the tomb (16:1).

While it is true that most of these triads are in Mark's passion account and may be due to his source material, it is equally true that in the more clearly redactional sections of his gospel Mark shows a proclivity for triads. There are for example, the three predictions of the passion in 8:31; 9:31; 10:33-34; the triadic format of the prologue: (1) John the Baptist (1:1-8), (2) the baptism of Jesus (1:9-11), (3) the temptation of Jesus (1:12-13); the three parables of 4:1-34; the three Apostles who accompany Jesus at the raising of Jairus' daughter (5:37), at the transfiguration (9:2), and at the agony in the garden (14:33). In ch 13 the apocalyptic discourse is divided into three parts (13:5-13; 13:14-23; and 13:24-37) and the exhortation to watch is given three times (13:33, 35, 37). In ch 11-12, Jesus engages in controversy with three groups of Jews: (1) the chief priests and elders (11:27-33), (2) some of the Pharisees and Herodians (12:13-17), (3) the Sadducees (12:18-27).

Other triads could be mentioned,[26] but the above suffice as confirmation of Mark's propensity for "thinking three". When this propensity is considered along with the hard evidence of the summaries as introductory summaries, the inclusions as frames for the narratives, and the three times repeated triadic pattern of (1) introductory summary, (2) Apostles, (3) narrative or instruction complex in each of the three sections of parts I, II, and III, it would appear to argue well for a definite and sophisticated Marcan structure.

There remain two observations to be made about the results of our study. The first concerns the extent of the Marcan prologue — whether it terminates at 1:13 or goes on to include and terminate with 1:14-15. The second concerns the placement of the Caesarea Philippi episode of 8:27-30 — whether with what precedes or with what follows.

---

25 Cf. T. A. Burkill, New Light on the Earliest Gospel (Ithaca: Cornell University Press, 1972) pp. 256-258; N. Perrin in H. Dieter Betz (ed.), p. 29 f; A. Farrar, passim.
26 E.g. The chronological arrangement of the passion narrative into two sets of three days: first three days — ch 11-13; second three days —ch 14-15.

With regard to the prologue, it now seems established that it terminates at 1:13. On internal evidence one can argue that 1:1-13 deals with John the Baptist and how the beginning of the proclamation of the good news came about. In 1:14ff we have the 'beginning' of how Jesus began to preach the good news. Mark 1:14-15 does indeed look back at John the Baptist in the words "after John had been arrested," but the whole intent of the passage is to summarize what is to follow — namely Jesus' preaching in Galilee. When the forward looking content of 1:14-15 is taken into consideration along with the triadic pattern of (1) introductory summary (2) Apostles (3) narrative or instructional complex which is consistently repeated throughout parts I, II, and III, it would appear true to say that one cannot leave 1:14-15 as part of the prologue without destroying the clearly triadic pattern that prevails throughout the remainder of the gospel.

The placement of 8:27-30 is more difficult. Even those who recognize the triadic pattern of parts I and II cannot persuade themselves to commit 8:27-30 to the section which begins at 6:6b.[27] They are joined by many others.[28]

Without prejudice to the significant part 8:27-30 plays in the gospel as a whole both in relation to what precedes and what follows, and without prejudice to the tradition history of the pericope and its possible earlier connection with the Petrine incident of 8:32-33, and going only by the literary evidence we have seen for the structure of Mark's gospel, it would appear far more likely that 8:27-30 should be attached to what precedes than to what follows.

There are several reasons for attaching 8:27-30 to the section that precedes. First, and perhaps most important, the Petrine pericope forms a clear inclusion with 6:14-16. It must therefore be the end of that section of the gospel. Second, the clear signs of Marcan redaction in 6:14-16[29] suggest Mark intentionally composed 6:14-16 (modelling it on 8:27-30) in order to create the inclusion. Third, the triadic pattern of 8:31-10:52 is perhaps the most clear-cut triadic pattern in the whole gospel. If 8:27-30 is taken to be the beginning of this section (8:27-10:52), then the symmetry of the pattern is broken at its very inception.

27 E.g., E. Schweizer, pp. 165ff; R. P. Martin, pp. 129f; N. Perrin, pp. 11ff; E. J. Mally, 42:50.
28 E.g., D. J. Hawkin, pp. 495ff; T. A. Burkill, pp. 251; A. M. Ambrozic, pp. 232ff; T. J. Weeden, pp. 64ff; M. Hooker, THE SON OF MAN IN MARK, pp. 178f; Brown, Donfried, Reumann (edd.), PETER IN THE NEW TESTAMENT (NY: Paulist Press, 1973) pp. 64-69; Q. Quesnell, pp. 127ff, joins those who see 8:27ff as a starting point and gives an imposing list of authors espousing the same opinion: Loisy, Lagrange, Lohmyer, Lightfoot, Ebeling, Percy, Sjöberg, Schniewind, Marxsen, Taylor, Schweizer, Joh. Schneider, Leon Dufour, etc. (ibid, 128).
29 Cf. E. Schweitzer, pp. 132-135.

Fourth, the triadic pattern of part I (1:14-8:30) is such that each section not only ends with an inclusion, as we have seen, but with a climactic episode. Thus, section A (1:14-3:6) ends with the climactic statement: "The Pharisees went out and at once began to plot with the Herodians against him, discussing how to destroy him" (3:6). Section B (3:7-6:6a) ends with the climactic rejection of Jesus by the people of his hometown Nazareth (6:1-6). It would seem we should expect some kind of climax at the end of section C (6:6bff). It is difficult to consider the cure of the blind man in 8:2-26 as a climax. Peter's profession of Jesus' messiahship, however, provides a dramatic climax not only for section C (6:6b-8:30) but for the whole first part of the gospel (1:14-8:30).

The long history of scholarship which connects Peter's profession of Jesus' messiahship with Jesus' rebuke of Peter in 8:32-34 is not easy to oppose. However, in recent years some authors have begun to dissociate the two at least on the basis of function.[30]

The function of 8:27-30 is now seen to be to serve as a proper and true testimony to Jesus' messiahship rather than to serve as a false testimony which has to be rejected by Jesus (presumably in 8:32-34). It has been pointed out by many that the messianic secret formula of 8:30 is not used in order to deny the truth of what has been professed. Indeed, in every case where the messianic secret formula is used in the gospel, it is used in relationship to what is true about Jesus. With regard to the truth of Peter's profession, it has been pointed out that the gospel begins with a statement about Jesus' messiahship, and that Jesus does not deny he is the Messiah when questioned by the Jewish authorities (15:61ff). Mark has no intention of denying Jesus' messiahship.

The proper function of 8:32-34, as of 9:33-34 and 10:35-37, has been shown to be to serve as a literary technique to point up the necessity of going beyond the profession of Jesus as Messiah to comprehend his passion, death, and resurrection as paradigmatic of Christian discipleship.[31] Jesus' rebuke of Peter in 8:32-34, therefore, should be seen as directed, not to Peter's profession of Jesus' messiahship in 8:27-30, but to his refusal to accept Jesus' statement concerning a suffering and dying Messiah in 8:31.[32]

---

30 Cf. Peter In The New Testament, pp. 68-69.
31 Cf. D. J. Hawkin, p. 500.
32 The author-editors of Peter In The New Testament (p. 69) make the point as follows: "In this interpretation the function of the Son of Man saying introduced by Mark in 8:31 is not a rejection of Peter's confession but a corrective to it by the addition of a note of suffering. Peter's confession is inadequate because he does not see that suffering is part of the career of the Messiah. It is only when Peter rejects this note of suffering that Mark (8:33) has Jesus rebuke him sharply by calling him Satan. The Satanic work of Peter is not in his confession of Jesus as Messiah but in his tempting Jesus toward a notion of messiahship that does not recognize the divinely ordained suffering and death of Jesus (see 1:13 for Satan the tempter)."

On purely literary grounds, therefore, there seems more than sufficient reason to attach 8:27-30 to what precedes and to consider it the climax of part I of Mark's gospel (1:14-8:30).

Eugene H. Maly

CREATION IN THE NEW TESTAMENT

In this paper we hope to explore the new meaning that Jesus Christ has given to creation, especially as that meaning is exposed in the magnificent Christological hymn in the Epistle to the Colossians. But before we come to that hymn some preliminary remarks are in order.

The New Testament takes for granted the Old Testament doctrine on creation, in particular the conviction that all things came ultimately from the one God. Thus, in commenting on divorce, Jesus notes that "At the beginning of creation God made them male and female" (Mk 9:6). Or He recognizes God's act of creation as one of the primary reasons why man must praise God, "Father, Lord of heaven and earth, to you I offer praise" (Mt 11:25).

But much more explicitly is creation seen in its salvific or soteriological aspect, thus developing the priestly author's observation that the work of creation was completed on the seventh day, which was the day which God blessed and made holy (Gn 2:3). Authors have noted this redemptive aspect of the creative act of God. In the New Testament Jesus is seen as acting in a similar way. This is most clearly stated in John's Gospel where Jesus, in referring to His Sabbath cures, remarks, "My father is at work until now, and I am at work as well" (Jn 5:17). Just as the Father "worked" on the Sabbath in the act of sanctifying, so is Jesus justified in curing the sick on that day since such cures are the work of making whole a creation that had been wounded by sin. Moreover, just as the Father's work of sanctification never ceases, since there is no mention of the close of the seventh day as there is of the others, so Jesus' work must continue. The history of the world is a history of salvation in which the Father's creative-redemptive activity never ceases. Now that history has taken on deeper dimensions through the salvific work of Christ.

The Sabbath cures narrated in the Synoptic Gospels seem to have the same import. Referring to the cure of the deformed woman in Luke 13:10-17, one author observes:

> The story emphasizes that Jesus healed on the Sabbath and that the healing fulfilled the true design of the Sabbath. The Sabbath is the day on which the work of creation was completed; and as such, it was sanctified by God. The Sabbath, therefore, is the appropriate day for a miraculous cure, when Jesus wants to commence the perfecting of the world. He is himself the initiation of the eternal

EUGENE H. MALY is Professor of Sacred Scripture, Mount St. Mary Seminary-of-the-West, Norwood, Ohio.

Sabbath Day of a world restored and brought to peace. It is in this sense that the letter to the Hebrews (4:9) later states that the people of God will finally attain to the great Sabbath rest.[1]

But it would seem that the most profound insights into creation were developed by the early Church in her reflection on a cosmic Christology, that is, on the relationship of the whole of creation to the risen Lord. There are several references in the New Testament writings, representing quite disparate traditions, to this relationship (e.g., 1 Cor 8:6; Heb 1:2, 10; Jn 1:3; Rev 3:14). Moreover, in each of these cases the relationship is referred to in a manner which quite manifestly indicates that it is a solid part of tradition, not a new doctrine just devised. In other words, the Church must have come quite early to the conviction of a cosmic Christology.

The one place where the doctrine is developed at some length is in Colossians 1:15-20. It therefore deserves our special attention. If the epistle is the product of Paul's mind, then it is a development of a thought that he had referred to in passing in his Corinthian correspondence (1 Cor 8:6). Even so, it is the conviction of the majority of scholars that the hymn is earlier than its present canonical form, indicating again the early development of this credal conviction.

We must begin with the formulation of the hymn itself:

He is the image of the invisible God, the first-born of all creatures. In him everything in heaven and on earth was created, things visible and invisible, whether thrones or dominations, principalities or powers; all were created through him and for him. He is before all else that is. In him everything continues in being. It is he who is the head of the body, the church; he who is the beginning, the first-born of the dead, so that primacy may be his in everything. It pleased God to make absolute fullness reside in him, to reconcile everything in his person, both on earth and in the heavens, making peace through the blood of his cross.

It should be noted that Paul is writing the letter in order to warn the Colossians about a dangerous teaching in their midst that is threatening to reduce the role of Jesus Christ to that of one of the angelic hierarchy. In this teaching other "powers" and "principalities" would be called on to help span the gap between God and His creation. According to one author the propaganda line would have been something like this:

All religions have their contributions to make, and so you can confine belief in Jesus Christ with the beliefs and practices of other cults. If you want the maximum insurance cover against the forces that

Press, 1971), Vol. I, p. 19f.
1 K. Schelkle, THEOLOGY OF THE NEW TESTAMENT (Collegeville, MN: Liturgical

control and endanger our existence, it is best to have a 'comprehensive policy' including what other Mystery religions have to offer.[2]

In other words, the hymn, with a few but important additions by Paul himself, is directed against a form of syncretism that would in the end eviscerate Christianity whose central confession is that Jesus is Lord.

Let us now examine the statements in the hymn in some detail. It begins with the profession that Christ is the image of the invisible God. This is an obvious allusion to Genesis 1:26f where man is said to be made in the image of God. But the addition of the word "invisible" and the whole context suggest that Christ is not just another man. Rather, He is the visible image of what God is invisibly. "As the 'image' of the invisible God, he does not belong to what was created, but stands with the creator who, in Christ, is acting upon the world and with the world."[3]

The second statement, "the first-born of all creation" (*prōtotokos pasēs ktiseōs*), could also be misleading. For one who did not know the Wisdom background of this concept, it could be understood (as it was by the Arians), as meaning that Christ was created first. But this is especially denied by the Old Testament Wisdom speculation that forms the background of the hymn. According to that speculation Wisdom is, indeed, said to have been created at the beginning of Yahweh's work (Pr 8:22) and "created before all things" (Sir 1:4), but the emphasis is decidedly on pre-eminence, not on creation, for Wisdom boasts that it was from eternity (Sir 24:9), was present with God when he made the world (Wis 9:9) and was the sharer of His throne (Wis 9:4). Consequently,

> With the description of the pre-existent Christ as the *prōtotokos pasēs ktiseōs* it must not be said that he was created as the first, and then the rest of creation followed. Rather it is much more a reference to his uniqueness whereby he is differentiated from all of creation. The author is speaking not of a temporal priority but of pre-eminence which is due him as the mediator of all creation. As the first-born he stands as the Lord of all creation.[4]

The following verse is the heart of the hymn's theology on the relation of Christ to creation. First of all, everything (and this is meant as all-inclusive as the words "in heaven and on earth" indicate) was created in him. This almost certainly points to Christ as the instrument or mediator of creation, as the background of the hymn suggests and as the following phrase "through him" makes clear. Christ, therefore, is the *archē*,

---

2 G. Thompson, CAMBRIDGE BIBLE COMMENTARY: LETTERS OF PAUL TO EPHESIANS, TO COLOSSIANS, AND TO PHILEMON (London: Cambridge Univ. Press, 1967), p. 121.
3 E. Lohse, COLOSSIANS AND PHILEMON (Philadelphia: Fortress Press, 1971), p. 48.
4 *Ibid.*

or primal principle for the creation of everything. Moreover, the same *panta,* or "all things", were created for him; that is, he is their goal or final purpose. This is a remarkable statement inasmuch as it defines the Christological nature of the creative act from the beginning. Hence, we can suggest the axiom "ktisiology presupposes Christology," meaning that the doctrine about creation presupposes that about Christ. It can also be noted in this verse that the aorist tense in the first part (*ektisthē,* "was created") suggesting a once-for-all action, is replaced by the perfect tense in the second part (*ektistai,* "were created;" there is no difference in the English translation), expressing the notion of continuing activity. Finally, Paul specifies certain entities which are included in "all things," namely, thrones, dominations, principalities, powers, which the Colossian teachers would have placed outside the sphere of Christ's influence. If they exist (and Paul does not deny it), they exist because of Christ. And if they were created through and for Christ, then *a fortiori* all else was, the Colossians could conclude.

Verse 17 has two parts, the first part describing the relationship of Christ to all things ("He is before all else that is"), the second describing the relationship of all things to Christ ("In him everything continues in being"). The phrase "before all else" can be taken in the sense of priority and so pre-existence, or in the sense of greater dignity. The former would seem to fit in better with the context and would be in accord with the statement in John's Gospel, "Before Abraham was I am." The word *pantōn* is without doubt neuter, not masculine. Thus this part of the verse proclaims the Lordship of Christ over all things. In the second part it is said that all things find their subsistence, their basic stand, their unity in Christ. The idea that all aspects of the cosmos find their unity in something is recognized in Platonic and Stoic philosophy. Also, Hellenistic Judaism used the same Greek word to express the basic stand of all of God's creation. And in Sirach 43:26 we read that " . . . by his word all things hold together." All of these ideas are brought together in Christ.

The first part of verse 18 contains a completely new idea, namely, the designation of Christ as head of His body, the Church. Before this the Church had been referred to as the body of Christ, as in 1 Cor 12, but there had been no direct reference to Him as its head. If Paul, or the author, took over an existing hymn, then the apposition "the Church" was probably added. In this case the original meaning of the *sōma* would have been the cosmos. The world or cosmos as a body is an early concept.
This mythological manner of conceptualization in which the cosmos appears as a body governed by its head provides the answer to man's search - man who is beset by worry and fear of the powers in the world and who asks how the world can be brought to its proper

order: Christ is the 'head' (*kephalē*) that governs the 'body' (*sōma*) of the cosmos; the cosmos is ruled and held together by this head. The universe is founded and established through him alone, i.e., in him alone is salvation.[5]
(The further question could be raised as to what normative value this pre-canonical meaning would have for us today.)

The canonical author, at any rate, by putting the words "the Church" in apposition with "the body," has historicized his contemplation of Christ. The Church thus becomes the "locus" of Christ's lordship over the cosmos. That the author has given an ecclesiological twist to what was a purely cosmological concept is evident. (And we might ask whether this could provide some basis for a broader understanding of Christology that would still be ecclesial.) But, since the Church is the community of those who are "called" out of the darkness of sin, it is clear that there is a soteriological note here, too. The immediate context confirms this soteriological aspect. The cosmic Christ who is the head of the Church is also the "first-born of the dead." In other words, in the biblical mentality He is not only the first to rise but effectively represents all the others; He is the *aparchē,* the first principle, the cause of the resurrection of others. Käsemann expresses this soteriological note very forcefully when he writes:

> The community in his body, inasmuch as it lives from the resurrection of the dead and wanders towards the resurrection of the dead. But that means, in the here and now, that it stands within the forgiveness of sins . . . Because it stands within forgiveness, it is new creation, the cosmic powers have nothing more to say to it, to give to it, or to ask of it. There is no way to the creation other than the way which passes through, and continues in, forgiveness. Every immediate attempt to break through, every attempt, that is, which does not derive from eschatology, turns into cosmology, into apostasy from forgiveness, into renewed slavery to the cosmic tyrants, who then take on the aspect of demonic powers.[6]

Verse 19 also has its share of difficulties, but the theology is more overwhelming than the difficulties. The verse can be translated: "It pleased (God) that all the fullness should dwell in him," or "It pleased all the fullnes to dwell in him." In either case, it refers to the fullness of deity, even if God isn't explicitly mentioned (cf. Col 2:9 where this is explicitly stated). The important word here is *plērōma,* which has a long pre-history. The *idea* is found already in the Old Testament: "Because the spirit of the Lord has filled the world, and that which holds all things together knows what is said" (Wis 1:7; note the context of holding to-

---

5 *Ibid.*
6 E. Kasemann, NEW TESTAMENT ESSAYS, quoted by Lohse.

gether). But there seems to be some dependence on the Hellenistic world, too, where *plērōma* was variously understood, at times in a kind of pantheistic sense: God himself becomes the fullness of all things. Our author, however, gives it a soteriological meaning in the use of the quasi technical word *eudokēsen*, "it pleased." The word is used of God's saving will in the Septuagint and is also used to express the divine election, for example of God's chosen one in Mark 1:11. In our hymn God's choice or election is associated with the dwelling of the *plērōma* in Christ.

> The emphasis is not on God's immanence, but on the cosmic effect of God's power working in Christ and in the Church. There is a possible influence of the Stoic idea of a universe filling and being filled by God. Later Gnostic systems made much of a teaching that God's *plērōma* was divided up and shared by a host of intermediaries. Paul may be counteracting a Gnostic tendency to trust in a number of intermediaries who shared God's power.[7] (Grassi, JBC).

There is but one intermediary precisely because of His unique relationship to creation.

In verse 20 the major theme is the reconciliation of *ta panta* "in his person" (literally, into him). There are a number of significant points that can be made here. First of all, the word "reconcile" is used only three times in the New Testament: here, in verse 22 and in Eph 2:16. In the last two cases it is used of reconciliation of persons. But the context of our passage certainly includes all of creation (an idea contained also in Rom 8:18ff), and so a secular or cosmic eschatology is proposed. The verse presupposes that the cosmic order had suffered a severe breach in its harmony and unity, and biblical revelation would determine this as having taken place because of sin. Something similar to this concept of reconciliation is found in John 12:32, where Jesus says that through His being lifted up (i.e., on the cross and in glory), He will draw all men to Himself. This is the usual reading, although there are good texts which read the neuter plural. This would be an interesting parallel to the Colossian text.

Secondly, the reference to Christ in verse 18 as the "first-born of the dead" suggests that the author does think of reconciliation through resurrection and glory (despite the probably later addition of "through the blood of his cross" which we shall see). "Heaven and earth" (in the pre-Copernican view) are brought together through this resurrection and thus are reconciled.

Thirdly, we can note the empasis on a realized eschatology here; there is no reference to the parousia eschatology, a reality yet to be attained. It is not that the author would exclude the latter, but the stress is

---

7 Joseph A. Grassi, "The Letter to the Colossians" in JEROME BIBLICAL COMMENTARY (Englewood Cliffs, N.J.: Prentice-Hall, 1968), p. 337.

on the proleptic manifestation of reconciliation in the person of Christ.

Lohse notes, fourthly, that this eschatological reconciliation estab-lished Christ's lordship over all, and that, because He is the mediator of reconciliation, He is also praised as the mediator of creation in the first part. Thus we have the axiom that protology presupposes eschatology.

Finally, a new idea is introduced through the expression "making peace by the blood of his cross." This is often taken as an addition to the original hymn by the Pauline author. The theology of glory of verse 18 ("first-born of the dead") gives way here to a theology of the cross, which is consonant with the rest of the epistle (cf. 2:14f). The two, how-ever, are complementary, not contradictory, as Phil 2:6-11 would indi-cate. Here the emphasis has the value of showing that, in the Christian conviction, true peace is achieved, not in some "heavenly drama" (Lohse), but in the very historical death of Jesus on the cross. Thus is the continuity between the historical Jesus and the risen Lord maintained.

If we may summarize the contents of this remarkable hymn, we say that it has profound eschatological, Christological, soteriological and ecclesiological dimensions. As far as the first is concerned, there is pre-sented both a cosmic or secular (which means all of creation) and a rea-lized eschatology. Christologically it establishes the Christocentrism of New Testament theology and indeed of all revelation. The soteriology is expressed both in the resurrection and in the crucifixion. Moreover, the soteriological drama involves all of creation. Finally, the Church is the arena in which this cosmic redemption is being worked out. Christ is its head, and His lordship, already established, will be mediated to the world through the Church.

This ancient hymn does not stand alone, though it does stand uni-quely, as illustrative of the completely new way in which Christians re-flected on creation. As in the Old Testament, there are still the three as-pects which have been proposed, namely, the secular, redemptive or soter-iological, and eschatological. But these three aspects have been joined by a fourth, the Christological, which completely re-orientates the con-sideration of creation. Among the other texts which state or imply this same re-orientation is, for example, Paul's statement in 1 Cor 8:6 that "for us there is one God, the Father, from whom all things come and for whom we live; and one Lord Jesus Christ, through whom everything was made and through whom we live." The author of the letter to the He-brews speaks of Christ as the One "whom he (the Father) has made heir of all things and through whom he first created the universe" (1:2). In describing Christ as the Word through whom "all things came into being" the author of the fourth Gospel alludes to the same conviction (1:3).

And the author of Revelation calls Christ "the source of God's creation" (3:14).

There is a remarkable feature of all these texts, not excluding the Colossian hymn we saw in some detail. As Karl Schelkle states it in his *Theology of the New Testament,*

> None of these places constitutes a first deployment or foundation of this Christology. Rather, it simply appears to have been in firm possession for a long time. In various locales of the Church, creeds and doctrine, building upon what was already accepted, applied the old teaching on creation to Christ, and carry it a step further in that they insert Christ into the traditional formula of faith, as the agent of creation.[8]

The primary referent in these passages is Jesus Christ, as Schelkle's observation indicates. There are still other passages in which the primary referent is creation or the creature man and in which Christianity's unique way of seeing creation is again demonstrated. These are particularly those passages which refer to the Christian as a "new creature" or a "new creation." Thus, in 2 Cor 5:17 Paul declares, "This means that if anyone is in Christ, he is a new creation. The old order has passed away; now all is new!" Affirming that all the differences of the old order have been obliterated by this new act of creation, he tells the Galatians, "It means nothing whether one is circumcised or not. All that matters is that one is created anew" (6:15). The newness, of course, is because of the Christ-dimension, as the author of the letter to Ephesians brings out: "We are truly his handiwork, created in Christ Jesus to lead the life of good deeds which God prepared for us in advance" (2:10). Other similar passages refer to the old man and the new man, to the outward man and the inward man. Again, the difference always is rooted in Christ.

How are we to understand this? Various scholars offer varying, but not necessarily contradictory explanations. C. K. Barrett remarks:

> In these passages, the 'new' or 'inward' man is not precisely Christ, as objectively distinct from the believer, nor, at the other extreme, is it a new nature, mystically or sacramentally bestowed upon and received by the believer, which he henceforth objectively and personally possesses. The terms, though applied primarily to the individual Christian, nevertheless . . . point also to the new community. Like the word 'image', they direct us to that place where the individual and corporate hope of mankind meet in the future in Christ. For Paul, 'Man' is a historical and individual term, for Jesus of Nazareth, who lived in Palestine in the first half of the first century and was crucified under Pontius Pilate, was the Man to come. But the

---

8 Schelkle, p. 49.

same word is also an eschatological and collective term, for it denotes the new humanity that is to be in Christ, and is already partially and inadequately adumbrated in Christians. The full conception of the Man to come can be disclosed only at the last day, when the heavenly Man appears with the holy ones who are conformed to his image.[9]

John Bligh, in his commentary on Galatians, sees a possible relationship between this new creation and the vision in Dn 7, where

man is reinstated as ruler over the beasts (cf. Gn 1:28; Ps 8:6-7) when the Son of Man receives dominion over every race and tribe and tongue . . . Christ, the fulfillment of this prophetic vision, is, in Paul's thought, the new Adam; he receives the Church as his bride; a new aeon is inaugurated, and human history begins again . . . [10]

Perhaps we can sum it up in this way. Christ *is* the newness because He is the second Adam, the perfect Man, the fully realized eschatological manifestation of what God had intended in creating at the beginning of time. This newness is at least incipiently communicated to man when he is newly and radically re-oriented to Christ through the act of faith or sacramentally united with Him in Baptism. Christ's newness is, as it were, contagious; it is incapable of being avoided if there is any contact with Him whatever. And while this contact is fundamentally affirmed in man who is able to give himself to Christ, no part of creation is innocent of some contact with Him since He is the Word of God who has taken on human flesh and thereby has irrevocably identified Himself with creation. That is why St. Paul can declare so boldly that all of creation will "share in the glorious freedom of the children of God" (Rom 8:21).

9 C. K. Barrett, FROM FIRST ADAM TO LAST (N.Y.: Scribners, 1962), p. 98f.
10 John Bligh, GALATIANS: DISCUSSION OF ST. PAUL'S EPISTLE (London: St. Paul's Publications, 1969), p. 465.

M. Lucetta Mowry

CHARISMATIC GIFTS IN PAUL

The resurgence of charismatic gifts within the Pentecostal movement during the last two decades is a religious phenomenon of unusual interest for psychologists, psychotherapists, anthropologists, clergy and biblical scholars.[1] In the history of religions a comparable explosion of spiritual fervor is the emergence of new religious sects in Japan which has been vividly described by the Japanese term, "the rush hour of the gods." The western counterpart is the neo-Pentecostal development regarded by some analysts as one which may be "the fastest growing single movement within Christianity today."[2] Its flood-like force has burst through the walls of traditional Pentecostal sects and penetrated such long-established ecclesiastical organizations as the Roman Catholic, Presbyterian, Lutheran and Episcopal churches. Within these congregations the neo-Pentecostals are challenging the effectiveness of formal ritual and expository sermons. These spiritually gifted individuals claim that the impact of the Holy Spirit on their lives cannot be expressed by means of rational concepts nor understood within the framework of usual experiences but by means of tongue-speaking or glossolalia which has been defined as "a form of unintelligible vocalization which has non-semantic meaning to the speaker."[3] Though some analysts of the contemporary phenomenon have commented on the divisive effect created by these claims of the spiritually gifted, they are inclined to appraise the occurrences of tongue-speaking sympathetically and

---

M. LUCETTA MOWRY is Professor of New Testament at Wellesley College, Wellesley, Massachusetts.

1 In a recent article R. W. Raskopf reviews four books on the Pentecostal movement each of which is written from a particular point of view and has an extensive bibliography on the subject. The four works are TONGUES OF MEN AND ANGELS by William J. Samarin; THE PENTECOSTALS by Walter J. Hollenweger; THE PSYCHOLOGY OF SPEAKING IN TONGUES by John P. Kildahl; and HOLY SPIRIT BAPTISM by Anthony Hoekema. See "Recent Literature on the Pentecostal Movement" by Roger W. Raskopf in the *Anglican Theological Review*, Series 2 (1973), pp. 113-118. Several recent articles on this subject are S. L. Bergquist, "Revival of Glossolalic Practice in the Catholic Church", *Perkins School of Theology Journal* XXVII (1973), pp. 32-37; A. S. Davis "Pentecostal Movement in Black Christianity", *The Black Church* I (1972), pp. 65-88; Walter J. Hollenweger, "Pentecostalism and Black Power", *Theology Today* XXX (1973), pp. 228-238; L. Lovett "Perspective on the Black Origins of the Contemporary Pentecostal Movement," *Journal of the Inter-denominational Theological Center* I (1973), pp. 36-47; B. Doyle, "Lutheran Pentecostals", *Christianity Today* XXVII (1973), pp. 44-45; Virginia H. Hine, "Pentecostal Glossolalia: Toward a Functional Interpretation", *Journal for the Scientific Study of Religion* VIII (1969), pp. 211-226; Felicitas D. Goodman, "Phonetic Analysis of Glossolalia in Four Cultural Settings," *Ibid.* pp. 227-239.
2 Raskopf, R. W., p. 118.
3 Hines, Virginia H., p. 211.

call attention to the therapeutic value for individuals who have received this gift of the Holy Spirit.

One of their claims is that tongue-speaking marks a revival of primitive Christianity when the fire of inspiration burned most brightly. They urge the churches to recapture that early zeal and enthusiasm. For the biblical historian this assertion raises three major issues. The first concerns an evaluation of the evidence from the record of the New Testament. The second involves an examination of the nature of spiritual gifts or charisms, especially that of glossolalia in the experience of the early Church. The biblical scholar also wishes to ascertain how the leaders of the early Church assessed the merits of these gifts for the life of the Church.

Evidence from the New Testament indicates that two of its authors speak of this religious phenomenon. Paul, the earlier of the two, discusses the subject extensively in 1 Cor 12-14. Several decades later Luke in his Acts of the Apostles tells of a chain of glossolalic experiences which, in his opinion, had great importance for the development of the Christian movement. The verdict of biblical scholars on the historical value of this evidence favors the Pauline description because Luke apparently has changed certain features along symbolic lines to suit the needs of his book. These needs are his understanding of the destiny of the Christian movement and the effect of Christ in that movement.[4]

Though this paper deals primarily with the Pauline evidence, it may be useful for our discussion to indicate what may lie behind the Lukan narrative. In spite of the fact that the evangelists, including Luke, do not portray Jesus or his disciples as ecstatics, it may very well be that the tension created by the appearances of the risen Christ to certain individuals and groups was heightened by the overtones of vindication and of fulfillment of personal and national hopes. Under the impulse of this tension the disciples may have left Galilee and returned to Jerusalem, the city where the Kingdom would first appear. There members of the Christian group were apparently caught up in the first of a series of ecstatic religious experiences. Though strange to this group, such experiences were not unknown in other circles such as that of the cult of Dionysus whose members practised and cultivated them.[5]

---

4 The Lucan references are Acts 2:1-42; 4:31; 8:14-17; 10:44-48; 11:15-17 and 19:2-7. The Pauline references are 1 Cor 12-14; 1 Thes 5:19-20; Col 3:16; cf. Eph 5:18-20. For a discussion of this material see E. Haenchen, THE ACTS OF THE APOSTLES, esp. pp. 166-175; R. F. Zehnle, PETER'S PENTECOSTAL DISCOURSE, esp. pp. 112-123; and Ira J. Martin, "Glossolalia in the Apostolic Church", *Journal of Biblical Literature* LXIII (1944), pp. 123-130.

5 In his article on *glossa* in THEOLOGICAL DICTIONARY OF THE NEW TESTAMENT, vol. I, pp. 722-23, Behm refers to Greek religious practices of the enthusiastic cult of the Thracian Dionysus, the divinatory manticism of the Delphic Phrygia, the Bacides and the Syblis which had associations with the esoteric, mysterious, magical and supernatural.

However one accounts for the sudden emergence of this religious phenomenon in the Christian community at Jerusalem it apparently was led to associate these occurrences of glossolalia with its eschatological hope for it seemed to have interpreted this new potentialized existence as the realization of life in the Kingdom of God. The life of the new age had dawned and the hope of the Kingdom had begun to be realized. It found support for this conviction in a prophecy of God to the effect that in the last days the Spirit of God was to be poured forth on all flesh. It would be, therefore, only a short time until prophecies would be fulfilled and until the cosmic cataclysm and the visible return of Jesus on the clouds would take place. The early community was also led to associate these experiences with the power of Jesus' person upon its life and to regard the Spirit as sent by him. Though one derives these impressions from the record in Acts, one needs to check them against the evidence which comes from Paul about another Christian community, the church at Corinth.

Before turning directly to Paul's discussion of the phenomenon of spiritual gifts at Corinth in 1 Cor 12-14, it is important to comment briefly on Paul's relationship with the Christian community there and on the circumstances which gave rise to Paul's remarks about charisms. The significance of Paul's correspondence with this church lies in its extensiveness and especially in revealing Paul at work as a missionary among his churches.[6] Paul's life was intimately linked with the Corinthian church (2 Cor 10:14b; 11:2; 2:1-4; 7:7-13a) and his correspondence with that community indicates that he was fighting for the preservation of his work and of his sense of integrity in Corinth. Though Paul characterizes the members of this church in the thanksgiving element of his introduction of 1 Cor (1:1-9) as individuals who had been enriched in all ecstatic and prophetic utterances and admits that these gifts served as a confirmation of their testimony to Christ, he also states that the ultimate question does not concern their gifts but their guilt (1 Cor 1:8). While Paul recognizes this congregation to be a very gifted one, he also views it as strong-willed, unsteady and still deficient in knowledge (1 Cor 1:18-2:5).

The immediate circumstance which gave rise to the writing of these chapters on spirtual gifts and others of 1 Cor was information received about the situation in Corinth (1 Cor 1-6) and questions raised by the church in a letter from it (1 Cor 7-15). 1 Corinthians is, therefore, not a doctrinal letter in the sense that those to the churches at Rome and in

---

6 Paul's Corinthian correspondence constitutes about two-fifths of the canonical material which may be ascribed to him. Originally this correspondence must have been more extensive and probably consisted of at least four letters. In 1 Cor 5:9, 11 he refers to a letter written before 1 Cor, a fragment of which may possibly be 2 Cor 6:14-7:1. In 2 Cor 2:4 he also mentions a "painful letter" which cannot be 1 Cor but may be 2 Cor 10-13.

Galatia are. Here Paul does not present an organized and systematic statement of the Christian faith but deals with ethical and practical matters. He does not deal with the issue of the relationship of Christianity to Judaism but with Christianity's contact with the Hellenistic world. In 1 Cor, then, he takes up practical considerations regarding factionalism which is imperilling the harmony of the community, immorality and incest within the church, litigations and law suits, and the problems about the advisability of mixed marriages, of eating food offered to idols, of the variety of spiritual gifts and doubts about the teaching on the resurrection.

The section of the letter dealing with spiritual gifts appears in the second part of the letter (1 Cor 7-15), the section in which Paul is answering questions raised by the congregation in a written communication to him (1 Cor 7:1). That Paul devotes three whole chapters to this subject is in itself an indication of the importance of the phenomenon of possession by the Spirit in the life of the early Church. From Paul's answer we would deduce that the Corinthians had asked two questions: how does one distinguish between Christian and non-Christian possession by the Spirit and which of several types of Spirit-possession is to be deemed as most valuable? As stated these questions suggest certain implications. The first question implies that in the life of the Corinthian Christians ecstatic forms of religious expression were not limited to the period after their conversion. They knew them from the pagan phase of their religious life as they well might for ecstacy and spiritual possession were typical expressions of the religious life of various pagan cults. The second question implies a limitation in the Corinthians' understanding of the extent and variety of spiritual gifts. They saw only the abnormal types and, as it appears from Paul's discussion, they wanted him to determine for them the relative value of speaking with tongues and prophecy. The request for such advice indicates, of course, their rationalizing procedure.

Paul has little difficulty in answering the first question (1 Cor 12: 1-3). Since spiritual gifts are an important phase of religious life, pagan or Christian, the Corinthians should be well-informed on that subject. As pagans they had been attracted to idol worship. Though the idols themselves were dumb, they had associated with them demons who could and did take possession of men and were the cause of ecstatic utterances. The Corinthians who were familiar with the phenomenon of spirit-possession needed, therefore, a criterion to differentiate between pagan and Christian spirit-possession. Paul's test is stated with respect to the nature of things said: "I want you to understand that no one speaking by the Spirit of God ever says 'Jesus be cursed!' and no one can say 'Jesus is Lord' except by the Holy Spirit." (1 Cor 12:3 RSV)

The second question regarding the relative merits of spiritual gifts is more difficult. Consequently, Paul gives his answer in a long and very carefully worked out section of this letter (1 Cor 12:4-14:40). For this reason one needs to follow his line of thought. He begins by admitting the variety of spiritual gifts and points to a larger range of diversity than the Corinthians had implied by their question (1 Cor 12:4-11). He first suggests that in addition to the variety of gifts there are varieties of service and of *energmatōn* (i.e., activities that call forth miracles or unusual deeds). He also states that behind the variety of functions and endowments there is a variety of divine being: Spirit, Christ and God. Since Paul can use these terms interchangeably (cf. Rom 8:9-11), he has not formulated a doctrine of the trinity as a basis for arguing unity in diversity but has expressed that unity in terms of function. Later in his argument he makes this clear by asserting that the Corinthians have not been given gifts for their private enjoyment but for serving the common good. After listing a richer variety of gifts under three main categories (the gifts of intellect, of faith and of utterance), the apostle concludes this initial phase of his discussion on the theme — that behind all diversity lies a unity to be discerned in the working of the same Spirit (1 Cor 12:8-11).

This theme suggests to him one of the most familiar analogies in ancient literature. The analogy of the body with its many members had been used by Greek rhetoricians to show how the one and the many may be reconciled. Though the analogy is appropriate for Paul's discussion, his application of this figure to the local condition at Corinth (1 Cor 12:14-26) is not carried out in a very happy or orderly fashion. The first point Paul wants to make of the analogy is that the body with its many members may be compared to the Spirit with the many spiritual ministries within the Church. The body, which is best visualized in congregational terms, is Christ himself.[7] The rite of baptism performed at the time of a convert's entrance into the Christian community and the drinking of one Spirit, probably associated here with baptism rather than with the celebration of the eucharist, are constitutive factors of this unity (1 Cor 12:13). The reference to baptism is quite appropriate in this context because baptism was traditionally the time of the bestowal of the Spirit and was regarded by Paul as a rite signifying a dying and rising with Christ and an incorporation into his body.

In his application of this analogy to the local condition at Corinth Paul seems to be concerned about two problems. On the one hand, some members of the congregation have apparently used the fact of their own

---

7 In Rom 12:4-5 Paul will also use the same figure in connection with gifts of the Spirit and the ministries of the Church. In Col 1:18 and 2:19, however, he adds a new element, namely that Christ is the head of the body.

capacities to cut themselves off from the rest of the church which has different capacities. Paul's answer to that problem is that the body requires all its members and that the members have no significance apart from the unity of the body. On the other hand, there is implied in the remark about the existence of a differentia between higher and lower members of the body another problem at Corinth (1 Cor 12:21-26). There seem to have been certain persons in the congregation who arrogated to themselves a status of special importance over others and thereby denied them a position of equal significance. Paul's comment on this situation stresses the fact that all parts of the body, even the weaker parts, are equally necessary. By being clothed these weaker and less honored parts are raised to a level of equalization and are not to be ignored or despised.

Finally, in his application of the analogy to the Corinthian church (1 Cor 12:27-31) Paul again asserts that each individual is a member of the body of Christ and that each individual has his function to perform within the community. Interestingly, his list of functionaries in the church implies a higher and lower order. He ranks apostles, prophets and teachers in the first three positions of prominence and puts at the end tongue-speakers and interpreters of those who practise glossolalia. If one applies his analogy to the list, one concludes that Paul is apparently suggesting that no single person can perform all needed functions and that the idea of variety should not become a barrier to participation in the work of the community. He does not intend, therefore, that negative conclusions should be drawn from his list. While not drawing negative conclusions it is at the same time amenable to the thought of diversity to desire higher gifts and functions (1 Cor 12:31). That had been the implication of the Corinthians' question: is prophecy or tongue-speaking the higher gift? Paul, however, prefers not to make such distinctions but rather to think of other categories. Hence he concludes this chapter with the thought: let me show you a better way to the perfection of the highest order of Christian status. This way is to desire the spiritual gift of love.

That Paul has expressed his ideas on love in a passage of considerable length (1 Cor 13) and constructed this section of his discussion on spiritual gifts with a keen sense of what makes good rhetorical prose indicates that he has given much though to the subject. An interpreter of his chapter on love, however, must beware of approaching it as though it were a sentimental encomium on affection and avoid coming to it with romantic ideas. Clearly the content of thought deals with ethical matters and spiritual gifts and the implied ideological setting throughout the chapter is theological.

This context is most skillfully stated in a section of his letter to the church at Rome (Rom 5:1-11). Here Paul has abandoned his earlier argumentative line of thought on the theme: what the opportunity of salvation by faith means, religiously and historically (Rom 3:21-5:21). After having established proof for his thesis he now becomes reflective. In this confessional mood he maintains that we as Christians stand in a condition of grace and are conscious of its occurrence through Christ. Not only have we got away from the specter of an angry God and come out of the darkness of despair into grace but we also have, in addition to peace, hope and joy (Rom 5:1-2). We, therefore, see where we are going in life but more than that we are able to triumph over frustrations, over hardships and over inner and outer difficulties (Rom 5:3-4). This is possible because God gives people in their relation to Christ a power of sanctification. Thereby Christ enables them to become capable of doing things they formerly could not do. In the Christian understanding of life, therefore, there are not only victories but also defeats and one's limitations are transmuted by Christ who gives men a power which they would not normally have. This power is God's love which has been poured into their hearts through the Holy Spirit, God's gift to them (Rom 5:5). Men, so endowed by His Spirit, can triumph over their despairs, handicaps and limitations of life.

From this general statement of what happens to dedicated Christians Paul goes on to one of the most profound declarations in his letter (Rom 5:6-11). He wants to state specifically why it is that Christians have assurance and what they believe to be the guarantee of their faith. Paul finds this assurance in the peculiar character of God as He works through Christ. Three times in this passage (Rom 5:6, 8, 10a) he makes an effort, as though he cannot say it well enough, to assert that this assurance is based on the death of Christ. The first point Paul makes is that contrary to and unintelligible by human standards Christ died for the ungodly (Rom 5:6-7). By human standards a man might give his life for people or causes which were worthy. Christ's death was not of this kind. It was not a death of martyrdom for those who meant something personally to the one who had sacrificed his life. The second point is that this death is an exhibition of God's love for men. The emphasis is on what God does through Christ (Rom 5:8-9, cf. Rom 3:25). Finally, that affirmation becomes important when men realize that the person who died was none other than God's own Son whom God gave to be a propitiation (Rom 5:10). Strange as it may seem that Christ as God's Son should have died for His enemies the event occurred because God wanted it that way. By human standards this act on God's part would seem to be damaging His own righteousness. The death of Christ, however, is an extension of God's love and is an expression of a profound paradox. While men were the enemy, He went out to save them. God pursues the enemy to be reconciled to Him. No person having any common sense would have done what God did. Clearly God's love is not common-sensical but is unlimited, costly and incomprehensible. Men, being who they are, can be reconciled to God only by Christ's death and his life (resurrection). Paul, therefore, concludes his reflection on men's situation with the ringing assertion that the mystery of God's pursuing love makes escape possible from their hopelessness and that He thereby shows them that they shall be as He is and they shall accomplish in another higher and perfect existence the hope of living and sharing in the glory of God (Rom 5:10 and 5:2). Having this hope of being redeemed from fleshly existence, they now rejoice in God through their Lord Jesus Christ, through whom they have received their reconciliation (Rom 5:11).

These thoughts about the character and quality of God's love make it abundantly clear that men by their own powers are unable to display a comparable love which prefers another's good to his own. They also provide the theological setting for Paul's comments about love in 1 Cor 13 and so give evidence that this chapter is no mere casual aside in his discussion of spiritual gifts. Love, as Paul understands it, is a spiritual gift and this point is made clear in the three sections of his chapter about love: its superiority to all other spiritual gifts (1 Cor 13:1-3), its nature (1 Cor 13:4-7) and its permanence (1 Cor 13:8-13).

In the first section on the superiority of love Paul uses four rhetorical, conditional sentences to speak of the relation of love to other spiritual gifts and of love as the most significant. The first gift Paul considers is speaking with tongues either of men or of supernatural beings (1 Cor 13:1). Though he does not condemn them, he says that they are valueless without the apostle turns to temple worship where the gong and cymbal were struck (Ps 150:5). The point of similarity does not lie in the loudness nor in the repetition but in the fact that the sound of the gong and cymbal is without melody. Speaking in tongues without love is equally without meaning. In 1 Cor 13:2 he deals with an intellectual and dynamic group of things: prophecy, knowledge of the hidden counsels of God (mysteries), all knowledge and mountain-moving faith (cf. Mk 11:23). Faith is spoken of here not in terms of the reception of the gospel (1 Cor 12:9) but of a miracle working faith. Without love even faith is nothing more than an external display and an exercise in exhibitionism. Like glossolalia and prophecy none of these gifts without love is significant. Finally, Paul considers those things which a person can give in the doling out of his property or in an act of self-immolation. The first is the kind of deed performed by a deacon and by giving what he has implies ascetic action. The second recalls a famous case of self-sacrifice at Athens in the days of

Augustus when a saint from India wished to make an exhibition of his religious ideas. Again, without love these demonstrations of dedication have no value without love. Love is superior, therefore, because it is profound, elemental, and basic, and is the essential ingredient in all acts.

In the next section (1 Cor 13:4-7) the apostle turns to the character of love itself. Again one finds a genuine rhetorical pattern in the parataxis of negative and positive elements which add to the effectiveness of the passage. Here, as elsewhere in his correspondence (cf. Rom 2:4; 2 Cor 6:6; Gal 5:22 and Col 3:12) Paul joins together the qualities of patience and kindness. Since God has been long-suffering and gracious toward men, they are obliged to show in their deeds the same attitude towards their fellowmen. Love does not allow a person to play the braggart nor to be inflated with a sense of his own importance. It does not display itself in tactless and selfish actions nor does it permit a person to yield to provocation. It restrains one from storing up resentment and from keeping an account book for the purpose of paying back with just retribution. Love does not rejoice in unrighteousness. It does not gloat over other people's ethical failures. This description of love, on the one hand, shows the effective range of Paul's experiences. On the other, it reveals what Paul means by love in its ethical dimensions. The nature of love is such that it does not allow itself to become hedged in by humanly constructed barriers such as selfishness and resentment. These act as barriers because they restrain the outflow of love to another and become the basis of separation from the other. Inherently love has that quality which sweeps away such barriers and expresses itself unconditionally even in extremely difficult situations.

In conclusion (1 Cor 13:8-13) Paul wishes to say something about the significance of love itself and particularly about its permanence. His opening phrase in Greek literally states that love never falls. The allusion depicts a man in the stress of battle who stands erect and does not fall under the blows of the enemy, or a tree which buffeted by a storm refuses to be uprooted. The Greek rhetoric suggests these metaphors and the power in them. In contrast to the stamina of love which stands against the ravages of time and hostility something does happen to the other great spiritual treasures. Love is permanent in itself but the treasures of ecstatic and revelatory experiences of God are not. Important though they may be they are nonetheless elements of the transient order of things. When the eschatological fulfillment takes place, they, therefore, will disappear. Paul underlines the boldness of his affirmation by specifying what he means by spiritual treasures. They are knowledge, even the type of religious knowledge in which the Corinthians took considerable pride, and prophecy, pre-

sumably oracular utterances from the time of Isaiah to that of current Christian prophets. These traditions of one's religious heritage are, in any case,
partial and not ultimate. Indeed, when the eschaton comes to usher in the
perfect and to inaugurate the age which will witness a transformation in
men's lives, their perfect comprehension will testify to the shabbiness of
their religious traditions and heritage. These will disappear but love will
weather all the storms of time including that of the coming of the eschaton
itself.

Paul now uses two metaphors to illustrate what that transformation involves (1 Cor 13:11-12). The first is that of a contrast between childhood
and adulthood which Paul uses to demonstrate the transition from the
lower to the higher. When one becomes mature, he can put in perspective
the significance of his childish intellectual proceses and impressions. The
second metaphor is that of the mirror which is another attempt to contrast
the present and the future. The metaphor implies two suggestions: that
one's relationship to things of the present is analagous to looking into a
mirror and that one's present situation is that of seeing an image dimly,
indefinitely or indistinctly. Furthermore, the image that one sees involves
not one's self but something indirectly as though the mirror reflected
something behind one's back. The time will come, however, when one will
see reality reflected clearly and directly. One realizes why Paul uses the
metaphor when he understands that Paul is speaking about spiritual reality.
Now one sees the spiritual only dimly or indistinctly through natural
reality (cf. Rom 1:19-23). The danger is that one becomes so enamored
of the dim image that he remains satisfied with that alone. Understandably
man, being who he is, is handicapped by being able to have only this
distorted view of reality. But there is another way man can comprehend
God's nature and will, that is through the oracles of the prophets. However, when the oracles were spoken or read, they were couched in the
enigmatic form of a riddle. Man's present knowledge of God and of himself is, therefore, only dim, indefinite, indistinct and partial. In the future,
however, it will be full and complete.

When Paul speaks of the transition from a lower to a higher state, he
is not speaking of an event which has its background in a developmental
procedure. His thought about the future involves being fully known and
God as the one who knows man fully. The ideas which God has about
man are complete and genuine. He knows man's needs so thoroughly that
He has made preparation for his salvation. To this end he established a
means of redemption and of propitiation because His knowledge involves
both an understanding of what man is and can be. Since man knows that
he is comprehended in God's knowledge, he knows that his imperfect

knowledge, either that of natural theology or revealed theology, will be complete in the future. This complete knowledge does not imply a growth of man's knowledge but the gift of absolute knowledge from God Himself.

Paul concludes his chapter on love not by comparing it with other spiritual gifts referred to earlier but with faith and hope. Before one can understand why the apostle has joined love (*agapé*) with the two concepts of faith and hope, one needs to summarize what he means by love. Clearly he does not have in mind two other significant Greek works for love, *eros* and *philia,* each of which has its separate connotation. *Eros* implies the desire of possessing something with passion and longing. *Philia* suggests a more placid quality and a strong intellectual flavor such as having a well-bred affection for something. *Agapé* is neither possessive love nor affection but rather an attitude of preferment that is expressed in concrete acts. That understanding of love in the New Testament and in 1 Cor 13 in particular is derived from a positive association with God. When God endows a person with spiritual gifts, that person is the object of God's love. This meaning of love does not have the overtones of sentimentalism nor of violence but of discrimination and choice. One comprehends the content and range of love when one realizes that God's intent is that of a saving will towards men. God can give men power which will cast out demons thereby showing His love for men by acts of preferment. The supreme act of God's love toward men, as we mentioned earlier, is to be seen in the death of His Son, Jesus Christ (Rom 5:6-11; cf. John 3:16). God performed this act not to save His face but because of man's needs. God's attitude is not conditioned by anything but His own goodness and is expressed in His action. Active preferment, then, is that factor in the character of God who has man in the grasp of His love (Rom 8:31-39).

Since this is the kind of love Paul speaks of in this passage, it is clear why Paul regards the spiritual gifts, so highly valued by the Corinthians, to be inadequate without love (1 Cor 13:1-3). If love has as its main ingredient the attitude of preferment, then tongue-speaking, prophecy and the comprehension of all mysteries are worthless unless they have a positive function for some one. The various spiritual gifts in themselves are merely vindications of the self and do not do something for some one. Paul's description of the inherent nature of love follows this same line of thought (1 Cor 13:4-7). If love involves preferment, it is obvious why jealousy, resentment and the like are not truly characteristic of love. Love, having this quality which places a person in a constructive relationship to another individual, is out-going in its desire to work for the latter's good whether circumstances are favorable or unfavorable, friendly or hostile.

Since love is characterized by this kind of outreach toward some one, it is possible to see why Paul in 1 Cor 13:13 has joined it with faith and hope. This triad has one thing in common. Faith, hope and love are all elements of an outreach which one expects to have realized. Faith expects something to be materialized and hope expects something to be possessed. These expectations will be fulfilled when the eschatological consummation takes place. Faith will disappear with vision and hope with realization. In the transition from the present to the future, however, one thing will not disappear. Love is the eternal factor because God's outreach to man is permanent and man's outreach to God will continue. "So faith, hope, love abide, these three: but the greatest of these is love" (1 Cor 13:13 RSV).

The importance of this chapter in Paul's correspondence cannot be underestimated. He was confronted by a situation in a church of the Gentile world which valued the ecstatic more than the ethical and the individual religious experience more than social responsibility. Though Paul at many points introduced new patterns of thought into the emerging Christian tradition, he reaffirms in this chapter, as elsewhere, the teaching of Jesus. At the heart of the gospel message is the merciful God who loves the just and the unjust, the evil and the good (Mt 5:44-48). What matters is the good deed, the concrete expression of an all-embracing love. It is still important, in Paul's opinion, to give food to the hungry, to offer the cup of cold water to the thirsty, to clothe the naked, and to visit the sick and imprisoned (Mt 25:35-36; cf. Rom 12-14). Those who have been truly endowed with spiritual gifts will, therefore, not allow themselves to be carried away by unproductive, emotional debaucheries nor to accent the existence of abnormal manifestations of the Spirit for Christians have been called to act freely through love to be servants of one another (Gal 5:13).

This very important exposition of love has laid the ground work for Paul to answer the question: which spiritual gift does one prefer (1 Cor 14)? His answer, as might be expected, is that gift which contributes what is fruitful and productive for the life of the community. Using this judgment as a criterion he tends to depreciate glossolalia and to value prophecy. Though Paul himself claims that he excels in the very gift which he depreciates, he does so because in the church the need is not for individuals who communicate esoterically with God but for those who contribute to the upbuilding of the congregation. Glossolalia does not contribute to the common good unless it can be interpreted. It is a pointless display of self-gratification to utter a series of unintelligible sounds. In fact, it is as meaningless for the congregation as though a visiting preacher gave the sermon in an unknown foreign language or as frustrating for an audience as though the flute and harp gave indistinct sounds, or as confusing for an army in battle as though the bugles gave forth only blurred sounds. Members of the Corinthian congregation have found that glossolalic prayers of thanksgiving are so incomprehensible that they do not know when to make the appropriate response of "Amen". Moreover, the practice of glossolalia has not built up the church by bringing new converts. When unbelievers enter the service of worship, they can only believe that they have found their way into an asylum for lunatics.

Paul prefers prophecy to tongue-speaking not only because of the negative factors exhibited in the latter practice but also because prophecy builds up the church and gives encouragement and consolation to its members. The basic resason is found in Paul's comment that the tongue-speaker edifies only himself while the prophet edifies the congregation (1 Cor 14:4). Paul believes that as far as his ministry is concerned he would not benefit the Corinthians by speaking in tongues unless he comes either as a prophet bringing a revelation of God's nature and will or as a teacher giving instruction in Christian knoweldge (1 Cor 14:6). For instructional purposes in the church he prefers speaking five words which make sense than uttering a glossolalic sermon of 10,000 words. In contrast to glossolalia, prophecy reaches out to the unbeliever and brings him into the church where he may be moved to repentance and become a worshiper of God (1 Cor 14:24-25).

Since Paul is thinking in congregational terms, he delivers some comments on the practice of worship in the Corinthian church. Its informality must have caused some anxiety for Paul who had become accustomed to a more orderly procedure during his earlier years when he worshiped in the synagogue. Because every member of the Corinthian church was free to speak as he was moved by the Spirit, chaos tended to characterize his adoration of God, who as Paul declared, was not "a God of confusion but of peace" (1 Cor 14:33a). Irregularities, appropriate possibly in the temple of Aphrodite on Acrocorinth and criticized by Paul, included women's participation in the service. With respect to the practice of speaking in tongues the major restriction was that everything should be done for mutual edification and nothing be done for private exhibitionism. In this connection Paul mentions five types of contributions for worship: a hymn, a lesson, a revelation, a tongue and an interpretation. Presumably the list is not exhaustive because he has not included prayers and readings from Hebrew Scripture. Interestingly, speaking in a tongue is permitted provided it is limited at three points. Only two or at the most three tongue-speakers may participate in a service and when they do so they are to speak in turn and their utterances must be interpreted. Paul, the ambassador of God, gives these directives the full weight of his authority. If those practising glossolalia do not adhere to these regulations, then the church will no longer recognize them as members in good standing.

The unequivocal nature of this command may seem unduly harsh. Because of the character of the Christian congregation at Corinth and of Paul's difficulties in attempting to explain to its members the significance of becoming a part of the Christian movement he felt the necessity of making this forceful demand. The situation of the Corinthian church may be explained in part by recent development in the city itself. In Paul's day Corinth was one of the wealthiest and most important cities of Greece. It had been a very rich and prosperous seaport until it was destroyed in the mid-second century B.C. About a century later it was revived by Julius Caesar who restored its commercial wealth and made it the capital of Achaia. Roman soldiers first settled there and were followed by Greeks and Orientals including Jews. It becomes a cosmopolitan city on the high road of commerce. Its citizens were not affected by Greek philosophy but had heard of oriental religions. Isis, Necessity and Demeter had their temples in Corinth. The cult of Isis was especially popular because religious equality was granted to women. Aphrodite with her temple on Acrocorinth, which rose more than 1800 feet above the town, was a symbol of the domination of the city by licentious practices.[8] There were also temples to Apollo and Ascelpius, and altars to such gods as Poseidon, Hermes, Artemis, Dionysus and Heracles. Religious associations dedicated to these deities, rather than the official cult, satisfied the need for fellowship among the uprooted, urban class of people at Corinth.

While these associations prepared the residents of Corinth for membership in the new Christian community, Paul found that converts baptized into the Christian association were ill-informed about what the change entailed. From 1 Corinthians one gets an intimation of the range of problems created by this situation. There were leaders of conflicting groups who were destroying the unity of the fellowship and persons who were guilty of moral wrong and had a minimal understanding of the connection between religious loyalty and ethical purity. There were also participants in law suits, those criticized by Paul because of their practices of marriage and of eating food offered to idols, the spiritual gifters and the anti-resurrectionists. Its members tended to twist Paul's teaching on Christian freedom in order to foster their desire for exemption from restricting regulations. They had failed to understand that the Christian faith had an inherent

---

8 Strabo in the GEOGRAPHY (VIII 6.60) states that Aphrodite had a thousand temple slaves, courtesans, whom both men and women had dedicated to the goddess. A familiar proverb stated that it was not for every man to visit Corinth. W. Schmithals in his book, GNOSTICISM IN CORINTH, ignores the significance of these oriental cults for the religious life of the residents of Corinth and maintains that Gnostic groups were solely responsible for pagan influences upon the Corinthian congregation.

moral standard.[9] In 1 Corinthians Paul endeavors to correct these misconceptions about Christian life and doctrine.

Since the pneumatic factor in this church shaped the character of the Christian community at Corinth, in 1 Corinthians Paul attempts to establish Christianity on the basis of a "demonstration of the Spirit and power" (1 Cor 2:4) rather than on a basis of a systematic statement of Christian doctrine (cf. Rom 1-8), or on the basis of eschatology (cf. 1 Thes). He siezes the first opportunity in his letter (1 Cor 2) to grapple with this approach to an understanding of the Christian faith and presents a profound and interesting conception of Christianity. In this passage he also lays the foundation for his appraisal of spiritual gifts and attempts to state what the "demonstration of the Spirit and power" means for the life and thought of the Church. Though this demonstration is antithetical to "plausible words of wisdom," the gospel which he proclaims is not absurd. It provides a type of wisdom available only to the *teleoi* (the mature or full-grown), a Greek term used for those initiated into the mysteries to distinguish them from the learners (uninitiated) about the mysteries. Since the Corinthians were familiar with the mystery cults and knew this distinction, Paul is apparently thinking of Christianity as a mystery religion or is using that analogy to explain the character of the Christian movement. He mentions by way of contrast two kinds of wisdom which Christian wisdom has surpassed: a "wisdom of this age," presumably the wisdom of philosophical schools, and a "wisdom of the rulers of this age," presumably a wisdom revealed by angelic powers. Compared with the teaching of the philosophers and the esoteric teaching of angelic powers Christian doctrine comes from a secret (*mysterion*) and hidden wisdom of God, the Power behind both non-Christian types of wisdom. Furthermore, this mystery revealed to the Christian is not one recently proclaimed by a prophet but is God's eternal plan revealed to Christians at His pleasure for their benefit (1 Cor 2:7). This plan made from the beginning of time, is to save men by faith and was accomplished according to the purpose of God, who transcends all lower deities, in the coming of Jesus Christ and the event of his crucifixion (1 Cor 2:2).

Paul develops the thought by turning to an interpretation of the significance of that event and to the means by which that significance was transmitted to the Christian community (1 Cor 2:8-16). The interpretation revolves on the meaning of "the rulers of this age" (1 Cor 2:8). Somehow angelic powers were responsible for Christ's crucifixion. Had they been aware of God's plan to save men through Christ's crucifixion "they would

---

9 Schmithals correctly points to this issue in the Corinthian church but over-simplifies a complex problem by arguing that this desire for freedom was primarily inspired by Gnostic groups (cf. GNOSTICISM IN CORINTH, pp. 218-245).

not have crucified the Lord of glory." To accomplish His plan God was compelled to keep it a secret. This interpretation involves a mythological conception of the forces of evil and dramatizes the effect of the cross in a conflict between God and evil powers. This conception differs, therefore, from that which stresses the propitiatory value of Christ's sacrifice, a notion which was intelligible in Jewish terms. This conception also makes the cross significant for the conquest of supernatural powers of evil rather than only for the justification of individual persons.

For the discussion of spiritual gifts in Paul we are particularly interested in the question about how this interpretation was transmitted to the Christian community. Paul asserts that the Spirit imparts to Christians this understanding of the Christian mystery. Implied in this assertion is a criticism of the Corinthian ecstatics who by means of their spiritual experience pridefully claimed complete comprehension of religious knowledge (1 Cor 12-14). Paul suggests by his assertion, however, that if the Corinthians had a more profound experience of the Spirit they would know what Christian wisdom really involved and would realize that God's Spirit is that aspect of God which alone has the ability to measure the mind of God and to plumb the depths of His thoughts. Moreover, the Corinthians should be cognizant of the fact that their ecstatic utterances were not the result of being possessed by any worldly spirit, nor even of possessing God's Spirit but of being possessed by His Spirit. This means that Christians who have received the gift of the Spirit at baptism, who have thereby been freed from the enslavement to sin and have been adopted as God's sons and made co-heirs with Christ, are nonetheless without property rights because they have actually become some one else's property (cf. 1 Cor 3:21-23). This paradox of freedom and servitude, comparable to the paradox of finding life and losing it, is a theme mentioned frequently by Paul and is alluded to in the last section of this chapter.[10]

The condition of the Christian as one endowed with the Spirit and its gifts of power, so Paul continues, is established on the basis of revealed wisdom (1 Cor 2:14-16). As a spiritual man the Christian is distinguished from the natural man who regards the Christian mystery as foolishness. Be that as it may, it is the spiritual man who is able to judge in the sense of discriminating and discerning values. Placed outside the range of the natural man's judgment, the Christian is a law unto himself because the Spirit has given him freedom and autonomy (cf. Gal 5:13-26 and Jn 3: 6-8). This autonomy is not the result of human effort but of having the mind of Christ which is to be understood as having something more than the sum total of Jesus' ethical teachings. It is having the kind of wisdom

---

10 For a discussion of Paul's views on the association of freedom with servitude see R. Bultmann's NEW TESTAMENT THEOLOGY, pp. 330-340.

which comprehends the intent of God's saving will as manifested in Christ's life, teaching, death and resurrection. The spiritually gifted Christian, then, is not one who enjoys the state of ecstacy but one who comprehends the working out of God's purpose and plan in their totality.

Though there may be aspects of Paul's thought on spiritual gifts which mark him as a man of his age, the main direction of his thought has a timeless quality which is applicable for any era of the Christian movement including our own. He urges the follower of Christ in every age to be open to the working of God's Spirit and to understand its power in the lives of men particularly as it is manifested in God's act through Christ which reveals His intent to redeem men from all evil. At the heart of that redemptive intent and action in and through Christ is God's love for men who in turn are to love God and man as fully as they have been loved. This love is to be expressed concretely in acts which edify believers and unbelievers and which exhibit an attitude of unrestricted good will even under circumstances that are unfavorable to its expression.

Jerome D. Quinn

MINISTRY IN THE NEW TESTAMENT

This paper offers an essay toward the history of Ministry[1] in the New Testament period and its documents.[2] The span of time stretches from the birth of Jesus of Nazareth to the death of the last apostolic witness, a, period of roughly three generations. The central generation, from the crucifixion of Jesus in about 30 AD to the fall of Jerusalem in 70 AD, is the most critical for this study, though it cannot be understood in isolation from the work and words of Jesus that preceded it nor the developments between 70 AD and the end of the first century.

JEROME D. QUINN is Professor of New Testament and Dean of The St. Paul Seminary, St. Paul, Minnesota.

1 This essay was originally published in LUTHERAN AND CATHOLICS IN DIALOGUE IV: EUCHARIST AND MINISTRY (Washington, D.C.: U.S. Catholic Conference, 1970), pp. 69-100. This revised and updated version retains a convention adopted in the previous publication: *scil.*, that "ministry" (lower case *m*, with or without the definite article) designates the ministry (*diakonia*) of the whole church insofar as the whole church has the task or service of proclaiming the gospel to all, unbelievers as well as believers. "The ministry of the church, thus defined, will be distinguished from the (or a) Ministry, a particular form of service — a specific order, function or gift (charism) within and for the sake of Christ's church in its mission to the world. The term Minister refers to the person to whom this Ministry has been entrusted." (*op. cit.* p. 9)

2 Two bodies of primary documentation are available for this study. The first is from Judaism and includes the materials from the library of Qumran, the so-called "Dead Sea Scrolls," and similar recent discoveries. With these materials we are able, as no one since 70 A.D., to document the interests and goals and ideals of a significant stratum of the Palestine Jewish community in the lifetime of Jesus and in the critical generation from his death to the fall of Jerusalem. To these we must add the works of Josephus and Philo as well as the most ancient stratum of the rabbinic materials.
The second body of documentation originates from the preaching and teaching of a new religious community, the Christians who appeared within Palestinian Judaism after the resurrection of Jesus. These literary materials began to appear well on in the forties of the first century and continued until the end of that century. Later generations of the Christian church gleaned from this literature a collection or canon of books that came to be defined as the New Testament. However, the remainder of these materials represented by the DIDACHE, the First Letter of Clement of Rome, and the Letters of Ignatius of Antioch, are indispensable for the historical inquiry as it seeks to recover the concerns to which the later documents of the New Testament spoke. The secondary documentation is both massive and growing. Whenever possible, French and German contributions have been cited in their English translations. The most comprehensive compilation and classification of the vast literature is in A. Guitard and R. Litalien, BIBLIOGRAPHY ON THE PRIESTHOOD: 1966-1968 and A. Guitard and M.G. Bulteau, INTERNATIONAL BIBLIOGRAPHY ON THE PRIESTHOOD AND MINISTRY (Montreal: Centre de Documentation et de Recherche 1969). The bibliographies incorporated into works of André Lemaire LES MINISTERES AUX ORIGINES DE L'ÉGLISE [Paris: Cerf, 1971], cited hereafter as MINISTERES; and "The Ministries in the New Testament," *Biblical Theology Bulletin* 3 (1973) pp. 133-166 cited hereafter as "NT Ministries") contain an excellent selection of the studies of biblical exegesis and theology on Ministry. J. Delorme (ed.), LE MINISTERE ET LES MINISTERES SELON LE NOUVEAU TESTAMENT (Paris: Seuil, 1974), a biblical and theological survey by a galaxy of French scholars, came to my desk as I completed this article. The few citations, under the abbreviation MMNT, hardly indicate the value of the work. The great THEOLOGISCHES WORTERBUCH ZUM NEUEN TESTAMENT, edited by G. Kittel and G. Friedrich, is available in an English version, edited by G.W. Bromiley as THEOLOGICAL DICTIONARY OF THE NEW TESTAMENT (Grand Rapids:

131   Jerome D. Quinn

I

It is incontrovertible that Jesus of Nazareth had followers in the period before the crucifixion. It is likewise beyond dispute that some of those persons (like Simon Peter) remained in the midst of the generation after the resurrection.[3] Behind and prior to questions that must arise about the Twelve, the apostles, the prophets, and the teachers, about the *episkopoi, diakonoi,* and *presbyteroi* of the first century churches, one must try to expose and explain how Jesus associated men with his work and word. What were the relationships between Jesus and these associates? How did he link himself with them and how did they conceive of and articulate their relationships with him? Did these relationships specifically differ from person to person or from group to group? Were they intended to develop, and, if so, how? The generation that followed the resurrection of Jesus was already posing these questions, though not from a primarily historical concern. The answers differed and provoked controversy then. They still do.

The Gospels and Acts, from the earliest strata (Mark, Q) designate those associated with Jesus as "disciples" *(mathētai).*[4] The term is not employed by the rest of the New Testament and T.W. Manson has noted that "it is . . . curiously rare in the utterances of Jesus himself."[5] It is evident from the varied uses of the term in Mark, Luke-Acts, and Matthew that a generation of theological reflection had already occurred.[6] As the historico-critical inquiry has inched its way back from this documentation certain characteristic elements of discipleship appear to be traceable to the

---

Eerdmans, 1964-1974). This translation (cited hereafter as TDNT) has, with one exception, not attempted to update the original articles. The reader should thus be aware that TDNT, I-III date from 1933-1938; IV from 1942; V-VI from 1954-1959, etc.

3 Robert P. Meye, JESUS AND THE TWELVE (Grand Rapids: Eerdmans, 1968), pp. 88-90 has pointed out that "New Testament scholars are wholly agreed that Jesus, as other teachers in the contemporary Jewish and Greek cultures, had a group of disciples to whom he particularly directed his teaching . . . Even those who cannot accept the historicity of the Twelve believe that Jesus had a circle of disciples who were in some way closer to him than all the rest." This study on "Discipleship and Revelation in Mark's Gospel" will be cited hereafter as Meye, JT. See H. Hahn (*ut cit.* fn 7). On the relation of Simon Peter to his fellow disciples and to the historical Jesus, see R.E. Brown *et al.,* PETER IN THE NEW TESTAMENT (Minneapolis/Paramus: Augsburg/ Paulist, 1973), cited hereafter as Brown, PETER.

4 K. Rengstorf, "*mathētēs,*" TDNT, IV, 415-460, especially 441-455. The "*mathētēs,*" i.e., one who is learning as a pupil, implies a teacher, "*didaskalos,*" and Meye, JT, 30-87, develops very persuasively the Markan portrait of Jesus the teacher.

5 T.W. Manson, THE TEACHING OF JESUS (New York: Cambridge University Press, 1935), p. 237 [cited hereafter as Manson, TJ]. Mark 14:14 and Luke 6:40 = Matthew 10:24-25 (Q) belong to the earliest traditions and Luke 14:26-27 = Matthew 10:37-38 (Q) may be a striking witness to the *ipsissima vox Jesu* if Manson's reconstruction of the Aramaic original is correct (237-240). The only remaining examples of the term *mathētēs* placed on the lips of Jesus are Luke 14:33 (L) and Matthew 10:42 (cf. Mark 9:41).

6 Cf. the summary of Meye, JT, 228-230, and footnote 70 below. The lengthier treatment of Sean Freyne, THE TWELVE: DISCIPLES AND APOSTLES (London: Sheed and Ward, 1968), should be supplemented from Brown, PETER, p. 77 fn 175, and Mark Sheridan, "Disciples and Discipleship in Matthew and Luke," *Biblical Theology Bulletin* 3 (1973) 235-255.

Sitz im Leben Jesu and to influence, if not control, the later developments. The first and in many respects the key historical memory concerning those most closely associated with Jesus' work was that he himself had initiated the relationship, that the invitation, indeed summons, into such an association was rooted in his expressed will.[7] His eye had searched them out[8] and his word surprised them at their everyday tasks. The Markan tradition expressed that word as *deute opisō mou* (Mk 1:17 = Mt 4:19) and again as *akolouthei moi* (Mk 2:14).[9]

Simon and Andrew, according to the Markan tradition, heard Jesus state his purpose for the command to come after him: "and I will make you become fishers of men" (Mk 1:17 = Mt 4:19, except for *genesthai*).[10] Their following is to issue in Jesus' own appointment or designation[11] for the task described metaphorically as fishing for men. That metaphor, as Wuellner remarks,[12] is "properly understood as a symbol for mediumship or partnership in the revelation event," in what is taking place in the works and words of Jesus of Nazareth. These men are summoned to listen to his words and to see his works, "to be with him" (cf. Mk 3:14) so that through their acts and words in turn the "revelation event" reaches others.[13]

The appointment and the task imply, indeed demand, an authority,

---

7 Cf. K.H. Schelkle, Discipleship and Priesthood (New York: Herder and Herder, 1965), pp. 9-32 (cited hereafter as Schelkle, DP). See also Ferdinand Hahn *et al.,* The Beginning of the Church in the New Testament (Edinburgh: St. Andrew, 1970), "Pre-Easter Discipleship," esp. pp. 10-21.

8 Cf. Mk 1:16, 19; 2:14 and Schelkle, DP, 10-11.

9 The tradition records for the sons of Zebedee simply *ekalesen autous* (Mk 1:20 = Mt 4:21). Their response is then described as *apēlthon opisō autou* (Mk 1:20), which in Matthew 4:22 becomes *ēkolouthēsan,* the term used to denote the response of Simon and Andrew as well as Levi (Mk 1:18 = Mt 4:20, and Mk 2:14 parr.). Thus the actions from the point of view of Jesus, the initiator, can be described as an imperative to come (cf. J. Schneider, *"erchomai,"* TDNT, II, 669) after (cf. H. Seesemann, *"opisō,"* TDNT, V, 289-292) or to follow (cf. G. Kittel, *"akoloutheō,"* TDNT, I, 210-215).These imperatives the tradition interprets as his *calling* them (cf. K.L. Schmidt, *"kaleō,"* TDNT, III, 487-491). No responding word appears from those so addressed. They are described as simply doing what they were asked, coming after or following Jesus himself, entering his company. The relationship with him is central and determinative, and there is no promise that it will ever be other than one of subordination.

10 That the metaphor goes back to Jesus' own word has been disputed (cf. R. Bultmann, History of the Synoptic Tradition, second edition [New York: Harper and Row, 1968], pp. 28, 386-387, [hereafter HST], and E. Schweizer, The Good News According to Mark [Richmond: J. Knox, 1970], p. 48). The reasons for skepticism seem to melt before the study of Wilhelm Wuellner, The Meaning of "Fishers of Men" (Philadelphia: Westminster, 1967), cited hereafter as Wuellner, MFM. He notes, "A primarily linguistic orientation can only list this metaphor along with others and conclude that Jesus used it explicitly for some elsewhere yet to be defined task of his disciples, and implicity for speaking of his own mission" (p. 135). Cf. Meye, JT, 100-110, and Hahn (*ut cit.* fn 7) pp. 13, 34.

11 Cf. H. Braun, *"poieō,"* TDNT, VI, 473-474; Schelkle, DP, 12-13; Meye, JT, 105.

12 Wuellner, MFM, 201.

13 Cf. Meye, JT, 103.

an "enablement."[14] Mark 3:15 and 6:7 witness to that author's belief that Jesus himself conferred an initial and limited authorization on certain associates in his historical ministry.[15] The text of Mark 6:12-13, 30 implies that the authorization extended not only to acts of exorcism but also to their preaching and teaching. Moreover, the mission charge of the Sayings Source appears to confirm the Markan narrative with its version of Jesus' word, "He who hears you hears me and he who rejects you rejects me, and he who rejects me rejects him who sent me" (Lk 10:16, cf. Mt 10:40).[16] This authorization to speak is, like the authorization to act, held in subordination to and dependence on Jesus himself.[17]

That Jesus actually called individual men into association with himself and his work, authorizing them to act and speak in his behalf, has thus far occupied this inquiry. One cannot avoid any longer the question of whether these individuals were also members of a group or groups that as such had a special association with Jesus. The Markan tradition remembers that the first persons that Jesus joined to himself came as pairs of brothers (Simon and Andrew; John and James, Mark 1:16-20) and the "mission" of Mark 6:7 sees these men and others sent out "two by two".[18]

14 W. Foerster, "*exousia*," TDNT, II, 569.
15 The *exousia* is explicitly ordered to exorcism and reminds the readers of Mark that the work of those "authorized" begins as did the work of Jesus, with an exorcism that manifested his own *exousia* (cf. Mk 1:27). The incident of Mark 9:17-18 indicates that the "enablement" was derived and limited. The contrary impressions of others, including the disciples (Mk 9:28), need not impugn the historicity of the authorization (*pace* V. Taylor, THE GOSPEL ACCORDING TO MARK [London: Macmillan, 1957], p. 303 [cited hereafter as Taylor, MARK]. That a criminal eludes a policeman would not lead one to think that the officer had not been duly appointed. Cf. Meye, JT, 178-181.
16 As T.W. Manson, THE SAYINGS OF JESUS (London: SCM, 1949), p. 78, [hereafter, SJ] has remarked, "The disciple represents in the fullest sense Jesus, and Jesus represents in the fullest sense the Kindom of God. What they offer is God's claim." Besides its synoptic parallels this saying is presented in yet another form in John 13:20 (cf. C.H. Dodd, HISTORICAL TRADITION IN THE FOURTH GOSPEL [New York: Cambridge University Press, 1963], pp. 343-347). That all of these lines of transmission go beyond the first generation Palestinian church (*pace* Bultmann, HST, 143, 147, 155, 163) into the teaching of the historical Jesus is historically credible. If indeed a form of the rabbinic proverb, "The one sent by a man is as the man himself" (cf. K. Rengstorf, "*apostolos*," TDNT, I, 415) was current in Jesus' day, it has been audaciously reworked and extended in this logion.
17 Mark 9:39 and 10:14 make clear that this authority to speak for Jesus can be abused and stands under his judgement (cf. Meye, JT, 180).
18 Why not singly but in teams? Mutual human support and security are surely involved, but that could be readily provided by a non-disciple, a member of the family or a friend. These men go out precisely as pairs of men who have been with Jesus and this simplest of groupings adds an element that has been described by Schelkle, DP, 80: ". . . this 'two by two' is . . . destined to give security to the message. If personal genius were what mattered, an individual left to himself might be capable of delivering the proclamation. Yet precisely this is not required: what is required is faithfulness to the assigned message. The message is guaranteed by this, that two keep each other in mind of it and vouch for each other in its preaching . . . " These pairs of men are witnesses of the revelation-event and what has happened in the words and work of Jesus. Their task is performed according to the laws of evidence accepted by Israel (cf. Dt 19:15). Thus, according to Luke 7:19, the Baptist sends "two of his

A grouping of three (that partially coincides with the pairs of brothers first called) emerges at Jesus' explicit initiative,[19] and a group of four is once glimpsed.[20] There are faint traces of groups of five and seven.[21]

Was there, finally, a group of twelve[22] that the historical Jesus associated with himself and his task? As a group, it is inherently no more improbable than the smaller groupings noted above and even the most astringent historical criticism is prepared to admit most of those. The evidence that the first and second generation churches believed that such a group existed is found in documentary strata as diverse as 1 Corinthians 15:5, the four gospels and Acts, and Revelation 21:14. Recent German criticism, however, has seen an influential minority arguing at length that the Twelve were the creation of the first generation church. Their thesis in turn has undergone a severe critique.[23] Ironically enough, the historicity

disciples" to hear Jesus cite his works and his preaching in answer to the inquiry that they have been authorized to make (cf. Jesus' own conduct in Mk 11:1 and 14:13). See Hendrick van Vliet, No SINGLE WITNESS: A STUDY ON THE ADOPTION OF THE LAW OF DEUT. 19:15 INTO THE NEW TESTAMENT (Utrecht: Kremink en Zoon, 1958) and J. Jeremias "Paarweise Sendung im Neuen Testament" in the Manson memorial edited by A.J.B. Higgins NEW TESTAMENT ESSAYS (Manchester: University Press, 1959), pp. 136-143, reprinted in Jeremias' ABBA (Göttingen: Vandenhoeck, 1966), pp. 132-139.

19 Mk 5:37; 9:2; 14:33. They witness the raising of Jairus' daughter, the transfiguration, and the Gethsemane prayer. Aain the ancient Israelite laws of evidence seem to determine the number.

20 Mk 13:3. This group of Peter, James, John, and Andrew coincides with the two pairs whom Jesus first called. The order of the names here, however, coincides with Mark 3:16-18. There seems to have been distinct pressure on the Markan tradition that dictated not only the names of "the three" but the order in which they were to appear. Andrew's blood relationship with Simon and the priority of his call before the sons also to be listed. That the sons of Zebedee were quite conscious of the special character of their relationship with Jesus in his ministry is evident from Mark 10:35-41. Bultmann (HST, 345) admits that here as well as at 5:37 and 13:3 "the naming of the disciples is original." Cf. Brown, PETER, pp. 59-60.

of Zebedee do not suffice to bring his name next to Peter's when James and John are
21 Mark 2:15 may refer only to those five called up to this point in his narrative. John 1:35-50 also associates five disciples with the earliest stage of Jesus' ministry. The Talmud, *Sanhedrin* 43a, also knows of that number. Note the list of five prophets and teachers at Antioch in Acts 13:1.

Mark 8:8 apparently knows of a group of seven for the number of those commissioned to gather the left-overs, would correspond to the number of baskets filled. The possibility of such a grouping would scarcely be worth mentioning if it did not also inexplicably occur in such diverse later witnesses as John 21:2 and Papias (*ap.* Eusebius, HE 3:39.4). Cf. also "the Seven" of Acts below and fn. 66.

Some other groupings are *ad hoc* and evidently stand in function of "the Twelve" (cf. "the ten" of Mk 10:41). The relation of the 70 (72) in Luke 10:1, 17 to the ministry of Jesus is too complex to be broached in this survey (cf. K. Rengstorf in TDNT, II, 634-635).

22 Cf. K. Rengstorf, "*dōdeka*," TDNT, II, 321-328; Jacob Jervell, LUKE AND THE PEOPLE OF GOD (Minneapolis: Augsburg, 1972) pp. 75-112; and the studies cited in Lemaire, "NT Ministries," pp. 140-141.

23 The studies of G. Klein, P. Vielhauer, *et al.* are cited in the bibliography of Meye, JT, 235-248. An English translation of W. Schmithals' work has appeared as THE OFFICE OF APOSTLE IN THE EARLY CHURCH (N.Y.: Abingdon, 1969). For a critique of these studies, see Meye JT, pp. 192-209; Freyne (as cited in fn. 6); J. Giblet, "The Twelve, History and Theology" in his THE BIRTH OF THE CHURCH (N.Y.: Alba, 1968), pp. 66-81.

of the betrayal by Judas appears to be the ineradicable taproot that anchors "the Twelve" in the history of Jesus.[24]

The group of three noted above and several of the pairs certainly existed within the Twelve. It is possible that several of the other groupings partially overlapped.[25] One would infer from this inclusion that the Twelve also were conceived of as "learners", as recipients of an authority to do and to teach what Jesus was doing and teaching. But one must still ask what it is that specifies and distinguishes the Twelve from the other groupings? The archaic logion of Matthew 19:28 (cf. Lk 22:28-30) conceives them as new leaders of the ancient Israelite amphictyony,[26] gathered around something greater than Solomon's Temple sanctuary (cf. Mt 12:42 = Lk 11:31-Q). They are all indisputably sons of Israel and yet they are a new beginning of the people of God. They are defined in terms of the twelve tribes of Israel from whom they have been chosen and to whom they are being sent. That mission will have reverberations to the end of history and the final judgement. God will accordingly seat them on thrones beside the "throne of glory" of the Son of man. There is no mistaking here the rich oriental and Old Testament imagery for royal rule.[27]

---

24 Thus "the Twelve" of 1 Corinthians 15:5 cannot be understood apart from the "he was betrayed" of 11:23. One may, of course, join the harmonizers and historicizers of the Western tradition and substitute "the Eleven" (perhaps from Matthew 28:16) but of course that number stands in function of "the Twelve" and is historically inexplicable apart from the betrayal by Judas (cf. Rengstorf, TDNT, II, 326, and Meye, JT, 202-204). In like manner, the archaic tradition recorded in Mark 14:10 tears apart every hypothesis into which it is sewed. Finally, the origin of the saying of Jesus reported in Matthew 19:28 (cf. Lk 22:28-30 [Q?]) must ultimately be assessed against the ineluctable scandal of the betrayal; for, " ... it is hard to see how the primitive Church could have invented a saying which promises a throne, amongst others, to Judas Iscariot" (T.W. Manson, SJ, 217). That Luke 22:30 has no "Twelve" before "thrones" (but has it before "tribes of Israel") is a parade example of the way this author has softened the edges of a logion that was acutely embarrassing.
A happy effect of this as yet unfinished debate has been to remind exegetes that one does not proceed from an a priori and perhaps irrelevant definition of a "group" or "body" of men whose existence is then verified (or denied) in first century Christian history. "The Twelve" are no more intelligible historically as an ad hoc committee convened by Cephas to prepare a report on the resurrection than they are as "a College of Cardinals systematising the doctrine, and superintending the organization, of the Primitive Church" (B.H. Streeter, THE PRIMITIVE CHURCH [New York: Macmillan, 1929], p. 42).
25 Perhaps the variations in the lists of the names of those who constituted "the Twelve" must ultimately be traced to the Sitz im Leben Jesu and a fragmentary memory of which persons in such smaller groups were actually numbered among the Twelve. Cf. Brown, PETER, p. 59, fn. 131.
26 Cf. K. Rengstorf, "dōdeka," TDNT, II, 321-322, 326, with Jervell (ut cit. fn. 22), pp. 93-94.
27 Cf. O. Schmidt, "thronos," TDNT, III, 160-167, esp. 164-165. He calls attention to the plural "thrones" in Daniel 7:9 as the vision of "one like a son of man" begins. The Qumran community of the "new covenant" had also a council of twelve (1 Q S 8.1) who represent the twelve tribes of Israel. They had, moreover, the function of judging and "reconciliation" and are described as a "foundation." A group of three priests is noted in the same text, but their relation to the "twelve men" is unclear. On the 4Q p Is d 54.11-12, cf. David Flusser, Qumran und die Zwölf" in C.J.

The central task of the ancient king and his court was judgment and this is precisely the issue of the work of the Twelve with Jesus. They are to rule[28] and judge[29] with him. If the Twelve are, in a famous phrase, "the eschatological regents,"[30] their rule is defined and specified by the one who shared his rule with them. They are the ministers of one who is to be crucified as "King of the Jews" (Mk 15:26) and the scandal of the cross is measure of their rule (cf. Mk 10:42-45).

There is evidence that the historical Jesus conceived and spoke of his death in terms of the levitical priesthood and sacrifice.[31] There is no question that the first Christian generation employed the vocabulary of Old Testament sacrifice and priestly office to express what Jesus had done on the cross, and the Letter to the Hebrews contains a full theological orchestration of the notes already heard for a generation.[32] It is not so often recalled that elements of this same levitical tradition are used in describing the role of the Twelve. Indeed, their very number as corresponding to the twelve tribes implies that the role of the sons of Levi in Israel found some counterpart in the task shared with the Twelve. The affirmation of Mark 3:14 that Jesus "appointed (*epoiēsen*) twelve," with its peculiar use of *poiein,* is to be read not only in continuity with the *poiēsō* of Mark 1:17 [33] but also with an eye to the use of this term for the appointment of priests for Israel.[34] In this light, the command of the his-

---

Bleeker (ed.) INITIATION (Leiden: Brill, 1965) 318-330, and A. Jaubert, "Le symbolique des Douze" in HOMMAGES A DUPONT-SOMMER (Paris: Adrien-Maisonneuve, 1971), pp. 453-460. There is no evidence for the direct influence of these Qumran materials upon the origin and development of the Twelve. Cf. the verdict of P. Benoit, "Qumran and the New Testament" in J. Murphy-O'Connor (ed.), PAUL AND QUMRAN (Chicago: Priory, 1968) pp. 14-16 and J. Fitzmyer, ESSAYS ON THE SEMITIC BACKGROUND OF THE NEW TESTAMENT (London: Chapman, 1971), 291-292, cited hereafter as Fitzmyer, ESBNT. Cf. fn. 52 below.

28 Cf. K. Stendahl, "Matthew," in PEAKE'S COMMENTARY ON THE BIBLE, edited by M. Black and H. Rowley (New York: Nelson, 1963), 790 and the citations there as well as F. Büchsel, *art. cit.* in fn. 29, p. 923. Rengstorf (*art. cit.* in fn. 26) apparently has misgivings about applying the term "rulers" or "leaders" to the Twelve. If, of course, those terms mean simply "despots" or "tyrants," the case is prejudged. That Jesus conceived of leadership or rule in quite different terms is evident (cf. Mk 10:42-45), but it is still leadership. That even among the Twelve there were those who had difficulty in grasping and implementing Jesus' concept of leadership is indisputable (cf. above fn. 17 as well as Mark 10:35-41), but *abusus non tollit usum.*

29 Cf. F. Büchsel and V. Herntrich, "*krinō,*" TDNT, III, 921-941.

30 R. Bultmann, THEOLOGY OF THE NEW TESTAMENT (London: SCM, 1952), vol. I, p. 37.

31 Cf. J.D. Quinn, "Propitiation," in LUTHERANS AND CATHOLICS IN DIALOGUE III: THE EUCHARIST AS SACRIFICE (1967), pp. 43-44.

32 Cf. Lemaire "NT Ministries," pp. 134-138, for a bibliography and his summary of the current state of the question on the sacerdotal and/or diaconal concepts of the Christian Ministry, as well as J.D. Quinn, "Apostolic Ministry and Apostolic Prayer," *Catholic Biblical Quarterly,* 33 (1971) 486-488 cited hereafter as Quinn, "Apos. Min.").

33 Cf. fn. 11 above, as well as Schelkle, DP, 112-116.

34 Taylor, MARK, 230, cites the LXX passages. The incident of the temple tax may be instructive for the way in which the Matthean church viewed the role of at least Peter

torical Jesus[35] at his last supper with the Twelve, "Do this *(touto poiēte),"* was an appointment to a ritual function that must be understood against the background of Israel's priestly worship.[36] Jesus' task of bringing the kingdom and rule of God was consummated by his priestly offering of his body on the cross. The Twelve whom he associated with himself in this task, he also designated to proclaim that death by repeating what he had said and done at his last supper with them. The cross again is the content and measure of the act which the word of Jesus empowered them to perform.

In summary, then, Jesus came to the cross after he himself had associated various individuals and groups with his work. He had authorized them to do and to teach what they had learned from him. One group, the Twelve, which included several of the smaller groups, he summoned specifically to share in communicating the rule, the judgment, and the sacrifice that he was bringing to the people of God. To single out these particular groups and some of their functions is not to deny that other men and women were associated with and were followers of Jesus. It is to say that Jesus designated some followers, as individuals and as groups, for a particular share in his work. The influence and development of these groups belong to the history of that first Christian generation which followed upon the resurrection of Jesus of Nazareth.

II

Within a few years after the resurrection, a distinction appeared among those who accepted Jesus as Lord. The first congregations of Christian believers had been believing Jews and remained recognizably such among their confreres. This study will designate these churches, found principally in Palestine and above all in Jerusalem, as Jewish Christian.[37]

(Mt 17:24-27: cf. J.D.M. Derrett, "Peter's Penny: Fresh Light on Matthew 17:24-27," *Novum Testamentum* 6 [1963], 1-15), and *infr.* fn. 45 and 47.

35 The *poiēte* command is witnessed to by Paul (1 Cor 11:24) and the longer text of Luke 22:19. According to J. Jeremias, THE EUCHARISTIC WORDS OF JESUS (London: SCM, 1966), pp. 237-255 (hereafter EWJ), it is "very probable that the command goes back to Jesus himself." I find his arguments for the longer text of Luke (pp. 139-159) convincing.

36 As Jeremias, EWJ, 249-250 notes: " . . . as can be seen from comparison with Exodus 29:35; Numbers 15:11-13; Deuteronomy 25:9 . . . ['Do this' is] an established expression for the repetition of a rite."

37 The title has been chosen deliberately with an eye to the continuing dialogue on this phenomenon and its development. The stimulating and controversial work of H.-J. Schoeps, THEOLOGIE UND GESCHICHTE DES JUDENCHRISTENTUMS (Tübingen: Mohr, 1949), represents one position. A more popular presentation of his principal conclusions and ongoing revision is available in his JEWISH CHRISTIANITY (Philadelphia: Fortress, 1969), cited hereafter as Schoeps, JC. The theological scope of the author's studies can be seen in his THE JEWISH CHRISTIAN ARGUMENT (London: Faber, 1963). His study, PAUL: THE THEOLOGY OF THE APOSTLE IN THE LIGHT OF JEWISH RELIGIOUS HISTORY (London: Lutterworth, 1961), is to be consulted on this topic. Another position is that represented by Jean Daniélou, THE THEOLOGY OF JEWISH CHRISTIANITY (Chicago: Regnery, 1964), cited hereafter as Danielou, TJC. An

Other congregations soon appeared (usually outside of Palestine) that received not only Jews but pagans directly into the company of Christian believers.[38] These "mixed churches" will be treated in Section III below.

The importance of the Jewish Christian church of Jerusalem is hard to overestimate. Every other Christian congregation, in the first generation, perhaps as far removed as Gaul and Spain,[39] felt the formative influence not only of Jewish Christians but also of the Jerusalem church. The Christian gospel was carried out into the *orbis terrarum* from Jerusalem by those eyewitnesses and ministers of the word whose national, cultural, and religious background was nothing if not Jewish. The Jerusalem church was the first *mater et caput omnium ecclesiarum*. Precisely because this enormously influential congregation was Jewish, it served as a bridge for the passage of Jewish elements into the life of the "mixed churches" outside of Palestine as well as a "brake" on the converts from paganism who brought no authoritative religious history into the Christian community.[40]

The oldest record of the Jerusalem kerygma (I Cor 15:3-7) explicitly links the appearances of the risen Jesus to both individual persons and to groups, to Peter and James as well as to the Twelve, five hundred brethren, and "all the apostles." Women were unable to give legally acceptable evidence in the Jewish world at that time, and thus have been excluded *de iure* from this record of official witnesses, though the oldest accounts of the resurrection note that *de facto* they were the first to see the risen Jesus.[41]

---

excellent summary of the present state of the question is that of M. Simon and A. Benoit, LE JUDAISME ET LE CHRISTIANISME ANTIQUE (Paris: Presses Universitaires, 1968), pp. 258-274, as well as the volume presented in honor of the late Cardinal Daniélou, JUDÉO-CHRISTIANISME, taken from *Recherches de Science Religieuse* 60 (1972) 1-320. This collection will be cited hereafter as JUD.-CHR.

38　There is no hard evidence for a congregation composed *only* of converts from paganism in the first Christian generation (*pace* W. Marxsen, INTRODUCTION TO THE NEW TESTAMENT [Philadelphia: Fortress, 1968], p. 32). At best one is dealing with churches in which the Jewish Christians are a minority. W. Marxsen, *ibid.*, pp. 97-100, would distinguish in the Roman church a third "stratum" of converts from paganism who had then more or less embraced Judaism. He calls them "proselyte Christians." For a critique of this position and others closely related to it, see R.J. Karris, "Rom 14.1-15.13 and the Occasion of Romans," *Catholic Biblical Quarterly* 35 (1973) 155-178.

39　Rm 15.24 and 2 Tm 4.10 (on the variant reading, see B.M. Metzger, A TEXTUAL COMMENTARY ON THE GREEK NEW TESTAMENT [N.Y.: American Bible Society, 1971], p. 649).

40　Even Paul finally clinches his varied argument for women keeping their heads veiled in the Corinthian worship-assemblies by saying. (1 Cor 11:16) "We recognize no other practice nor do *the churches of God*." The latter phrase certainly includes, if it does not specifically designate, the Palestinian Jewish Christian congregations (cf. 1 Thes 2.14). Cf. J. Jervell (*ut cit.* fn. 22), pp. 33-34 on 1 Cor 14:36.

41　J. Jeremias, JERUSALEM IN THE TIME OF JESUS (cited as JTJ hereafter) London: SCM, 1969), pp. 374-375. Cf. fn. 18 above on the concern for legally unimpeachable witnesses, as well as the emphasis of Acts 1.21 that one of the *men* (*andrōn*) who have followed Jesus is to be chosen to fill out the Twelve. On the origin of the formula 1 Cor 15:3-7, see R. Brown, THE VIRGINAL CONCEPTION AND BODILY

The Pauline citation above presupposes elements in the societal structure of the most archaic Jerusalem church which also surface in the Acts of the Apostles. The narrative of Acts 1:13-14 proposes[42] that the first gatherings of believers in Jerusalem were for prayer and the author differentiates three groups within the assembly. He first lists by name eleven persons, beginning with Peter. He then notes "the women and Mary the mother of Jesus" and finally "his brothers."[43] Each of these groups had had some encounter with the risen Jesus, but this does not seem to be the principle of differentiation from the rest of the assembly, for at least two men outside these groups, Joseph Barsabbas and Matthias, had also seen the Lord. On the other hand, even within the group of the brothers of Jesus, there is evidence only for James having seen him risen.

Luke, immediately after describing an already differentiated community at prayer, narrates another act of this Jerusalem congregation, undertaken at Peter's initiative and before the Pentecost experience of the Holy Spirit. This is the election of Matthias to bring the Twelve back to its full complement.[44] Luke envisions certain qualifications for the can-

---

RESURRECTION OF JESUS (Paramus, N.J.: Paulist, 1973), pp. 81-96, noting that J. Jeremias replied (*Zeitschrift für die Neuentestamentliche Wissenschaft* 57 [1966] 211-215) to those who challenged his evidence for the original Aramaic language behind this formula.

42 Luke-Acts is, of course, a primarily theological exposition. It is not scientific history, but does contain "material from the rich tradition concerning the time of the apostles" (J. Munck "Primitive Jewish Christianity" in M. Simon [ed.] ASPECTS DU JUDÉO-CHRISTIANISME [Paris: Presses Universitaires de France, 1965], p. 83). As Munck points out, Ernst Haenchen has denied the existence of such a rich tradition in his ACTS OF THE APOSTLES (Oxford: Blackwell, 1971), pp. 81-90, 117-121, 159-165 (cited hereafter as Haenchen, ACTS) and elsewhere (cf. fn. 65 below). J. Jervell (*ut cit. fn.*, 22) pp. 19-39 has marshalled demonstrative evidence for existence of such traditions. The studies of C.K. Barrett both take up and qualify Haenchen: LUKE THE HISTORIAN IN RECENT STUDY (London: Epworth, 1961, and reprinted, Philadelphia: Fortress, 1970); NEW TESTAMENT ESSAYS (London: SPCK, 1972) pp. 70-100 (cited hereafter as NTE); "Pauline Controversies in the Post-Pauline Period," *NT Studies* 20 (1974) 229-245. H.J. Cadbury, THE BOOKS OF ACTS IN HISTORY (London: Black, 1955) and the studies of A.N. Sherwin-White would considerably qualify Haenchen's thesis. Thus the latter in his ROMAN SOCIETY AND ROMAN LAW IN THE NEW TESTAMENT (Oxford: Clarendon, 1963), p. 189, can say, "For Acts the confirmation of historicity is overwhelming. Yet Acts is, in simple terms and judged externally, no less of a propaganda narrative than the Gospels, liable to similar distortions. But any attempt to reject its basic historicity even in matters of detail must now appear absurd."

43 Cf. Mk 6:3 = Mt 13:55 — James, Joses, Simon, Judas. Luke-Acts never identifies any one person with the title "the brother of the Lord." Indeed the use of the same term in a different sense in the very next verses (Acts 1:15-16), the way in which James is named at Acts 12:17, and the listing of "his brothers" in last place, after the women (Acts 1:14), would all indicate that the author was not eager to exalt this group in the Jerusalem church.

44 The historicity of the incident and its significance is convincingly expounded by K. Rengstorf, "The Election of Matthias" in CURRENT ISSUES IN NEW TESTAMENT INTERPRETATION, edted by W. Klassen and G.F. Snyder (London: SCM, 1962), pp. 178-192. A lengthier German form of this study appeared in *Studia Theologica* 15 (1961) 35-67. C.K. Barrett, NTE, pp. 78-79, also recognizes here "An historical

didates (a number are presumed). They must be men; they must have accompanied not only Jesus but the original Twelve from the time of John's baptism. These conditions would exclude the group of women as well as the members of Jesus' family. Finally, the candidate must have seen the risen Jesus. The whole assembly then offered two candidates and after prayer, cast lots to determine who would succeed to Judas' place (*topon;* al. lect., *klēron*) among the Twelve.[45] That "place" Luke designates as "this Ministry" (Acts 1:17, 25: *diakonias tautēs*),[46] "his office" (1:20: *episkopēn autou*),[47] "apostleship" (1:25: *apostolēs*),[48] and becoming a "witness" (1:22: *martura*)[49] with the remaining eleven to the resurrection of Jesus. The terminology is that of Luke and it bears moreover the weight of a generation of Christian reflection on the phenomenon of the Twelve. The historian still must attempt to discern the functions of the original structure in the first years of the Jerusalem church and determine which of its germinal elements (if any) made it possible for the generation following to apply the terminology of Ministry, superintending

---

tradition about Matthias, which . . . [Luke] used probably without fully understanding its original significance." The Qumran parallels have been noted by Fitzmyer, ESBNT, pp. 296-298.

45 Acts 1:15-26: it is significant that choice by lot (*klēros*) was a practice of the priestly tradition in Judaism in designating those who would exercise the priestly ministry. Cf. Fitzmyer, ESBNT, p. 297, who also notes the link with military service; J. Jervell (*ut cit.* fn. 22) p. 107, fn. 37, and Y. Aharoni, "Arad: Its Inscriptions and Temple", *The Biblical Archaeologist* 31 (1968), p. 11. Luke begins his gospel with the note that "according to the custom of the priesthood it fell to him [Zecharia] by lot (*elache*) to enter the temple of the Lord and burn incense" (Lk 1:9). Cf. Jeremias. JTJ. 201-202, and W. Foerster, "*klēros*," TDNT, III, 758-764, esp. 761, 763, as well as H. Hanse, "*lagchanō*," TDNT, IV, 1-2, and H. Koester, "*topos*," TDNT, VIII, 205.

46 Cf. H. Beyer, "*diakonia*," TDNT, II, 87-88. The significance of the demonstrative, *tautēs*, should be noted in Luke's phrase. To be numbered among the Twelve is to have more than *diakonia* in general; it is to have *this* particular Ministry which he will further specify as "*apostolē*" (1:25).

47 Citing LXX Psalm 108:8. Cf. H. Beyer, "*episkopē*," TDNT, II, 606-608.
The Old Testament served as a kind of theological dictionary for the terminology used to designate an essentially new phonomenon. Here the official prayerbook of Judaism is employed to provide a term that will describe the function of those who led and directed the prayer of the first Christian communities (cf. the comments below on Acts 6:1-4 and Quinn, "Apos. Min.," pp. 487-488.

48 Cf. K. Rengstorf, "*apostolos*" and "*apostolē*" TDNT, I, 407-447. More recently, see R. Brown, "The Twelve and the Apostolate," JEROME BIBLICAL COMMENTARY (Englewood Cliffs N.J.: Prentice-Hall, 1968) 795-799 (hereafter cited as JBC) as well as his PRIEST AND BISHOP (Paramus, N.J.: Paulist, 1970) pp. 47-73 (cited hereafter as Brown, PR BP). The American edition of C.K. Barrett, THE SIGNS OF AN APOSTLE (Philadelphia: Fortress 1972) has been enriched with a bibliography of the studies by Barrett and others on this question (see esp. pp. 1-4 and 143-144). Besides R. Schnackenburg's "Apostolicity: the Present Position of Studies", *One in Christ,* 6 (1970) 243-273 (cited hereafter as "Apostolicity"), see his "Apostles Before and During Paul's time" in W.W. Gasque and R.P. Martin (ed.), APOSTOLIC HISTORY AND THE GOSPEL (Grand Rapids, Mich.: Eerdmans, 1970), pp. 287-303 (cited hereafter as "Apostles Before").

49 Cf. H. Strathmann, "*martus*," TDNT, IV, 474-504 and esp. 492-494 on the Lukan use of the term.

office, witness, and apostleship to the Twelve. The group was evidently considered of decisive importance to those earliest days[50] and there is no question of the leadership of Peter among them, both within the community as well as when the Twelve addressed themselves to their primary task, the conversion of Israel.[51] Their original title was singularly modest, simply the number, *twelve*.[52] Moreover Luke remembers that on occasion two of their number, Peter and John, functioned as a pair in proclaiming the gospel (Acts 3:1, 11-12; 4:13, 19) to unbelieving Jews as well as in ministering to a new congregation of believers (Acts 8:14).[53]

An internal crisis overtook the expanding Jerusalem church within this period, a few years after Pentecost. With it came a profound clarification of how the Twelve functioned *vis-à-vis* the Jerusalem congregation (as distinguished from their function for unbelieving Israel). According to Acts 6:1ff., inequities had occurred in the giving of relief to the poorest members of the church, the widowed women. In the face of the resultant grumbling, the Twelve (Acts 6:2)[54] assembled the congregation[55] and proposed to turn over what had apparently been one of their responsibilities, the distribution of food to the poor. This, they proposed, should be entrusted to seven men chosen by the assembly and then commissioned

---

50 In this respect the witness of Acts 1:13-14, placing this group first among the three noted and recording eleven names, is in agreement with Paul and the kerygma of the Jerusalem church (1 Cor 15:5). The central fact that this notice presupposes is their having seen the risen Jesus. Paul also knows that the title *apostolos* and the term *a postolē* can be applied to at least one of their number (cf. Gal 1:18-19; 2:8).

51 Again the witness of Acts (cf. 1:13 15; 2:14 etc.) is that of Paul (note the position of Cephas in 1 Cor 15:5 as well as Gal 1:18; 2:8). See Rengstorf and Barrett (*ut. cit.* fn. 44) on the conversion of Israel as historically the frst priority of the Twelve as it had been of their master. On the way in which Luke articulated the emergence of the mission to the gentiles, see Jervell (*ut cit.* fn. 22) pp. 41-74 and S.G. Wilson, THE GENTILES AND THE GENTILE MISSION IN LUKE-ACTS (Cambridge: the University Press, 1973).

52 The Qumran documents illustrate how first century Palestinian Judaism understood that number as the studies of Flusser and Jaubert (*ut cit.* fn. 27) indicate. In view of the connotations of the lots in Acts 1.26 (cf. fn. 45), one notes the Qumran description of their twelve in terms of the precious stones on the high priest's breastplate and the Urim and Thummim of the priestly tradition. Where Ezechiel 48:30-34 assigns the names of the twelve tribes to the twelve gates of his visionary Jerusalem, a new scroll from the Qumran area puts twelve gates, similarly named, in both the outer and middle courts of its projected temple, as noted by Y. Yadin,, "The Temple Scroll," in D.N. Freedman and J.C. Greenfield (ed.) NEW DIRECTIONS IN BIBLICAL ARCHAEOLOGY (Garden City, N.Y.: Doubleday, 1969), p. 146. Rev 21.12-14 follows Ezechiel here, associating the gates and foundations of the heavenly *city* with the names of "the twelve tribes of the sons of Israel" and of "the twelve apostles of the Lamb" Of course the new Jerusalem in the vision of Rev (21.22) has no temple," for its temple is the Lord God, the Almighty, and the Lamb."

53 Cf. fn 57 and 83 below.

54 This is the only time that Acts employs *hoi dōdeka* as a technical phrase to designate the group which Jesus had associated with himself, though the phrase occurs in this sense six times in his gospel (cf. fn. 60 below).

55 *To plēthos*, a phrase that resembles the use of *hrbym* at Qumran (Fitzmyer, ESBNT, pp. 290-291).

by the Twelve to this service. The Twelve reserved to themselves "preaching the word of God" (Acts 6:2) and proposed to devote themselves "to prayer and to the ministry of the word" (Acts 6:4: i.e., to the preaching to the Jews, and a leadership in the Christian assemblies for worship and the study of the Old Testament scriptures).[56]

The author of Acts emphasized the function of the Twelve in the worship of the earliest Jewish Christian church, for not only did the members of that congregation participate in the public worship of the temple (Acts 2:46) but also a pair from the Twelve are depicted in Acts 3:1 as about to participate in "the prayer"[57] of Judaism, the evening oblation of the lamb (cf. Ex 29:39 ff.) in the temple. Acts 6:1-5 presupposes that a certain leadership in "the prayer" of the Jerusalem church had been reserved to the Twelve, which would accord with the notice that the first converts "devoted themselves to the apostles' teaching and fellowship, to the breaking of bread and (the) prayers" (Acts 2:42). For Luke the *klasis tou artou* refers to the eucharistic meal[58] and his reader is invited to infer that the Twelve were carrying out the command, "Do this . . . ", which Luke had previously recorded in his narrative of the last supper.[59]

Luke, of course, is not unaware that "the apostles" are a wider group than the Twelve.[60] He may well imply that a function given to the Twelve was capable of being shared with others. Indeed, the fact that Matthias was now numbered among the Twelve, sharing their Ministry, certainly means that he was to function with them not only in "preaching the word" but also in leading "the prayer" of the community. He shared not only a Ministry to unbelieving Israel but also to those Israelites who had repented and been baptized (cf. Acts 2:5, 14, 22, 36, 38-41).

---

56 For this interpretation of *hē diakonia tou logou*, cf. B. Gerhardsson, MEMORY AND MANUSCRIPT (Lund: Gleerup, 1964), pp. 240-245, 331.

57 *Hē proseuchē*: cf. F.F. Bruce, THE ACTS OF THE APOSTLES (London: Tyndale, 1952), p. 103, cited hereafter as Bruce, ACTS). Such *communicatio in sacris* is noted even for Paul (Acts 21:23-27).

58 Cf. the materials assembled by J. Behm, *"klasis,"* TDNT, III, 726-743. The interpretation followed here is that of J. Dupont, "The Meal at Emmaus," in J. Delorme *et. al.*, THE EUCHARIST IN THE NEW TESTAMENT (Baltimore: Helicon, 1964), pp. 105-121, and also of J. Jeremias, EWJ, 118-122. For the latter the four phrases of Acts 2:42 "describe the sequence of an early Christian service" (p. 119). *Contra* Haenchen, ACTS, p. 191, cf. p. 263.

59 Cf. fn. 35 above and Brown, PR.BP., 40-41.

60 Cf. the Lukan usage in Acts 14:4, 14 (see Barrett, NTE, 80-81, on the Western text here) as well as his narrative of the last supper, where in the context one reads of "the Twelve" (Lk 22.3), "my disciples" (Lk 22.11), and "the apostles" (Lk 22.14). Luke-Acts (like Mark) never employs the *phrase*, "the twelve apostles." Matthew does so only once (10.2), though he speaks several times of "the twelve disciples" (cf Brown, PETER, p. 77 fn. 175). Cf. the observations in fn. 54 above as well as 67 below.

Significantly, Luke places the dispute about precedence within the leadership immediately after the command to repeat the supper action and the betrayal prophecy (22. 24-27). Leading the eucharist and leading the community, mean leading to the Crucified, with the judgment that implies.

The crisis that precipitated the creation of this body, witnesses to another form of sharing, precisely because these men are not to be counted among the Twelve but rather the Twelve are representd as entrusting a function that was expected of themselves to another group which received again a modest appellation, the Seven (Acts 6:3; 21:8).[61]

Acts does not name these men *diakonoi,* though they were chosen with an eye to the "daily distribution *(diakonia)*" of 6:1 and this service *(diakonein,* 6:2) is distinguished from "the Ministry *(diakonia)* of the word" (6:4) reserved to the Twelve. The Seven were staffed from a minority group within the Jerusalem church, the Hellenist Jewish Christians.[62] Their names are all Greek. The qualification for their task is not that they had seen the risen Jesus but that they be "full of the Spirit and wisdom" (Acts 6:3). They receive their office in a setting of worship which apparently specifies the significance of the imposition of hands by "the apostles."[63] The Qumran documents have revealed no parallel thus far to this structure in the Jerusalem church.[64] Moreover, it is striking that the Seven are never depicted as exercising the function for which they were chosen.[65] Instead they exercise a form of Ministry which the Twelve had reserved when they appointed the Seven. Stephen preaches Jesus as Lord in the Jerusalem synagogue worship-assemblies. Philip later preaches in Samaria and then along the Mediterranean coast until he settles in Caesarea. He is the only one of the Seven who receives a title indicating his function and that title is "the evangelist" (Acts 21:8), i.e., one who preaches the good news about Jesus as the Christ.[66]

---

61 Cf. Haenchen, ACTS, 260-263, and Brown, PETER, 46-47, fn. 108. For a quite different approach see E. Schweizer, CHURCH ORDER IN THE NEW TESTAMENT (Naperville: Allenson, 1961), pp. 70-71 (cited hereafter as Schweizer, CONT).

62 Cf. J. Fitzmer, ESBNT, 277-279. A. Apiro has argued that the "Hellenists" were Samaritan Jewish Christians in J. Munck, THE ACTS OF THE APOSTLES (N.Y.: Doubleday, 1967), pp. 285-300. C.H.H. Scobie, "The Origins and Development of Samaritan Christianity," *New Testament Studies* 19 (1973) pp. 390-414, has a review of the evidence to date for this hypothesis (pp. 391-400).

63 On this title in Acts 6.6, cf. fn. 60 above. It is not clear in this text that *only* the apostles imposed hands (Brown, PR.BP., 55). But if not, certainly the Seven were brought before them by the rest of the community and the apostles are to be numbered among the community as a whole which imposed hands. See fn. 74 on the endowment of the Seven with the Spirit.

64 Cf. P. Benoit, "Les origines apostoliques de l'Épiscopat selon le N.T." in H. Bouessé and A. Mandouze, L'ÉVÊQUE DANS L'ÉGLISE DU CHRIST (Paris: Desclee de Brouwer, 1963), pp. 34-35 (cited hereafter as Benoit, Épiscopat; this full dress, critical article should not be confused with a considerably earlier, more popular exposition, reprinted in this author's ÉXEGESE ET THEOLOGIE [Paris: Cerf, 1961], vol. II, pp. 232-246.

65 Cf. E. Haenchen, "The Book of Acts as Source Material for the History of Early Christianity," in L. Keck and J. Martyn (ed's) STUDIES IN LUKE-ACTS (New York: Abingdon, 1966), p. 264 (cited hereafter as Keck, STUDIES); Schweizer, CONT, 49 with fn. 162; and Barrett, NTE, 108-109.

66 Luke does not say this preaching of the Seven was done without the approval or supervision of the Twelve. In fact, Peter and John are dispatched to Samaria to review Philip's work (Acts 8:14-17) and Peter later appeared in Caesarea also, to do

The way in which the Seven understood and preached the gospel now precipitated an external crisis for the Jerusalem church. With the assassination of Stephen "a great persecution arose against the church in Jerusalem, and they were all scattered throughout the region of Judea and Samaria," and then Luke notes, "except the apostles" (Acts 8:1). The storm had broken over the Hellenist front of the Jerusalem congregation. The Seven were scattered (providentially as events proved) while the Twelve remained, apparently because the orthodoxy (or orthopraxy)[67] of the latter in the eyes of their fellow Jews was still intact.[68] The gospel was carried to Samaria and the Mediterranean coastal towns; Christian churches were formed in Galilee and Damascus (Acts 9:31) and then in Phoenicia, Cyprus, and Antioch (Acts 11:19). In all of this missionary work the gospel was addressed only to Jews. Peter alone had dared to admit gentiles directly into the church and even he had to answer for it at length before the Jerusalem church (Acts 11:1-18).

At last, in Antioch, in the early forties, the gospel was addressed to the gentiles as such (Acts 11:20) and the first mixed congregation outside of Palestine appeared and prospered. As the author of Acts wished it understood, the Jerusalem church sent down a Cypriot Levite whom the apostles had renamed Barnabas (Acts 4:36) to inspect this new kind of Christian church and he was more than satisfied with it. For help in ministering to it he sought out a convert from Tarsus, a Jew named Saul (Acts 11:25-26) to whom the risen Jesus had once appeared and spoken (cf. Acts 9:17, 27). With this pair, deliberately formed, a Ministry of teaching in a "mixed church" began.[69]

---

what apparently Philip (then residing in that city, Acts 8:40; 21:8) did not feel free to do, i.e., admit a gentile family into the Christian community. It is not often noted that it is as the leader within a group of *seven* Jewish Christians that Peter preached to Cornelius (Acts 10:23, 45 and 11:12). Cf. fn. 73 below.

67 The Seven as a group were no more "permanent" than the Twelve (cf. Jervell [*ut. cit.* fn. 22], p. 95) and the martyrdom of Stephen did not require a replacement among the Seven any more than the later martyrdom of James, son of Zebedee, called for a replacement among the Twelve (cf. fn. 24 above). Luke's readiness to let individuals and structures disappear without explanation has challenged the ingenuity of his commentators (cf. Barrett, NTE, pp. 80-82 and Brown, PETER, pp. 40-41 fn. 91). Particularly illuminating is Schuyler Brown, APOSTASY AND PERSEVERANCE IN THE THEOLOGY OF LUKE (Rome: Pontifical Biblical Institute, 1969), pp. 82-97, on "The Apostasy of Judas."
On the orthodoxy/orthopraxy distinction, A.D. Nock noted " . . . that Judaism was at all times a religion of orthopraxy and not a religion of orthodoxy" (EARLY GENTILE CHRISTIANITY AND ITS HELLENISTIC BACKGROUND [N.Y.: Harper & Row Torchbook, 1964] x; cf. W.D. Davies, "Torah and Dogma: A Comment," *HTR* 61 April, 1968), 87-105, and Schweizer, CONT, p. 40, fn. 116).

68 Cf. Schweizer, CONT, p. 42, fn. 126 and Haenchen in Keck, STUDIES, 262-264.

69 Haenchen, ACTS, 370-371, would discern minimal "concrete material" behind this Lukan narrative, but cf. fn. 42 above. The pair continues in the narrative from Acts 11.30 throuh 15.36-39. At first apparently Barnabas is taken as leader and named first (11:30; 12:25; 13; 1, 2, 7). Then Paul is given priority (13:43, 46, 50; 14:20;

The appearance of Paul, entering a position of leadership in one of the newly founded churches, makes it imperative at this point to summarize the function of a group of men, numerically undefined, that were called, from the earliest days of the Jewish Christian church, *hoi apostoloi,* "the apostles."[70] As noted above, "all the apostles" figured in the most archaic record of the Jerusalem kerygma as a group to whom the risen Jesus appeared (1 Cor 15:7). Whereas Paul never even intimated that he should be considered one of the Twelve, he did insist tirelessly that he was truly to be counted, even though as least, among "the apostles" (1 Cor 15:8-10). He did not begrudge members of the Twelve the title "apostle" or an "apostleship' (Gal. 1:17-19; 2:8). But he was convinced that he also belonged to a wider circle that had received this title and task.

In his earliest surviving letter Paul described himself, Silvanus, and Timothy as "apostles of Christ" (1 Thes 2:7) and the postcript to Romans (16:7) greeted an Andronicus and a Junias "who were men of note among the apostles and . . . in Christ before me."[71] Paul had no qualms about styling himself *apostolos* and spent no little time vindicating his right to that title and his Ministry as an authentic *apostolē* to the gentiles. What constituted this group into which Paul came? What functions did its members have antecedent to Paul?

Recent studies have indicated that Paul did enter a distinct and recognized group and that one expected to find its members in the neighborhood of Jerusalem in the very first decade after the resurrection. There seems to be little question that the appearance of the risen Jesus to those men, in the eyes of their Jerusalem confreres, qualified, identified, confirmed, and even authorized them as *apostoloi.*[72] Association with all or part of Jesus' earthly ministry appears to have been irrelevant to their status as apostles. As their title implies, they were understood and received as men who had been "sent", as authorized witnesses and missionarieis of the risen Lord. Since

---

15:2, (*bts*), 22, 35), though the previous arrangement recurs in significant contexts (14:12, 14; 15:12, 25). When this pair separated it was for Paul to form with Silas and Barnabas with John Mark two further pairs.

70 The further inquiry as to whether Jesus used the term *apostoloi* or its Semitic equivalent for the members of any of the groups associated with him before the crucifixion will not be broached here, though its outcome would not be unlike that for *mathētēs* (cf. Section I above, esp. fn. 4-6).
It has been argued that the Christian use of the term *apostolos* originated in the Antiochean congregation (see Lemaire, "NT Ministries," p. 142 for the proponents of this hypothesis). On the other hand, the record of the appearance "to all the apostles" transmitted in 1 Cor 15.7 and Paul's declaration that after his conversion, he did not immediately go up "to Jerusalem to those who were apostles before me" (Gal 1.17, cf. 19) still favor the Jerusalem church as the first locale for the use of the concept if not for the use of precisely that Greek term.

71 On these passages, see Schnackenburg, "Apostles Before . . . " pp. 290-296.

72 Thus Schnackenburg, "Apostles Before . . . " p. 292. On what follows, see also his "Apostolicity," pp. 247, 252-253.

their "mission" was perceived as primary and central, the way was open for men who had not seen the risen Jesus (e.g: Timothy, Andronicus, Junias) to be styled *apostoloi* in the world of the Hellenistic mission. Their converts were the "authentication" of their mission. By the time Paul had preached in Thessalonica, this concept could be taken for granted. Even when his own apostleship was under attack he still appealed to the evidence of the churches that had resulted from his preaching, but to this he emphatically prefixed what was in the Jerusalem church the *sine qua non* and foundation of apostleship, his encounter with the risen Lord (1 Cor 9.1-2; cf. 15.7-10).

Before the founding of a church in Syrian Antioch, Jesus had been regularly proclaimed as Lord and Christ only to the sons of Israel, whether in Palestine or abroad, whether by the Twelve or by the Seven or by the apostles (Acts 11:19-20).[73] When the mixed congregation at Antioch sent out Barnabas and Paul on a systematic mission to the pagans, they extended the concept of *apostolē* as fundamentally as had the election of Matthias or the action of the Seven in proclaiming the Christ to yet unbelieving Jews without having themselves seen the risen Jesus. Accordingly, in that first mission from Antioch, Luke deliberately and for the only time in Acts styled both Barnabas and Paul *apostoloi* (Acts 14:4, 14).[74] the way in which Paul in particular developed the content of *apostolos* and *apostolē,* stamping it indelibly with his own style,[75] belongs to the history of Ministry in the mixed churches (section III below).

---

73 Peter heading a group of seven (cf. fn. 66 above), had preached to the gentile household of Cornelius (Acts 10:1-11:18) at a moment that is difficult to anchor chronologically. The missionary orientation of the Twelve was not altered, for Peter acted as part of another group. What had been an extraordinary incident became years later a precedent (Acts 15.7-9). Cf. Brown, PETER, 43-45.

74 In the theology of Luke, the special and lasting endowment of the Seven with the Spirit and wisdom may be equivalent to an encounter with the risen Jesus, for as D.W. Smith (WISDOM CHRISTOLOGY IN THE SYNOPTIC GOSPELS [Rome: Angelicum, 1970, unpublished dissertation], p. 260) has noted, " . . . several passages from Acts (cf. 10:14 with 10:19) parallel the Spirit with the glorified Jesus in such a way that Jesus seems to become present to his Church through the Spirit which is his gift . . . ". The anarthrous "full of Spirit and wisdom" of 6:3 becomes in the description of Stephen (6:5) "full of faith and the Holy Spirit" which in its turn and with a slight variation becomes the description of Barnabas "full of Holy Spirit and faith" as he is dispatched by the Jerusalem church to the new congregation of Antioch (Acts 11:24). Barnabas in his turn appears to need Saul with him in the Ministry to the Antiochean congregation because of the mission which the latter had received from the risen Jesus. They began as a pair of teachers (Acts 11:26: *didaxai*); in Acts 13.1 they are called "prophets and teachers." Finally, in Acts 14:4, 14, they both receive the critical title "apostles" (cf. Section III and fn. 100-103 below). The progression can scarcely be accidental (cf. 1 Cor 12:28-29), particularly since in 14:3 " . . . Luke says of Paul and Barnabas, word for word, the same as he had said of the Twelve in 5.12" (Haenchen, Acts 4:20). Thus, for all the use of a source at this point, the author is not mechanically reproducing it without thought for his own concept of apostleship (cf. Brown, PR.BP., p. 50, fn. 31).

75 Schnackenburg, "Apostolicity," p. 250.

Toward the mid-forties of the first century, two events precipitated another crisis for the Jerusalem church. The first mentioned by Luke was a famine;[76] and the second was an outbreak of persecution that struck at the leading members of the Twelve. James, son of Zebedee, was beheaded and Peter was imprisoned to await the same fate. Both events occasioned new organizational developments within the Jerusalem church.

With the famine there appear for the first time Christian *presbyteroi*[77] (presbyters, elders) among the Jewish Christians of Jerusalem. The structure was certainly borrowed directly from the organization of contemporary orthodox Judaism. The evidence of Acts is persuasive. The term *presbyteroi* occurs eighteen times in that book. On its first occurrence it has the ordinary sense of "older men" (Acts 2:17 = Joel 3:1). After that a very significant distinction appears. The term is used first to describe an influential body of men within Judaism as such.[78] Then with Acts 11:30 it is used to denote an influential body within the Jerusalem Christian congregation itself. Thus there are Jewish *presbyteroi* and Jewish *Christian presbyteroi*. We first meet the latter as administrators[79] of the famine relief fund that the mixed congregation of Antioch sent up "by the hand of Barnabas and Saul."

The reader of Acts is immediately struck by the fact that these *presbyteroi* received the gift and not the Twelve. Luke immediately explains by noting the second contemporary crisis. The central leadership had been under attack: one of its members was already dead; Peter himself had narrowly escaped death. He fled the city and there is reason to believe that the others had already taken a similar course, for the parting word of Peter to the Jerusalem church was, "Tell this to James and to the brothers" (Acts 12:17). This statement implies that the leadership of the Jerusalem church had been left in the hands of the family of Jesus, for this James seems to have been the oldest of the "brothers of the Lord."[80] Again there

---

76 Acts 11:28: the event figures also in Josephus (ANT. 3.15.3 and 20.2.5 as well as 20.5.2) and Suetonius (CLAUDIUS, 18.2).

77 Cf. G. Bornkamm, "*presbyteros*," TDNT, VI, 651-680 (esp. 662-663), and Fitzmyer, ESBNT, p. 295, as well as Lemaire, MINISTERES, *passim*. and "NT Ministries," pp. 146-147.

78 Acts 4:5, 8, 23: a group on a par with "rulers, scribes, and high priests" (cf. P. Benoit, ÉPISCOPAT, 19-25 *et passim*). Lemaire, MINISTERES, p. 49 has suggested that the Barabbas attached to two different personal names in Acts 1.23 and 15.22 is the very archaic Aramaic term for "son of the elder," in the sense of "member of the group of elders" (cf. the Hebrew, "son of the prophet" etc.).

79 These *presbyteroi* seem to be exercising the Ministry to the poor which the Seven had once exercised in the Jerusalem church (cf. Brown, PETER, p. 46, fn. 108).

80 If the Letter of James with its Jewish Christian and even Palestinian origin does indeed date from the fourth decade of the first century, it not only witnesses to the prestige and influence of this leader in the Jewish Christian churches (Jas 1.1), but also to the existence of a class of "teachers" (among whom the author includes himself: Jas 3.1) as well as *presbyteroi* who exercised a Ministry of healing in the con-

is no indication that this action of sharing their function with another group dissolved or compromised the authority and primacy of the Twelve and Peter. As noted above a distinct stratum within the Jerusalem congregation, present from its beginnings, was constituted by the members of Jesus' family who were, of course, like him, of Davidic descent.[81] James apparently enjoyed a certain primacy among them not only by primogeniture but also because the risen Jesus had appeared to him (I Corinthians 15:7).[82]

Within a few years of the famine, at the time of the Jerusalem "council," Peter (as Acts 15 narrates events) took the initiative and proposed the case for the "apostles," Barnabas and Paul, before their fellow apostles and the Jerusalem *presbyteroi*. It was James, however, who spoke for the Jerusalem church and its *presbyteroi*.[83] He proposed the compromise which made possible a *modus vivendi* between the Palestinian Jewish Christian

---

gregation(s) to which the epistle was directed (Jas 5.14-15). See J. Haar, DER JACOBUSBRIEF (Stuttgart/Göttingen: Klotz, 1971).

81 The sharing out of leadership functions with "the brothers" at this point is not basically different from the first sharing of the *diakonia* of the Twelve with the Seven. It may be more than a coincidence that when Paul paid his first visit to the Jerusalem church, he already met a pair, Cephas and James, each of whom was apparently a leader in his own group (i.e. the Twelve or the family of Jesus) in the Jerusalem congregation (Gal 1:18-19). Cf. fn. 67 above on the question of replacement among the Twelve or the Seven. Fitzmyer, ESBNT, 113-126; S.E. Johnson, "The Davidic Royal Motif in the Gospels," *JBL* 87 (June, 1968), 149; and D.C. Duling, "The Promises to David . . . ," *NT Studies* 20 (1973), 55-77, as well as K. Berger, "Die königlichen Messiastraditionen des NT," *ibid.*, 1-44, are helpful for understanding the concern about the Davidic tradition among the Jewish Christians of the first generation.

82 H. von Campenhausen, JERUSALEM AND ROME (Philadelphia: Fortress, 1966), pp. 3-19, presents the arguments against there ever having been a "caliphate" or a hereditary succession in leadership in primitive Christianity. Cf. Brown, PETER, p. 47, fn. 109.
The use of later models, exotic or commonplace, from the history of religion, has perhaps impeded an assessment of the admittedly fragmentary evidence for one of the methods of providing leadership that was tried in the first and the beginning of the second century (cf. fn. 24 *ad fin.*)

83 Galatians 2:9 witnesses to a group of three, James, the brother of Jesus, as well as Cephas and John, surviving (?) members of the trio within the Twelve, who appear to be leading the Jerusalem church and are styled ironically by Paul as "pillars." That term may be an actual citation of the terminology already employed by the Jerusalem congregation (cf. their use of *pistis* in Galatians 1:23). The dating of Paul's visit in Galatians 2:1 is so vexed that the historian can scarcely affirm more than that such a trio functioned in Jerusalem before 50 AD and that it bears an obvious resemblance to the trio within the Twelve. Cf. J. Fitzmyer, "A Life of Paul" (p. 218) and "The Letter to the Galatians" (pp. 239-240, JBC, and Brown, PETER, 49-55. Perhaps it should be remembered that the trio of Jerusalem "pillars" met with a trio from Antioch, Paul, Barabas, *and Titus* (Gal 2.1). Titus was surely present as something more than an exhibit of a convert from paganism. He was a gentile convert who shared the Ministry of Paul (note the emphatic *Titos, ho syn emoi, Hellēn ōn*). The "pillars" approved the Jewish Christian Ministry of Paul and Barnabas to the gentiles (cf. the *hēmeis* of Gal 2.9). They did not give the right hand of fellowship to Titus. They had found acceptable a Jewish Christian Ministry to the pagans. They did not commit themselves with respect to such a Ministry by a convert from paganism. See C.K. Barrett, "Titus," in E.E. Ellis and M. Wilcox (ed.), NEOTESTAMENTICA ET SEMITICA, Edinburg; Clark, 1969), 1-14, esp. 4-6, for other suggestions on the career of this figure.

church and the mixed churches now being organized in the Roman world at large, especially by Paul and Tarsus.

During the next decade, James' leadership continued, and, as Gal. 2:12-13 makes painfully clear, his prestige and that of his congregation extended as far as Antioch.[84] On Paul's last trip to Jerusalem (again with a collection) in about 58 AD, he had an official audience with James "and the *presbyteroi* were all present" (Acts 21:18). Paul reported on the success of the mission among the gentiles and demonstrated with the collection the real unity that those mixed congregations had with the Jewish Christian church of Jerusalem. James in his turn explained how successfully the compromise of the previous decade had worked for the mission to the Jews. "You see, brother, how many thousands there are among the Jews of those who have believed; they are all zealous for the law" (Acts 21:20).[85] The Twelve had been driven from Jerusalem, but apparently even the most suspicious had been unable to undermine or impugn the orthodoxy of James. Thus under his leadership the Jerusalem church had been able to win many more from Israel to belief in Jesus. James then cited the slanderous rumor that Paul despised the law and taught his *Jewish* converts to apostatize. In order to give it the lie, he suggested that Paul participate publicly in the worship of the temple and Paul agreed readily. The plan miscarried. Paul was imprisoned and eventually carried off to Rome for trial. By this time the days of the Jerusalem church were numbered. Palestine was in political chaos, and, in AD 62, James himself was murdered at the instigation of Ananus, the Sadducean high priest.[86] By AD 66 the great revolt had erupted. In the next four years it resulted in ". . . the destruction of Jewish and Christian communal life . . ."[87] in Palestine. The Jewish Christian churches, and above all the Jerusalem church, were caught between the millstone and the grinder. Their pagan contemporaries treated them as Jews and thus as traitors to and revolutionaries against Rome. Their orthodox Jewish confreres considered them

---

84 Cf. Brown, PETER, 26-32, 47-55.

85 Historically speaking the compromise of James was as unimpeachably apostolic in its motivation as the mission of Paul. The portrait of "this last Davidian and this first curialist . . . this fearsome ecclesiastical politician" (E. Stauffer, NEW TESTAMENT THEOLOGY [London: SCM, 1955], p. 34) is quite overdrawn. The "gentiles", the heirs and beneficiaries of Paul, have tended to forget that the conversion of Israel was a practical, pressing, and critical concern for that first generation church (as it had been the first concern of their Lord). The delay in the conversion of Israel posed far deeper questions of theology and apologetics than the delay of the parousia. To take up a famous image, the latter is a secondary crater in the vast problem of the fate of Israel (cf. Wuellner, MFM, 206). Cf. Jervell (*ut cit.* fn. 22), pp. 185-207, on "James: the Defender of Paul," in Luke's plan.

86 Josephus, ANTIQ., 20.9.1 (197-203).

87 W.F.Albright, HISTORY, ARCHAEOLOGY AND CHRISTIAN HUMANISM (New York: McGraw-Hill, 1964), p. 57.

not only heretics but now in addition "pacifists and defeatists."[88] Eusebius says that the Jerusalem church fled across the Jordan into Pella.[89] Meanwhile Palestine was sealed off from the *orbis terrarum,* until in 70 AD the Jewish nation had been annihilated and Jerusalem was in ruins. Jewish Christianity survived into the following generation, but as the *magni nominis umbra,* wilting and dying like a great tree whose roots have been slashed. As late as the reign of Domitian, we have some evidence that the Jerusalem church was still led by another surviving "brother of Jesus" (Simeon; Simon). This experiment with a hereditary form of leadership apparently atrophied and disappeared with Jewish Christianity itself.

III

The mixed churches that had begun to appear thirty years before the fall of Jerusalem as a happy side-effect of the mission to the Jews, were by 70 AD (and more by default than by their own design) the guardians and interpreters of the gospel of Jesus Christ.

It had been Paul's systematic and brilliant apostleship to the gentiles that had raised in acute, practical form the question of the identity of the church over against Judaism. But he was indeed a premature birth. In his activity and in his correspondence he presented the theological rationale for the radical independence of the Christian faith, but he was in no position (nor did he intend) to tear apart the chrysalis of Judaism within which the first generation churches were developing.

Powerful opponents were never persuaded by Paul's ideas or arguments, but they died, and Paul's new ideas conquered (as valid new ideas do) by surviving their opponents — not by convincing them.[90] It was not Paul's theology but the armies of Vespasian and Titus that ripped away the chrysalis of orthodox Judaism. It was Paul's theology that made it possible for those mixed congregations of the second generation to rescue that which was of intrinsic value from the shambles of Palestinian Christi-

---

88 W.F. Albright, THE ARCHAEOLOGY OF PALESTINE (Baltimore: Penguin, 1960), pp. 240-242 (the quotation is on p. 241).

89 H.E., 3.5.3. The historicity of this notice has been the object of an ongoing critique by S.G.F. Brandon since the publication of his THE FALL OF JERUSALEM AND THE CHRISTIAN CHURCH, second edition (London: SPCK, 1957). His arguments have, by and large, not been found demonstrative. Cf. M. Simon (*ut cit.* fn. 37), p. 271 and his "La Migration à Pella" in JUD CHR. (*ut cit.* fn. 37) 37-54, as well as B.C. Gray, "The Movements of the Jerusalem Church During the First Jewish War," *Journal of Ecclesiastical History* 24 (1973) 1-7.
The excavations that have begun at Pella may eventually shed some light on the earliest Christian history of a church that produced the apologist, Aristo (c. 140), and to which the Letter to the Hebrews may have been addressed (thus H. Cazelles, NAISSANCE DE L'EGLISE [Paris: Cerf, 1968], pp. 108-109). R. H. Smith, PELLA OF THE DECAPOLIS (Wooster, Ohio: College of Wooster, 1973) I, should be consulted. *Testimonia* related to the first Christian century are on pp. 41-46.

90 The language is that of Max Planck, discussing the development in mathematical science in recent generations.

anity and to survive an age of transition.

The mixed churches of the first generation were to a great extent the result of the apostolic Ministry of Paul. The apostleship itself developed under the pressure of his experience and thought; yet precisely because of the Jewish-Christian background of Paul and other apostles as well as their own Jewish-Christian members, the social structuring of the mixed churches reflected that of the "churches of God" in Judea. New elements were introduced into the structure of mixed congregations and older ones were modified, because of the converts from paganism and the pressure that arose from their living cheek by jowl with converts from Judaism.

From the Pauline correspondence one can discern something of the nature and character of Paul's apostolic Ministry — a powerful, personal, and detailed control over every aspect of the Christian life of his foundations.[91] His churches were his children in Christ (1 Cor 4:14-17; Gal 4:19; 1 Thes 2:7-12), the chaste spouse that he was presenting to his Lord (Cor 11:2). The imagery attests not only to the heroic charity that impelled him but also to the unique and exclusive bond of the churches with the apostle himself. He was not only founder but model and final arbiter for these foundations, and he reserved to himself judgement on other apostles who entered his domain (cf. 2 Cor 11:4-5). He did not conceive his apostleship as ending with the conversion of his hearers; he remained their apostle after they became believers (1 Cor 9:2). Moreover, he addressed them as both prophet and teacher,[92] with "the authority (*exousia*) that the Lord had given" him for upbuilding the church (2 Cor 13:10; cf. 10:8).

As the Twelve shared out functions of leadership with other groups in the Jerusalem church, so Paul associated others with the tasks of his apostleship. The working in pairs and trios which is conspicuous in the Pauline correspondence has also been remembered in the traditions utilized by the Acts. These "co-workers (*synergoi*)" of Paul shared not only in administrative functions[93] but in the properly apostolic tasks of proclaiming the gospel to unbelievers[94] and the further teaching of the congregation. Of Timothy, the Apostle wrote to the Corinthians, ". . . he is doing the work of the Lord *as I am*" (*hōs kagō*: 1 Cor 16:10; cf. 4:17) and earlier

91 Cf. A. Jaubert in MMNT (*ut cit.* fn. 1) 28-31 and P. Grelot, *ibid.*, pp. 34-46.
92 Cf. M. Bourke, "Reflections on Church Order in the New Testament," *CBQ* 30 (October, 1968), 493-511, esp. 494-501 (cited hereafter as Bourke, *CBQ*).
93 Acting as messengers (1 Thes 3:6 of Timothy), and supervising finances (2 Cor 8:16-19, 22-23 of Titus and "the brother"). A glimpse of a functionary in the entourage is provided by Romans 16:22.
94 2 Corinthians 1:19 states this of Silvanus, Timothy, and Paul proclaiming (*kēruchtheis*) Jesus Christ, the Son of God, to the Corinthians upon their arrival among them. The use of the first person plural in 2 Corinthians 3 - 4 and 6 in describing the Ministry Paul shared is in striking contrast to the first person singular of his defense of his personal apostleship (2 Cor 11 - 12). Cf. B. Rigaux, LES ÉPITRES AUX THESS. (Paris: Gabalda, 1956), pp. 77-80, "L'Emploi des 'nous' et des 'je'."

Paul had included him along with Silvanus when he wrote to the Thessalonians that ". . . we might have made demands as apostles of Christ" (1 Thes 2:7).[95] These co-workers must regularly have administered the baptismal rite (cf. 1 Cor 1:14-17).

The way in which Paul with his aides structured the communities that he founded is much less clear.[96] From the first of his extant letters (dating from about 51 AD) we read, "But we beseech you, brethren, to respect those who labor among you and *are over you in the Lord*[97] and admonish you, and to esteem them very highly in love because of their work." The Greek term for "those who are over you," literally "those who have been set over you," may advert to the Thessalonians having a part in the choice of their leaders. In any case it is a leadership that the apostle acknowledges and supports.

In correcting and instructing his Corinthian converts, Paul apparently bypassed the local leadership[98] and addressed the congregation as a whole.

---

95 Thus Timothy in 1 Thessalonians 3:2 is "our brother and *God's servant (synergon tou theou)* in the gospel of Christ, to establish you in your faith and to exhort you." Paul's co-workers in his apostolic tasks are God's co-workers (cf. 1 Cor 3:9 of Paul and Apollos, "We are God's fellow workers"). Cf. G. Bertram, *"synergos,"* TDNT, VII, 871-875. On 1 Thes 2.7, see fn. 71 above. For a discussion of cretian ministerial titles in Paul see E.E. Ellis, "Paul and His Co-Workers," *New Testament Studies* 17 (1971), pp. 437-452.
The written evidence of Paul's style in leadership and teaching is the epistolary itself, and it is striking that, excluding the Pastorals, only three letters are dispatched under the name of Paul alone (Galatians, Romans, Ephesians). All the remainder are sent as the communications from two or three together (thus Paul, Silvanus, and Timothy for 1 and 2 Thessalonians; Paul and Timothy for 2 Corinthians, Philippians, Colossians and Philemon; Paul and Sosthenes for 1 Corinthians). In the light of the evidence noted in the previous paragraphs, one simply cannot dismiss this as a superficial formality. It has its significance not only for the Pauline (and first generation) concept of the apostolate and the sharing of this Ministry but also for the exegesis of many a passage in which the first person plural occurs. Critical analysis of the letters has not perhaps been critical enough in "the quest for the historical Paul."
96 "Since the apostle is the pre-eminent figure, and since he, Paul, is the principal director of the community, offices of guidance other than his are of relatively slight importance," Bourke, CBQ, 503.
97 *pröistamenous hymōn en kyriōi*, 1 Thes 5:12-13. Cf. B. Reicke *"pröistēmi,"* TDNT, VI, 700-703, who remarks, "the reference is to officebearers though not to a technical title."
98 Though one must weigh 1 Cor 16.15-16 with its reference, in Levitical terminology (Ellis, *ut cit.* fn. 95, 450), to Stephanas' household, "first fruits (*aparchē*) of Achaia," who "have devoted themselves to the service (*diakonia*)" of the congregation. Paul there urges the Corinthian believer "to be subject to such men and to every fellow worker and laborer (*synergounti kai kopionti*)." The latter terms again are central to Paul's vocabulary for the apostleship and those who share its task (cf. F. Hauck, *"kopos,"* TDNT, III, 827-830; Bertram, *ut cit.* fn. 95; and J. H. Elliott, "Ministry and Church Order in the New Testament: A Traditio-Historical Analysis (1 Pt 5:1-5 & parallels)," *CBQ* 32 (July, 1970), pp. 381-382.
Since Stephanas was the leader of the trio that came to consult Paul in Ephesus (1 Cor 16:17), it is possible that the local leadership was actually with Paul as he dictated the letter (1 Cor 1:16 certainly sounds as if Stephanas was given the chance to look over the first draft). There would thus be no reason to counsel the leaders of the Corinthian church in writing. They had appealed the problems of their congregation directly to Paul and now Paul in turn directs his letter to the church, but not

In 1 Corinthians 12:4-6 (immediately after his treatment of the Lord's supper) he turned to the question of the unity of that church amid its varied gifts, services, and works.[99] In summarizing his argument (12: 27-31) he remarked emphatically that "God has appointed in the church first apostles, second prophets, third teachers, then workers of miracles, etc."

The three-fold Ministry of the word, which Paul here singled out as in some sense distinct from the following charismata and functions, belonged to the apostleship as well as the local congregation.[100] Yet this was not simply an umbrella, missionary structure, for the prophets and teachers in the Corinthian congregation were surely part of the local church. Somewhat later Ephesians 4:11 inserted "evangelists" and "pastors" into the archaic triad, between "prophets" and "teachers," witnessing to a further development in the structuring of Ministry.[101]

The triadic "order" may have derived from the way in which the mixed congregation at Antioch structured its leadership. The very archaic tradition behind the list of five "prophets and teachers" in Acts 13:1, included two, Barnabas and Saul, whom Acts 12:26 had previously described as simply teaching and to whom Acts 14:4, 14 gave the title, "apostles."[102] Thus, whereas all were not apostles or prophets or teachers (cf. 1 Cor 12:29), a given person could receive several charisms for the building up of the church. The Ministry of the Christian prophet was

without saying, "Give recognition to such men" (1 Cor 16:18). Cf. A. Jaubert, MMNT, (*ut cit.* fn. 1), p. 18, fn. 3.

In the next generation, in still another letter to the Corinthian congregation, it appears that 1 Clement 42:4 understood that Stephanas' household did lead the Corinthian church when he notes that the apostles "preached from district to district and from city to city, and they appointed their first fruits (*aparchas*), testing them by (*or* with regard to) the Spirit, to be bishops and deacons (*episkopous kai diakonous*) of future believers." The Pauline use of *aparachē* here is striking (cf. G. Delling, *s.v.*, TDNT I, 484-486). The passage of course should be read along with I Clement 44 and that author's concept of succeeding to the apostles.

99 Some have assumed that the Corinthians were Paul's ideal or model congregation or church. The evidence might well be read otherwise. If Paul ever favored a church as approaching his "ideal" that at Philippi would be among the strongest contenders for the honor. Curiously, that is the one Pauline congregation where we know that there were leaders called *episkopoi* and *diakonoi* (cf. Bourke, *CBQ,* 501, 502).

100 Cf. Danielou, TJC, p. 350, and Bourke *ut. cit.* in fn. 92 above.

101 Cf. C.K. Barrett, THE FIRST EPISTLE TO THE CORINTHIANS (London: Black, 1968), p. 295 (cited as Barrett, FIRST COR hereafter). If the Jerusalem prophet Silas = the Silvanus of 1 Thes 1.1; 2 Thes 1.1; 2 Cor 1.19, the way in which Paul linked the apostolic (1 Thes 2.7) and the prophetic Ministry may have its earliest documentation. H. Merklein DAS KIRCHLICHE AMT NACH DEM EPHESERBRIEF (Munich: Kösel, 1973) was inaccessible when this study was written.

102 Acts 11.27 described "prophets" coming down from Jerusalem to the Antiochean church after sketching the way in which Barnabas and Saul began to teach there (cf. fn. 74 above). Four out of the five Antiochean prophets and teachers had Jewish names. (X. Leon-Dufour, THE GOSPELS AND THE JESUS OF HISTORY [London: Collins, 1968], p. 174), and again (cf. fn. 83) a certain hesitation about admitting gentile converts to a Ministry may be in the background.

linked to the assembly for public worship, the official prayer, and within that gathering he exhorted the faithful to respond at this moment to the word of God as it had come in the Old Testament and the teachings of Jesus. The Jewish Christian teacher, on the other hand, probably functioned in somewhat the same way as his Jewish counterpart, transmitting a more systematic *didache* in a non-liturgical setting.[103]

These charisms, including apostleship, were conceived by the author of Acts as functioning not only *for* the church but also *through* the church. Thus the Jerusalem conference of apostles and *presbyteroi* dispatched its direction as that of the Holy Spirit as well (Acts 15:23-29), and their letter went down accompanied not only by two "apostles," Barnabas and Paul, but also by a pair of prophets, leading (*hēgoumenous*) men, Judas Barsabbas (the presbyter!) and Silas (Acts 15:22, 32). Previously in Acts 13:2-3 the Spirit had been described as commanding the leadership of the Antiochean church, in its assembly for public worship, to set aside two men, already charismatically endowed, for another divinely given "work" (*to ergon*). The assembly itself then sent Barnabas and Saul on their mission. Again the tie between apostle and prophet surfaced when Paul and Barnabas separated and Paul chose the prophet Silas to share his work (Acts 15:40). In Acts, as in Paul, all ecclesial leadership is a gift (charism) of the Spirit and there is no contradiction between office and charism, between institutional leaders and charismatics, between Law and Spirit.[104] This is not to say that there was no ordering, no priority among the charisms, for the triad of apostles — prophets — teachers had an explicit order within it and it took precedence over the other gifts and services with which the Corinthian congregation was familiar, among which were those of the "helpers" and "administrators" (1 Cor 12:28). In Rom 12:8 the *proïstamenos* (cf. 1 Thes 5:12-13) is noted as one who has received a charism that he must use with zeal.[105] In Phil 1:1, written perhaps half a dozen years after this, Paul and Timothy explicitly greeted

103 For the observations here and below, cf. E.E. Ellis, "The Role of the Christian Prophet in Acts" in Gasque and Martin (*ut cit.* fn. 48), pp. 55-67, and the superb article by E. Cothénet, "Prophetisme et N.T." Dictionnaire de la Bible, Supplément (Paris: Letouzey, 1972) VIII, 1222-1337, esp. 1286-1287.

104 Cf. H. Conzelmann, "*charisma,*" TDNT, IX, pp. 402-406, and Cothénet (*ut cit.* fn. 103) 1264-1267 and 1301-1303 for a history and critique of the obsolete systematic (and non-scriptural) antithesis between institution and charism. See also Lemaire, "NT Ministries" pp. 138-139, 156-157.

105 Cf. Reicke, *ut cit.* fn. 97. Barrett, First Cor, pp. 295-296, notes that the helpers "May foreshadow the work of deacons . . . , whose main task in the early church was that of ministering the church's aid to the needy," and administrators "that of bishops . . . , the name sometimes given to those who presided over the church's affairs (cf. Rom 12:8). There were local ministries (cf. Phil 1:1), in contrast with the peripatetic ministry of apostles and secondary to the ministry of the word exercised by prophets and teachers."

the *episkopoi* and *diakonoi* of the Philippian church.[106] The local and surbordinate leadership that had been present from the beginning and that had been designated as it developed with several general titles now had names linked to it that would remain constant while the development continued.

With this the evolution of the structures in the mixed churches has been traced up to the outbreak of the Palestinian revolt. The star of Jewish Christianity had begun to set. Furthermore, the leadership of the first generation was now being thinned at every level, in mixed as well as Jewish Christian congregations. The imprisonment of Paul was as sharp a setback to the mixed churches as the assassination of James was to the Jerusalem church and the Jewish Christians. The martyrdom of Peter, perhaps in 64 AD, was grim news for both.

The last stratum in the Pauline correspondence, the Pastoral Epistles, may have begun with a few brief despatches from the Pauline entourage, as late as 67 AD. In the form in which they have come down to us (dating from cir. 85 AD),[107] the *episkopos* appears (only in the [generic?] singular: 1 Tm 3:2; Ti 1:7) and *diakonoi* as well (1 Tm 3:8, 12). But now for the first time another term for a Minister occurs in the Pauline corpus. The Pastorals speak of *presbyteroi* (1 Tm 5:17, 19; Ti 1:5). The technical term and the organization have been seen in the Jewish Christian congregation in Jerusalem. With the Pastorals the *presbyteroi* have become part of the leadership in the churches of the *orbis terrarum*. It is possible that not only the title and structure had come from the Jewish Christians but that some of the very persons who bore the title had belonged to the now fragmented Jerusalem church. The functions of these *presbyteroi* seem to have coincided for all practical purposes with those *proïstamenoi* that Paul put in charge of his churches from the beginning. Luke, of course, actually called the leaders of the Pauline foundations *presbyteroi* (Acts 14:23) but he probably applied the term to men whose function corresponded to what was current when he wrote this volume in the second Christian generation. Indeed at one point he says that the *presbyteroi* of Ephesus came to hear Paul's farewell speech (Acts 20:17). He then cites what may be an earlier source and there these same hearers are

---

106 Cf. E. Best, "Bishops and Deacons . . . ", STUDIA EVANGELICA (Berlin: Akademie, 1968), IV, pp. 371-376.

107 On the vexed questions of the dating and authorship of 1-2 Tm and Ti, see C. Spicq, LES ÉPITRES PASTORALES (Paris: Gabalda, 1969), cited hereafter as EP, and the translation of M. Dibelius and H. Conzelmann, THE PASTORAL EPISTLES (Philadelphia: Fortress, 1972). The hypothesis within which I submit my observations is that Luke drafted a first form of these letters under Paul's direction c. AD 67. He then re-edited them after completing Luke-Acts and attached them as the hird "volume" to that work, c. AD 80-85: cf. J. Quinn, "P46 — the Pauline Canon?" *CBQ* 36 (1974), fn. 36.

called *episkopoi* (Acts 20:28).[108] Thus the members of a structure known in the Jerusalem church as *presbyteroi* correspond with the leaders in the mixed congregations known as *episkopoi.* The coincidence was, however, not total. For all the ambiguities of the data, we still can say that all *episkopoi* were *presbyteroi* but all *presbyteroi* were not *episkopoi,* somewhat as all the Twelve were apostles but not all apostles belonged to the Twelve. In the relatively undeveloped and strongly Jewish Christian congregations envisioned by Titus, the *presbyteroi* were practically equated with the *episkopos* (a generic singular?). In the more developed and mixed church envisioned by 1 Timothy, the qualifications for the *episkopos* — *diakonoi* (3:2-13) are strikingly similar to those for the Cretan Ministry (Ti 1:5-9). However, apart from the episcopal and diaconal Ministry, 1 Timothy 4:14 knows of *presbyteroi,* organized and functioning as a body, a *presbyterion.* 1 Timothy may thus be a witness to an early stage in the amalgamation of the Jewish Christian presbyteral Ministry with the episcopal-diaconal model employed by the mixed churches.[109]

The closest parallel to the Christian *episkopos* in the structure of a Jewish community is the *mebaqqer* ("overseer" — the literal sense of the Greek term also) among the devout Jews gathered at Qumran. There "the *mebaqqer* is an interpreter of the law, a preacher and pastor and the officer most closely concerned with the initiation of novices."[110] The parallel to the Christian *episkopos* is striking but unfortunately no direct link with Qumran can be adduced.[111] If ever the Qumran "overseer" were associated with the aides that corresponded to the "deacons" of the Pastorals, the case for direct borrowing would be more than a hypothetical possibility.

The development of the deacons and their functions constitutes a study in itself. Some have seen this Ministry as rooted in the work of those who assisted the apostles; others have seen its prototype in the relation of the Seven to the Twelve. It is significant that the first century texts explicitly link *diakonoi* with *episkopoi,* but not with *presbyteroi.* One would infer that the deacons were conceived of originally as assistants to and immediately subordinate to the *episkopos* and not to *presbyteroi.* The first evidence

---

108 Contrast Bruce, ACTS, p. 377 with Haenchen, ACTS, p. 590. J. Dupont, LE DISCOURS DE MILET (Paris: Cerf, 1962), pp. 28-29 would admit *"l'essentiel de la pensée de l'Apôtre."* He is impressed by the resemblances to the language of the Pastorals.

109 Cf. J. P. Meier *"Presbyteros* in the Pastoral Epistles," *CBQ* 35 (1973) pp. 323-345. 1 Clement never speaks of a *presbyterion;* Ignatius a few years later (and in Asia Minor) does so frequently. On the other hand Ignatius speaks only of the *episkopos* where I Clement never uses the term in the singular, except for God, though apparently considering *episkopoi* as largely synonymous with *presbyteroi.* (1 Clement 44.1, 4 and 5). Like the Pastorals, 1 Clement associates *diakonoi* immediately and only with *episkopoi,* whereas in Ignatius they are separated from the *episkopoi* by the *presbyteroi* and are apparently subject to the latter (*ad Magn.* 2.1).

110 C. K. Barrett, THE PASTORAL EPISTLES (Oxford: Clarendon, 1963), p. 58.

111 Cf. Fitzmyer, ESBNT, pp. 293-294 and Benoit (*ut cit.* fn. 52), p. 16.

for a hierarchy in three steps, with *presbyteroi* subordinate to an *episkopos,* and diakonoi subordinate to *both,* appeared in Asia Minor at the beginning of the second century.[112]

The generation following the fall of Jerusalem thus saw a continuing and by no means unilinear development of Ministry in the mixed churches.[113] It is notable that even in this period the New Testament documents do not explicitly name those who conducted the eucharist.[114] Even in the previous generation, as noted above, one can only reasonably infer that the Twelve and the apostles carried out the supper command of Jesus as they presided over the Christian assemblies for worship. Similarly one can only infer that they shared this function with others as they certainly shared their apostolic Ministry of preaching and teaching. It is possible that in the older Jewish Christian churches the Ministry of prophets and teachers included leading the eucharist[115] whereas in the mixed congregations the *presbyteroi-episkopoi* eventually emerged with this function.[116]

The laying on of hands to designate men for and establish them in apostolic Ministry was certainly employed on occasion in the first generation (Acts 6:6 of the Seven; 13:3 of Barnabas and Paul). The Pastorals alone remember that Paul as well as the *presbyterion* had so ordained Timothy (1 Tm 4:14; 2 Tm 1:6). The imposition of hands, with its precedents in the Old Testament, was probably adopted originally by the Jewish Christians of Palestine, whence it came into the mixed churches.[117]

---

112 Cf. *Didache,* 15.1 and fn. 109 above, as well as Lemaire, MINISTERES, pp. 185-186, and "NT Ministries," pp. 144-148. Spicq, *EP,* I, 74-77, 456-463, treats the *diakonoi* in the Pastorals.

113 For the various forms of Ministry that can be glimpsed in the later documents of the New Testament, see Lemaire, "NT Ministries," pp. 148-161 and the studies cited there.

114 The only individual ever named as presiding is Jesus himself at the original supper, though, of course, Paul scarcely intended to exclude himself when he made his appeal to "the cup of blessing which *we* bless" (1 Cor 10:16; the observation is Bourke's, *CBQ,* 507) and Luke thought of Paul as leading the "breaking of the bread" in Acts 20: 7, 11.

115 Cf. *Didache* 15.1 and perhaps 10.7, though the type of leadership in eucharistic worship involved here eludes precise definition (cf. Bourke, *CBQ,* 508: Brown, PR.BP., p. 19: Cothénet [*ut cit.* fn. 103], col. 1276, 1286-1287, 1301, 1310, 1327, 1333). The sacerdotal terminology applied to prophets, "your highpriests" (13.3: *archiereis*), who are to receive for their support "first fruits" (*aparchēn*: cf. fn. 98 above), appears to apply to the *episkopoi-diakonoi* who "conduct the Ministry (*leitourgousi . . . tēn leitourgian*) of the prophets and teachers for you" (15.1).

116 *Didache* 15.1 seems to witness to a church (or churches) where the older Jewish Christian structure was being phased out in favor of the *episkopoi-diakonoi* (*Didache* never speaks of *presbyteroi*). By the time of I Clement 44.4 there are *presbyteroi-episkopoi* in the Corinthian church "who have blamelessly and holily offered the sacrifices" (of the episcopate). A few years later, in the churches of Asia Minor, the *episkopos* or one whom he has appointed (*epitrepsēi*) is to preside at a "valid" (*bebaia*) eucharist (Ignatius, SMYRN., 8.1 and Bourke, *CBQ,* 508-509).

117 Cf. E. Lohse, *"cheir,"* TDNT, IX, pp. 424-434, esp. 428-429 and 433-434; Bourke, *CBQ,* 504-505; Meier, *ut cit.* fn. 109 above.

The more generic *katastēsēis* of Titus 1:5 leaves room for other means of appointing the *presbyteroi* of Crete,[118] and of course there is no indication of the way in which Titus himself was appointed by Paul to his function.

Finally, the Pastorals depict not only Timothy and Titus but also the persons whom they in turn associated with their Ministry as teaching, witnessing to and guarding the faith, and directing the churches.[119] With this stage in the sharing of the apostolic ministry, the phenomenon designated by "apostolic succession" is present in all but name.[120]

IV

In summary, from this brief survey of the development of Christian Ministry in the first century, the following points are noted.

1. The Ministry of the church is ultimately rooted in the way in which the historical Jesus called disciples, and particularly the Twelve, to share his task.

2. The elements of both appointment by the risen Jesus and sharing of functions with others are characteristic of the Ministry of the Twelve and of the apostles from the earliest days of both the Jewish Christian and mixed churches. The functions for which those who had not seen the risen Lord are designated include proclamation of the gospel to unbelievers as well as teaching and directing communities of believers.

3. Ministry in its various forms is a gift (charism) of the *Spirit,* and exists, as do other *charismata,* for the upbuilding of the church.

4. The means of appointment, the *how* of designation, apparently admitted of considerable variety, and it is quite possible that several different means of ordination flourished simultaneously in different apostolic churches.

5. The sharing of apostolic Ministry is the historical matrix from which succession to the apostolic Ministry emerged. It is important to note that just as the original apostles' sharing in the Ministry of the Twelve did not make them one of the Twelve,

---

118 As does the *cheirotonēsantes* (cf. Lohse [*ut cit.* fn. 117], 437) of Acts 14:23. 1 Timothy 5:22 also mentions a laying on of hands in the context of *presbyteroi,* but it is not altogether clear that the author is referring to a designation for this Ministry (cf. Spicq, EP, I, 546-549).

119 Cf. Bourke, *CBQ,* 505-506.

120 And within a few years of the final edition of the Pastorals, 1 Clement 44.2 employs the critical verb when he says " . . . they [our apostles - Peter and Paul?] appointed (*katestēsan*) those who have already been mentioned [the *episkopoi* and *diakonoi* of 42.4], and afterwards added the codicil that if they should fall asleep, other approved men should succeed (*diadexōntai*) to their ministry (*leitourgian*)."

so the sharing of a Silvanus and a Timothy in the apostolic Ministry of Paul did not make them apostles in every sense of that term. In like manner, the successors of the apostles are *successors,* not apostles. There was an untransmittable, personal qualification for the apostle as there was for being numbered among the Twelve.

6. There is a pattern of bifurcation and differentiation in the development of first century Ministry. It is a leadership *both* by groups (of two, three, seven, twelve; *apostoloi;* prophets; teachers, *episkopoi; diakonoi; presbyteroi*) *and* by single individuals even within the groups (Peter; Paul; James; Titus in Crete; Timothy in Ephesus; the *episkopos*). Moreover the groups themselves are the result of a certain division of the Ministry (the Twelve and the Seven; apostles-prophets-teachers; *episkopoi-diakonoi*) in which one group has a priority of precedence over another.

7. Though there was development in Ministry in the first century, it was not unilinear. It is historically more exact and eventually more instructive theologically to respect the differences in structuring the Ministry that existed simultaneously in different churches (Jerusalem; Corinth; Ephesus; Rome, etc.)

8. The appointment to the specifically eucharistic Ministry is governed by the observations in no. 2-4 above. There is no evidence in the New Testament that every baptized person was *ipso facto* enabled to preside at the eucharist.[121] This is not to say, however, that this Ministry could be bestowed only on certain believers. The New Testament does not envision any priestly caste or clan from which those who are to undertake specific Ministries must be chosen, though there are hints that this was a concern in some quarters in the first-century churches. The Ministry assigned to women is still debated.[122]

9. Certain antitheses of later theological schools appear to have been of little if any concern for those who wrote the first century documents: e.g. the charismatic vs. the institutional;[123] the local vs.

---

121 Cf. J. H. Elliott, THE ELECT AND THE HOLY: AN EXEGETICAL EXAMINATION OF 1 PETER 2:4-10 AND THE PHRASE BASILEON HIERATEUMA (Leiden: Brill, 1966), and particularly the summary on pp. 219-226.

122 Cf. Lemaire, "NT Ministries," p. 163-164. J. Reumann, "What in Scripture Speaks to the Ordination of Women?" *CTM.* 44 (1973), pp. 5-30, who addresses the question from a modern Lutheran viewpoint, contains an excellent bibliography. From a Catholic viewpoint, see H. Denis and J. Delorme, MMNT (*ut cit.* fn. 1), pp. 505-511 and the index *s.v.* "*Femmes.*"

123 Cf. fn. 104 above.

the missionary Ministry;[124] the sacerdotal vs. the Ministerial view of ecclesial order.[125] If inquiries within such a problematic have become quarrelsome and sterile, it may signal their distance from the actual biblical data and concerns.

124 In this connection, it must be emphasized that the texts certainly know of Ministries that *we* would classify as local or missionary. These are, however, not conceived of within an antithetical dialectic. One missionary Ministry can be contrasted with another (cf. Gal 2.7-8; 2 Cor 11.12-13) and one local church with others (1 Cor 11.16; 14:33-34). A missionary apostle can confront a "local" prophetic Ministry (1 Cor 14:37-38). In no case, however, is the itinerant vs. the locally fixed character of the Ministry critical for ascertaining the *theological* value of a Ministry or its work. There is, indeed, theological reason to believe that *every* Christian Ministry is "missionary". The case for that is not proved or refuted with a map and scale of miles.
125 Cf. Lemaire, "NT Ministries," pp. 134-138, 157-158: Quinn, "Apos. Min." pp. 484, fn. 25 and 26; pp. 486-487; J.M. Tillard, "What Priesthood Has the Ministry," *One in Christ* 9 (1973), 237-269, esp. 242-267; Grelot, MMNT (*ut cit*. fn. 1), pp. 53-54. Brown, PR.BP., pp. 16-19, has observed that the first generations of Christian believers saw themselves as a *renewed* but not a *new* Israel. They did not condemn and reject the priesthood of Israel any more than they rejected the Jerusalem temple and its worship. Their very reluctance to apply the term *hiereus* to anyone but Jesus (and even to him only "according to the order of Melchizedek" Heb. 5.6, 10 *et pass.*) meant that the Christian Ministers were not really in competition with the Levitical Ministry of Israel. Perhaps the very archaic practice of designating their leadership groups by number (cf. above fn. 21, 22, 24, 61, 66, 67) or simply by the names of the persons was the precipitate of this attitude. In any case, the goal of the first Christian generations was the goal of their Lord, to convert and renew the whole nation of which they were members. The destruction of the temple and ending the public worship of the priests of Israel was done by the Roman legions, not by the Jewish Christians. It was only hesitantly, as the Jewish Christian mission atrophied and the possibility of the conversion of Israel faded (cf. fn. 85 above), that the Ministers of the churches (consisting now mainly of converts from paganism) began to be seen in terms of the priests of Judaism and finally to be designated *hiereis* or *sacerdotes*. The hesitancy was more pastorally than dogmatically motivated in its origins.

Cyrus H. Gordon

UGARIT AND ITS SIGNIFICANCE

The twentieth century has witnessed the discovery of many important archaeological finds in the Near East and elsewhere, but probably
none has eclipsed the cuneiform tablets found at Ugarit between 1929
and 1973.[1] The material itself is impressive in quality and quantity, but its
date and provenance make it particularly interesting. The tablets were for
the most part inscribed from about 1400 to 1200 B.C., as the Bronze Age
was closing and the Iron Age about to begin. The Amarna Period with all
its internationalism produced the backdrop for the emergence of the Greeks
and the Hebrews as people on the stage of history. By around 1200 B.C.
the migrations of various groups, including the Sea Peoples, foreshadowed
events that were to reverberate in Homer and the Bible. The Trojan War,
the fall of the Hittite Empire and of Ugarit, the Hebrew Conquest of
Palestine, the mass migration of Philistines from the Aegean, the appearance of the Aramean states, etc., are more or less contemporary, and can
hardly be unrelated. The tablets from Ugarit illuminate the restless period
that ushered in the early history of the Greeks and Hebrews.[2]

Being an important North Syrian coastal city, in maritime contact with
the Aegean, Ugarit attests to links between the West Semitic and Aegean
spheres. An Akkadian tablet is a charter for a ship trading between Ugarit
and Caphtor (= Crete).[3] Archaeological and artistic materials also point
to close ties between Ugarit and the Aegean. The mythological tablets from
Ugarit confirm this by the role of Kothar-wa-Hasis in the Ugaritic pan-
theon. He is the god of arts, crafts and architecture with his atelier on
Caphtor. This is the way mythology states that Ugarit looked to Crete as
the center of its material culture. At that time the greatest artistic center in
the East Mediterranean was Crete.

Kothar-wa-Hasis is a compound name, all of whose elements are
Semitic. We know of specific ties between Ugarit and the Aegean sphere
that became Greek. For example, the solar deity at Ugarit is špš, with the
labial stop – p – instead of the labial nasal – m –, and is feminine. As
Michael Astour[4] has pointed out, Pausanias (2:25:10) records that the

CYRUS H. GORDON is Gottesman Professor of Hebraic Studies at New
York University, New York City.

1 About seventy tablets are said to have been accidentally unearthed by the Syrian Army
while seeking building materials for fortifications during the 1973 October War.
What has happened to the tablets is not yet known.
2 A history of Ugarit, reign by reign, is supplied by Mario Liverani, STORIA DI UGARIT
(Rome, 1962).
3 Jean Nougayrol, LE PALAIS ROYAL D'UGARIT III (Paris, 1955), pp. 107-8.
4 Michael Astour, HELLENOSEMITICA (Leiden, 1965), p. 103, n.l.

ancient name of a site near Epidaurus was Sapyselatôn reflecting the dis-
tinctively Ugaritic *špš elt*" the goddess Špš". While there is not yet any
general agreement on the linguistic identification of Minoan Linear A, it
contains so many Semitic words and grammatical elements that some scholars maintain that Minoan is Semitic.[5] What is clear is that the non-Greek
"Eteocretan" language written at Cretan sites such as Praisos, Dreros and
Psychro between 600 and 300 B.C. is West Semitic with strong Aramaic
affinities. There are definitely some words (e.g., *kl* "all", *u* "and") common to Minoan and Eteocretan. More revealing would be the establishment
of the linguistic continuity of the formulae for dedicating engraved stones
from Minoan to Eteocretan, which has been proposed[6] but still awaits
general acceptance.

Ugarit has yielded many administrative tablets dealing with guild per-
sonnel.[7] The guilds extended not only to the practitioners of the conventional arts and crafts, but also to the categories of priests and military
specialists. Presumably most if not all of the guilds were hereditary, though
adoption could make it possible for an outsider to be initiated under special circumstances. The guilds were mobile because their services were in
demand. Two priestly guilds were common to Ugarit and Israel: the *khmn*
and *qdšm*. At Ugarit both were eminently respectable. In Israel, the *qdšm*
were officially condemned but not eliminated until the reform of Josiah.[8]
As far as we can now tell, the distinctive terminology of the priesthood in
Israel was the Levitical factor.[9] The priests specialized in techniques to win
over the gods to their devotees. This did not generally involve what we
would call theological beliefs. It had rather to do with knowing how to
offer sacrifices properly, and how to facilitate communications between
gods and men through oracles, interpretation of dreams and omens, and
conveying prayers in ways acceptable to the gods. For these reasons, priests
such as *khmn* were international rather than denominational.

Two texts from Ugarit are clasified as epics, rather than myths.[10] They
are known as the Epic of Danel (or Aqhat)[11] and the Epic of Kret. Danel
is portrayed as a virtuous ruler, dispensing justice;[12] and Kret is repeatedly
called a *mlk* "king". Both are concerned with progeny, particularly a son to

---

5 See my Evidence for the Minoan Language [EML] (Ventnor, N.J., 1966). The
Semitic identification of Minoan is now being actively espoused by Jan Best of the
University of Amsterdam.

6 EML, p. 29, par. 124.

7 Cyrus Gordon, "Ugaritic Guilds and Homeric *Demioergoi*," The Aegean and the
Near East (Studies presented to Hetty Goldman) (Locust Valley, N. Y.,
1966), pp. 136-143.

8 2 Kings 23:7.

9 Not only the Levites but also the official priests were in theory supposed to be de-
scended from Levi. Note the terminology in Deuteronomy 17:9, 18; Ezekiel 43:19,
44:15 where the legitimate priests are called "The Levitical Priests".

carry on the royal line. This has clarified an aspect of the Patriarchal narratives in Genesis. The latter are (among other things) royal epic. Not only is there a pervasive concern with the birth of the right son to carry on the line, but Genesis 17:6, 16 plainly states that Abraham and Sarah are the progenitors of kings. Actually the narratives bring out the royal character of the Patriarchs in various ways. Genesis 14 represents Abraham as possessing his own army and heading up a coalition that defeats another coalition of kings. What has obscured the kingship of Abraham is the fact that he is on the move and not like the familiar kings of city states or of empires. He is in some ways like the kinglets who form parts of the Achaean or Trojan coalitions in the Iliad. It is interesting that his title of *nśy'* in Genesis 23:6 is rendered *basiléus* "king" in the Septuagint. This translation is supported by the use of *nśy'* as a title of heirs to the Davidic throne from Solomon (1 Kgs 11:34) down into post-biblical times when it is applied to exilarchs. That the Septuagint translators sensed the meaning of *nśy'* in Genesis 23:6 may be due to the fact that they knew not only the Bible but also Homer, and they realized that the heroic ages of the Greeks and Hebrews had something in common vis-à-vis the institutions of both peoples in subsequent eras.

The most basic level of continuity from Ugarit to all subsequent stages of Western Civilization is brought out by the order of the alphabetic letters used at Ugarit. Although the Ugaritic ABC has thirty letters, the twenty-two that constitute the Phoenician-Hebrew alphabet, are already in the same sequence in the Ugaritic alphabet.[13] It is furthermore possible that the Greek and Latin alphabets retain one feature that is present in the Ugaritic, but lost in the Phoenician-Hebrew alphabet; namely, the letter *u* which appears after *t* in Ugaritic, Greek and Latin. There is reason to believe that *u* (unlike the subsequent letters in the conventional form of the Greek alphabet) was original, and not a late addition created for the Classical Greek alphabet.[14]

A few tablets from Ugarit (e.g. texts 57 and 74) are written from right to left (like Hebrew) in a shorter form of the Ugaritic ABC. In this shorter alphabet, *ḥ* falls together with *ḫ*, and *ṯ*, with *š*, as in Hebrew The short ABC approximated, if it did not indeed agree with, the Hebrew in number and order of the letters. Tablets in this shorter alphabet have

10 The texts are in my UGARITIC TEXTBOOK [UT] (Rome, 1965; reissued with Supplement in 1967).
11 The literary texts from Ugarit are translated in my UGARIT AND MINOAN CRETE (New York, 1966; reissued in paperback, 1967).
12 2 Aqht: V: 4-8.
13 UT, p. 12, par. 3.2.
14 EML, p. 17, par. 54.

been found at sites to the south in Phoenicia (Sarepta[15]) and Israel (Mount Tabor, Taanach and Beth-Shemesh),[16] strongly suggesting a tie-in between Ugaritic and Phoenician-Hebrew literacy. That the relationship was not limited to the ABC but extended to the spread of a literature, is indicated by a number of factors. For example, the name of Danel's son Aqhat, appears in the biblical genealogies as Qht, the son of Levi. The popularity of the Epic of Danel is borne out by the mention of Danel by the exilic prophet Ezekiel (14.14, 16), who lists Danel with Noah and Job as virtuous men of old who came through catastrophe with their children. The epilogue of Job tells us that Job came through his ordeals with his children.[17] That Noah survived the Deluge with his children is familiar from Genesis. The extant portions of the Ugaritic Epic of Danel imply that Danel came through his trials with Aqhat brought back to life. The Epic of Danel was apparently known to the Hebrews in both the Patriarchal and exilic periods.

The linguistic proximity of Ugaritic and Hebrew is so close that the languages share not only many individual words but pairs of synonyms, conventionally used to parallel each other in the stichs that constitute the verses. The following are examples of the many pairs of words used to parallel each other in both literatures:[18]

’hlym "tents"	||	mšknwt "tabernacles"
’yb "enemy"	||	ṣr "foe"
’lp "1000"	||	rbbh "10,000"
’rṣ "earth"	||	ʿpr "dust"
byt "house"	||	ḥsr "court"
ḥlb "milk"	||	ḥm’h "butter, cream"
ydʿ "know"	||	byn "perceive"
ksp "silver"	||	ḥrwṣ "gold"
ʿwln "eternity"	||	dr dr "everlastingness"
ʿnh "answer"	||	šwb "reply"

So close are the two branches of West Semitic, that parallel pairs of two-word phrases can be shared by Ugaritic and Hebrew: ṭl (h)šmym "dew of (the) heavens" \|\| šmny (h) ’rṣ "fat of (the) earth".

Perhaps the most pervasive contribution of Ugaritic to Hebrew linquistics, has to do with the prepositions b and l, both of which have the

---

15 Found, but not yet published, by J. B. Pritchard. I know of this tablet through information kindly supplied by David Owen.

16 One was also excavated at Tell Soukas, in Syria, south of Ugarit.

17 His seven sons and three daughters mentioned before the catastrophe (Jb 1:2) are restored (i.e., brought back to life) in the epilogue (42:13).

18 For simplicity sake only the Hebrew forms are cited here: see UT, p. 145, par. 14.3, for the Ugaritic alongside the Hebrew. For further examples, see the detailed opus edited by Loren R. Fisher RAS SHAMRA PARALLELS I (Rome, 1972).

19 See UT, p. 92-93, par. 10.1.

meaning "from" in addition to their familiar uses.[19] Since *mi(n)* "from" is virtually absent from Ugaritic, *b* "from" and *l* "from" are common. But in Hebrew where *mi(n)* normally expresses "from", there are nevertheless many survivals of *b* "from" and *l* "from" that remained misunderstood until the impact of Ugaritic was felt. Thus the Masoretes emend *b* "from" to *m* in the *qrê* in *ḥrḥq m'd b'dm (qre: m'dm) bᶜyr* "very distant from the city Adam" and in *wycsrhw — bmlk (qrê:mmlk)* (2 Kgs 23:33) "he stopped him from ruling". Of the many examples of *l* "from" we single out one historically significant illustration; 2 Kings 14:28 relates that Jeroboam II restored Damascus and Hamath *lyhwdh* "from Judah" into Israel. Obviously the northern Kingdom of Israel could not be restoring still more northerly areas of Syria to, for or from the southern Kingdom of Judah. At that period there was a powerful Kingdom of Judah whose capital was not Jerusalem but Sam'al (now Zinjirli) in the northwestern corner of Canaan.[20] 2 Kings 14:28 informs us that the biblical author was excerpting the Chronicles of the Kings of Israel. In the northern Kingdom of Israel, it was then well known that Sam'alian (not Jerusalemite) Judah had dominated Damascus and Hamath, and that Jeroboam II had recovered those areas from Sam'alian Judah. For two and a half millennia the readers of the biblical books of Kings, with their Jerusalemite Judean orientation, did not understand the passage, and no sense could be made of it without changing the text and thereby losing the intended meaning. The Assyrian annals and the inscriptions of Sam'al have provided us historical background concerning northern Judah, and Ugarit has enabled us to understand the prepositions so that we can translate the passage correctly, exactly as it stands in the Masoretic text. Jeroboam II recovered from Sam'alian Judah, territory that had once belonged to David and Solomon.

Ugaritic and Hebrew literatures are not only close to each other linguistically, but also in prosody. The same poetic structures are frequently shared by both.[21] A familiar parallel is Ugaritic text 68:8:

ht . ibk (9) *bᶜlm*	"now, thine enemies, O Baal,
ht . ibk tmḥṣ	now thine enemies shalt thou smite,
ht . tṣmt ṣrtk	now shalt thou destroy thy foes"

with which Psalm 92:10 may be compared stylistically:

ky hnh 'ybyk yhwh	"for lo thine enemies, O Yahweh,
ky-hnh 'ybyk y'bdw	for lo thine enemies shall perish,
ytprdw kl-pᶜly 'wn	all doers of iniquity will be scattered"

In both of these tristichs, note that in the first stich, the divine name is lacking, but the verb is there. In both versions the same noun for "foes" is

---

20 Cyrus Gordon, THE ANCIENT NEAR EAST (New York, 1965), p. 219.
21 Hebrew prosody should be restudied comprehensively against the background of Ugaritic prosody.

used and repeated in the first two stichs. In the final stich of both versions, a different verb and a synonym for "foes" appear.

The late Professor Cassuto felicitously described the Hebrew Bible as new wine in old bottles. The language and literary devices were old; Israel adopted them after the Conquest and during the Settlement, and proceeded to use them as the medium for expressing the new messages of the Bible.

Nowhere is the content of the Bible more distinctive than when it consciously opposes the values of Canaan as expressed in the religious texts from Ugarit. In the Baal Cycle, Baal mates with a heifer and sires a bull calf.[22] Variations of this pagan cult reverberate as the Golden Calf in Sinai, and as the Golden Calves worshipped at Dan and Bethel. That it went with bestiality in the fertility cult is natural enough. In any case, Leviticus 18:23 prohibits copulation with animals precisely because it was an abomination wherewith the older inhabitants of the Promised Land had defiled themselves and the Land (vss 24-25). The Bible clearly expresses its opposition to the old values that are now recorded from the Canaanite point of view in the Ugaritic tablets.

The biblical prohibition against transvestism can now be explained as opposition to what was sacred in Canaan. In the Epic of Danel, the murder of Aqhat is avenged by his sister Pughat, who wears a man's garb and wields a man's sword.[23] It is interesting to note that Deuteronomy 22:5 not only outlaws transvestism, but also the bearing of men's weapons by women. Again Ugarit provides the background against which Israel reacted.

More significant is the origin of the Tenth Commandment against coveting. Since coveting cannot be treated as a legal offense (and there is no punishment for it in the Bible or in any other code of laws), its inclusion in the Ten Commandments used to pose a problem. However there is now an explanation, for in the Ugaritic tablets the god Baal is repeatedly described as a coveting god. The same word (*ḥmd* "covet") is applied to him in texts 75 and 2001, where he covets land and animals, as in the Tenth Commandment. One of the main episodes in the Baal Cycle concerns his craving a house because the other gods have houses.[24] He wants and gets one bigger and better than theirs. The Canaanites admired gods and men who were able to take what they coveted. Anath covets the wondrous bow which Aqhat refuses to sell her. Accordingly she has him murdered so that she can filch the bow.[25] When Ahab could not prevail upon Naboth to sell him his vineyard, Ahab as a Hebrew could do nothing but

---

22 67:V:17-22; 76:III:33-37.
23 I Aqht:206-7.
24 51:IV:50 - VII:27.
25 2 Aqht:VI:16-47; 3 Aqht:obv. & rev.
26 I Kings 21.

drop the matter. But Jezebel approached things differently.[26] Like her goddess Anath, Jezebel had Naboth murdered and then proceeded to confiscate his property for her husband Ahab. Jezebel's conduct was heinous from the standpoint of Hebrew values, but not from the Canaanite view-point. If we say that Ahab felt the sentiments of the Tenth Commandment, we should also perceive that Jezebel was as good a Canaanite as Ahab was a Hebrew. She did what was expected of the powerful vis-à-vis the weak who had the temerity to resist, and her deed can be described as *imitatio deorum;* she did what her goddess Anath had done according to the sacred Canaanite texts from Ugarit. The tragedy of the union between Ahab and Jezebel was not that a good man had the misfortune to be wed to a bad woman, but rather that husband and wife adhered to opposing value systems. Ahab's religious values had developed in conscious opposition to Jezebel's religious heritage.

A specific detail in Hebrew ritual is of interest in this connection. Leviticus 2:11 forbids the use of honey as a burnt offering. Inasmuch as honey is not forbidden by Hebrew rules of ritual purity, it is curious that it is banned ceremonially in Leviticus 2:11. Ugaritic provides an explanation, for honey is specified as an offering in the Epic of Kret:165. The sacrificial use of honey in Canaanite ritual would be enough to justify banning it in Israel.

The chronology of the Patriarchal Period is still subject to wide disagreement. Some prefer a Middle Bronze date, while others favor a Late Bronze chronology. This is not the place to align all the opposing arguments. "Logical" reconstructions, by drawing on what supports them and disregarding everything else, often look better than they really are. But this much may be said in favor of a late date for the Patriarchs: in the ancient literatures the closest parallels to the institutions of the Patriarchs come from the Amarna Age and slightly later. For instance the Nuzi tablets of the fifteenth and fourteenth centuries provide the closest set of parallels to the laws and customs of the Patriarchs.[27] The Ugaritic tablets provide the same emphasis as the Patriarchal narratives on the theme of securing divine aid for the birth of the right son to carry on the royal line.[28] We also have from Ugarit, Akkadian tablets to the Ugaritic King Niqmepaᶜ (ca. 1336-1265) from the Hittite Emperor Hattusilis III (ca. 1282-50) regulating the activities of his merchants from the city of Ur(ra) who were operating in Ugarit.[29]

The mercantile interests of the Patriarchs are reflected in Genesis. We

---

27 See my "Biblical Customs and the Nuzu Tablets" in THE BIBLICAL ARCHAEOLOGIST READER II, edited by E. F. Campbell and D. N. Freedman (Garden City. N.Y., 1964).
28 It pervades the epics of both Danel and Kret.
29 Published by Jean Nougayrol, PALAIS ROYAL D'UGARIT IV, (Paris, 1956), pp. 103-5.

need not stress the statement that Abraham pays Ephron the Hittite 400 shekels of silver "current for the merchant" in Genesis 23:16 because the text does not explicitly say that Abraham was a merchant. Two other passages definitely imply that the Patriarchal family had mercantile interests. When the Shechemites want to induce Jacob's family to settle with them, mercantile privileges are offered (Gn 34:10, 21). Later, Joseph, before revealing his identity to his brothers, tells them that if they can establish their reputation for honesty, they can trade throughout Egypt (Gn 42:34). This implies that trading was known to be one of their main interests. Their possession of cattle does not contradict their mercantile activities; Harry Hoffner has called attention to a Hittite text in which merchants have with them cattle as well as precious stones and metals.[30] Merchants could trade in cattle, as well as use them for transportation and as a source of means of subsistence.

In the reign of King Niqmepaᶜ of Ugarit, there were complaints against the merchants of Ur(ra) who were operating under the aegis of Hattusilis III. The Hittite monarch accordingly sent a tablet regulating his merchants' activities in three ways. First, they were to ply their trade and collect what was owned to them. Second, they were not to stay in Ugarit throughout the year. After the harvest season they were to move on for the winter. Thus permanent residence was forbidden. Third, the merchants of Ur(ra) were not to acquire real-estate in Ugarite. Accordingly, they were to (1) transact their trade, but they were prevented from unduly exploiting the community by being obliged to forgo (2) permanent residence and (3) owning real estate.[31] It is striking that when the Shechemites want to induce the family of Jacob to join them, they offer precisely the three items (Gn 34:10, 21) spelled out by Hattusilis concerning his merchants of Ur(ra); trading rights without which they could not function economically, and two privileges normally denied such foreign merchants: permanent residence and purchasing real-estate. It may be added that Abraham's buying real-estate in Genesis 23 is stressed partly because foreigners were not ordinarily allowed to acquire it.

The phonetic identification of Ur = Ur(ra) is of more than passing interest. Urfa in southern Turkey is according to tradition the Ur where Abraham was born. The Syriac name of the city was Orrhai, which is close to the Akkadian spelling *Ur-ra*.[32] It would be going too far to insist that Orrhai/Urfa is the very Ur(ra) whence Hattusilis' merchants came. There were many Ur(ra)s named after Sumerian Ur, probably because they had

---

30 The cuneiform tablet is known to Hittiologists as KBO XII:4 = ABot 49.
31 For further details, see my "Abraham of Ur", in Hebrew and Semitic Studies (presented to Godfrey Rolles Driver), edited by D. W. Thomas and W. D. McHardy (Oxford, 1963), pp. 77-84.
32 Variant spellings include Ú-ra, Ú-ri, Ú-ri-e and Ú-ur-ri; see my "Abraham of Ur", p. 83, nn. 1, 2, and 3.

been founded as commercial colonies of that city in its heyday around 2000 B.C. Other Urs are mentioned in the Nuzi and Alalah tablets. The location of Orrhai is suitable for a site in the realm of Hattusilis. Moreover, the strong connection between Orrhai and Aramaism is interesting because the language (Gn 31:47) and homeland (Gn 24:10; 25:20) of the Patriarchs are Aramean.

While the tablet of Hattusilis does not throw light on Abraham personally, it does place him in a historic context, among the royal merchants of Ur(ra) operating on mobile missions in Canaan.

The date of the Hattusilis tablet (first half of the thirteenth century B.C.) does not prove that Abraham is to be dated that late, for (as mentioned above) the mercantile colonies of Ur must have begun at the dawn of the Middle Bronze Age (ca. 2000 B.C.). However, the fact that Abraham is not a Sumerian or Babylonian but an Aramean (cf. also Dt 26:5) from Ur of the Chaldees does suggest a late date. Moreover, the respect shown to Abraham in Genesis 23 by a Hittite enclave suggests that Ephron and Abraham both owed allegiance to the Hittites. Otherwise it is hard to understand why the Hittites of Hebron tell Abraham "thou art an exalted prince in our midst" (Gn 23:6).

Perhaps the most significant aspect of the Ugaritic tablets is the light they cast on the Greeks and the Hebrews as they were emerging as ethnic factors of consequence in the East Mediterranean. The most striking evidence of this is in the epics of Homer, Ugarit and Genesis that are rooted in the closing part of the Late Bronze Age. All three sets of texts deal with royal epic. Moreover all three have built into them what we may call the Helen of Troy motif: the theme of a beautiful bride that the king must retrieve from a foreign court. Helen is recovered by her husband King Menelaus of Sparta from the court of Priam of Troy. King Kret marches with a great army to retrieve[33] his wife Hurrai from King Pbl's court in distant Udum. Abraham must recover the beautiful Sarah from the courts of Pharoah and of King Abimelech of Gerar.

That Ugarit has radically changed the nature of Old Testament studies is generally recognized. That it sheds important light on the Mycenaean Greeks and therefore on the earliest cultural history of Europe, is becoming increasingly evident.

---

33 The text (Krt:14) states that Kret's wife had departed (*tbʿt*). Some authors interpret this to mean that a first wife had died, and that Hurrai was therefore a different woman. However, the verb *tbʿ* is elsewhere always used in the literal sense of "to depart" and is never a euphemism for "to die".

George Ernest Wright

THE SIGNIFICANCE
OF AI IN THE THIRD MILLENIUM B.C.*

Much has been written concerning the archaeology of Ai in relation to the Biblical tradition of the site's conquest according to Joshua 7-8. This paper proposes briefly to concern itself with the Early Bronze Age city. Fooliwing the uncompleted excavations of 1933-1935,[1] a joint American expedition is to conduct its fourth season of excavations at the site in 1969, the other seasons having been in 1964, 1966 and 1968.[2] Under the direction of Joseph A. Callaway of Southern Baptist Theological Seminary, the site's chronology has become clear and awaits only the detailed publication of the evidence for the Director's present conclusions to be sustained.

The Early Bronze City and Fortifications

Neither the biblical name nor the modern name represents the site's ancient name in the Early Bronze Age. Indeed, it is possible, if not probable, that Hebrew *hâ-'ay* and Arab *et-Tell* are related in the sense that they mean approximately the same thing, "the ruin." In any event, it is clear that the original name and presumably the traditions of the city's great era were forgotten during the approximately twelve or thirteen hundred years when the site lay vacant between the mid-third millennium and the brief Israelite occupation during the twelfth and eleventh centuries.[3]

The late GEORGE ERNEST WRIGHT was Parkman Professor of Divinity at Harvard University, Cambridge, Massachusetts, and at the time of his death was President of the American Schools of Oriental Research.

---

* I wish to acknowledge my indebtedness to two Harvard graduate students: Lawrence E. Stager for assistance in gathering the data, and Fr. Carney E. Gavin for the plans in Figures 4 and 5. I am also under obligation to Thomas D. Newman for correcting my mathematics in a number of places.

1 Owing to the untimely death of the excavator, Mme. Judith Marquet-Krause. For her main preliminary report, see "La deuxième campagne de fouilles à Ay, 1934," Syria 16, 1935, pp. 330-333. Her volume, LES FOUILLES DE 'AY (ET-TELL), 1933-35, (Paris 1949) was posthumously publishel by her husband, Yves Marquet, its main content being the excavation register. See for full summary Pere L. H. Vincent, "Les fouilles d'et Tell-Ai," RB 46, 1937, pp. 231-266.

2 See Joseph A. Callaway, "The 1964 'Ai (et-Tell) Excavations," BASOR 178, 1965, pp. 13-40. The preliminary reports of the 1966 and 1968 seasons have not been formally published, but have been carried in ASOR Newsletter, No. 2, ("The 1966 'Ai Excavations") for 1966-1967, and in ASOR Newsletter, No. 5, ("The 1968 'Ai Excavations").

3 For the comparatively small Iron Age village, see Callaway, BASOR 178, pp. 22-28, the ASOR Newsletters cited above, and for a rather unusual attempt to deal with the site's traditions in Joshua as related to the Iron Age strata, see Callaway, "New Evidence on the Conquest of 'Ai," JBL 86, 1968, pp. 312-320.

The first fact to be stressed with Professor Callaway is that Ai in the third millennium was a phenomenon for which no reason or explanation is readily apparent. It was far larger than most scholars had considered, far more powerfully fortified than would be generally expected for such a seemingly insignificant geographical spot in the hills - and there is no known water supply within the vicinity of the tell!

The earliest large groups of pottery found at 'Ai are from three tombs, B, C, and G, dating to Early Bronze I.[4] Whether they date at the beginning or before that period (de Vaux and Kenyon) or at its middle (EB IB) appears simply a terminological problem, since all scholars give an absolute date for them the period ca. 3000 B.C.[5] The first small fragments of house walls on the tell appear to the excavator as later, perhaps from the very end of EB I (ca. 2900 B.C.), but this is yet to be precisely determined.[6]

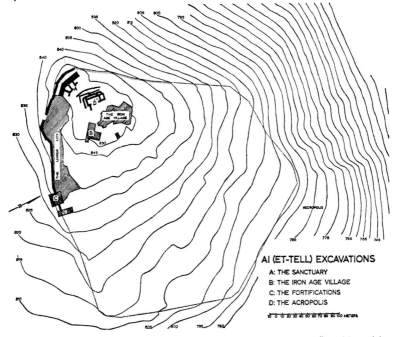

Fig. 1. Contour plan of Ai with sites under excavation in 1964-1968. [In this article we are primarily interested in Site A at the west. This plan appears in ASOR Newsletter, No. 5, 1968-1969, p. 3]

---

4 See now Joseph A. Callaway, POTTERY FROM THE TOMBS OF AI (London 1964).
5 See, for example, this writer's, "The Problem of the Transition Between the Chalcolithic and Early Bronze Ages," ERETZ ISRAEL 5, 1958, pp. 37*-45*; K. Kenyon, ARCHAEOLOGY IN THE HOLY LAND, (New York, 1960), pp. 88-90, and JERICHO I, (London, 1960), pp. 4 ff.; R. de Vaux, CAH[2], Fascicule 46, London 1966, p. 5.
6 From a private letter of Professor Callaway to the writer, November, 1968.

At the beginning of EB II an entirely new city was erected at one time, comprising some 110 dunams (ca. 10.1 hectaares; 27.5 acres) (see Fig. I). Houses were built on bedrock or on a surface just above the rock leveled with packed earth or marl. Of particular importance are the great size of the fortifications. The first wall was 3.25 m. wide and surrounded the whole city. During the same period, if not at the same time, it was felt necessary to strengthen it by adding Wall B running parallel to it on the outside. This double wall, with narrow passage between, is comparable to the Early Bronze fortification[7] on the west side of *Tell Ta'annek,* and possibly also at *Tell el-Far'ah* (biblical Tirzah).[8] In any case, at Ai the two walls together made a fortification on the south side of some 7.50. width (ca. two dozen feet: in Site C), and still standing over two meters in height. Elsewhere the Early Bronze fortifications are said to be eight m. wide, and still standing seven m. high (Site H), while a gate was discovered in the southeast corner (Site K), and an even larger gate complex appears to be emerging on the south side (Site J) overlooking the Wadi Asas, which cuts its way eastward into the Jordan Valley.

The tell slopes higher as it proceeds westward until its highest point is reached at 856 m. above sea level. Here the city's most significant building was erected, while the fortifications at this, evidently the most vulnerable, point are tremendous. At first, according to the evidence of the 1968 campaign, two huge towers and probably a gate existed here in EB II. In EB III a massive tower of solid masonry was erected over these remains, some 15 m. in width (60 ft.) At Site C on the south side in EB III Wall A was constructed against the outer face of Wall B, which itself was repaired, widening the fortifications still further. Indeed, it can be argued, as Peter Parr has done,[9] that here as at a number of other EB sites there was gradually created a rocky glacis around the lower slopes while the giant tower stood at the most dangerous point, the west.

The Rooms Termed "The Sanctuary"

Immediately inside and erected against the western fortifications are some nondescript rooms which Mme. Marquet-Krause named "the sanctuary." In a feat of marvelously meticulous stratigraphical work, Professor Callaway has cleared up the stratigraphical problems of the area.[10]

Sometime after the first fortification, Wall A, had been erected and rubbish had collected against its base, "Sanctuary B" was constructed. It

---

7 Paul W. Lapp, BASOR 173, 1964, pp. 10-14.
8 R. de Vaux, RB 55, 1948, pp. 553-4; 58, 1951, pp. 421-22; 62, 1955, pp. 563-564 and Fig. 15; and 69, 1962, pp. 212-231 and accompanying plates.
9 So Peter J. Parr, "The Origin of the Rampart Fortifications of Middle Bronze Age Palestine and Syria," ZDPV 84, 1968, pp. 18 ff.
10 See BASOR 178, pp. 16-21.

consisted of two roughly rectangular rooms. The second or southern of these rooms is called an "Altar room" because it contained a roughly semicircular stone structure which was believed to be an altar. A heavy layer of brick debris, broken pottery and calcined limestone covered the floors - evidence of the city's destruction, presumably at the end of Early Bronze II (ca. 27th cent.). "Sanctuary A" was erected on the ruins of the earlier rooms. The northernmost room in this case contained a raised podium erected against the fortification tower (Wall B), which Mme. Marquet-Krause believed to be an altar.

Presumably the interpretation of these rooms as a "sanctuary" was suggested by their contents. Mme. Marquet-Krause's interpretation is as follows:

The main entrance into the "sanctuary" was at the south in the eastern end of Wall E (see Fig. 2).[11] In Room A II the earthern floor was covered with burned debris 70 to 80 cms. in thickness. Without any suggestion as to the reason for the conclusion the original excavator says that the whole structure, composed of three parts, is a type of Semitic sanctuary. The entry in Wall E opens into the first room (A II in Fig. 2) which is 8.50 m. long by 6 m. wide. An alignment of flat stones, covered by cement, formed a bench along part of the east and north walls (P and H). In the middle of the room two incense stands were found; they were rectangular, without bottoms but with squared openings on each side, and round jar-like necks and rims which presumably held bowls for the incense - unless the vessels were for libations. Between them was a piece of carbonized wood, 1.25 m. in lengtth, which Père R.P. Vincent suggested was the symbol of the goddess Asherah (!).[12] The room contained a number of pottery vessels which may have contained liquid offerings and food of various types, since animal bones existed in the debris. An ivory handle, "belonging without doubt to a ritual knife," was also found in the room.

Proceeding northward into Room A III, one notes study stone walls covered with cement. In the southeast corner was a bench (N) on which were a dozen small bowls, in the words of the original excavator, "prêtes à recevoir les offrandes." On the west side were a series of three small bins. But most important to Mme. Marquet-Krause was the tiny area in the southwest corner which is called "a holy of holies" with "altar" J, 1.70 m. long and 70 cms. high, of stone covered with cement. In it was a small niche containing a goblet, polished over a red slip, and one-half of "a small votive bed." On the "altar" and on the floor of the small room

---

11 See SYRIA 16, 1935, pp. 329-336. As is evident in Callaway's plan (Fig. 2), he found no evidence of such a door in Wall E at the point in question. He did find two phases in "Sanctuary A", however, and an entrance, blocked in the latest phase, existed in Wall E at the western end next to Wall A.

12 Why this and not a piece of roofing beam is not eplained.

were a large number of ceramic vessels and some imported Egyptian ala-
baster bowls, dating in type from the Early Dynastic period.

Further north are wall fragments (A IV) which the original excavator believes to have belonged to the "sanctuary". She speculates that there
were once three rooms in A IV which once constituted a second "sanctuary",
the southeastern room probably being another "holy of holies." Professor
Callaway did indeed find a door in the first phase of Wall M against the
tower Wall B, which was blocked up in its second phase.

To this writer the "sanctuary" interpretation of the rooms in question
is to be credited to a very active imagination. The structures, lacking special
architectural form, contain bins and "benches" and small platforms which
normally would be taken for domestic installations elsewhere. That small
structures in each of the two phases are to be conceived as "altars" is an
extremely problematic position. We obviously cannot conceive ancient
temples as containing "altars" comparable to those tables or structures
which form the focus of worship in certain modern churches. Altars for
literal sacrifices would have to be outside in sacred open courts. Within,
the most one could expect would be small incense altars, but there is no
suggestion that there was evidence of the burning of incense. The only
suggestion of cultic significance in these rooms is the presence of the two
ceramic stands in Room A II, which *may* have held bowls for incense, or
they may have been libation stands. The small piece of a ceramic bed
probably has some cultic significance. Yet during the Iron Age, at least,
such objects are frequently found in private homes.

The most that one can say for the rooms in question is that they were
storerooms for a quantity of vessels. The small bench along part of the
walls of Room A II recalls the benches which are a regular feature of the
contemporary private homes of Early Bronze Arad.[13] Thus, if the rooms
were for some public, rather than private, purpose, perhaps one at most
could suggest that they served as storage for vessels used in the large
public building a short distance to the east. While one cannot deny flatly
that the structures were *not* a "sanctuary" or "sanctuaries," one *can* say
that there is no evidence whatever for the fanciful interpretations of the
original excavator, and the burden of proof falls upon those who think
otherwise, keeping in mind what we now actually know of religious architecture (see below).

The Building Termed "the Palace" or "Citadel"

Directly west at the tell's highest and most visible point is clearly the
main building of the city (Fig. 3), Here again Professor Callaway's care-

---

13 See Ruth Amiran in: Amiran and Aharoni, ANCIENT ARAD (Introductory Guide to
   Expedition Held at the Israel Museum, January-April, 1967: Israel Museum Catalogue
   No. 32), pp. 9-10 and Fig. 6.

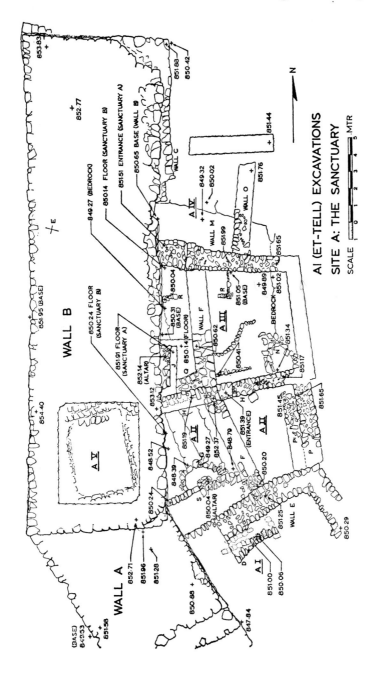

Fig. 2. The Ai citadel (Wall V) and so-called "Sanctuary" erected against it.
(From BASOR 178, 1965, p. 17, Fig. 2.)

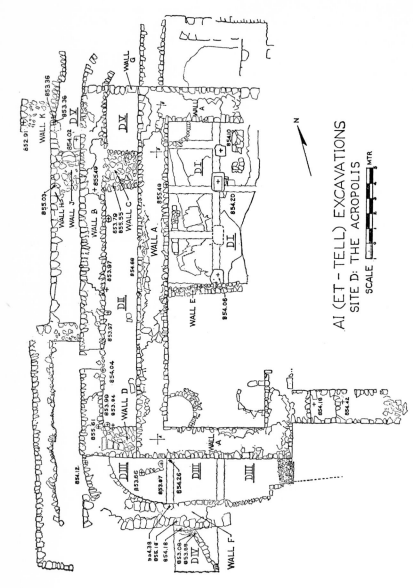

Fig. 3. The main building at Ai in EB II–III; it is located a short distance east of the structures shown in Fig. 2. Cf. Fig. 1. (From BASOR 178, 1965, p. 32, Fig. 12.)

ful probing in an already excavated structure has clarified most of the problems of phasing the various walls. Two main periods of the building exist in Early Bronze II and III, respectively, the second being better built but a duplication of the first.

As is well known, the building is a long-room or rectangular building with entrance in the middle of the long side, facing east (Wall A). This is surrounded by a protective wall which curves around the rear corners (Wall B). The latter, badly tilted in the destruction of the first structure, was buttressed by an additional protective wall (H) erected to sustain it, at least in the area of Wall J. Wall K, mostly eroded, evidently served as a similar added fortification for the first building. Pillar bases existed in Area D II; the one specifically mentioned by Callaway belonged to the first phase of the building, indicating roofing of the corridor area in EB II.

The main room of the building (DI) is a large open space, ca. 20 m. long by 6.60 m. wide, which was roofed with the assistance of four or five pillars in the center. Those of the first phase were roughly rounded or squared blocks (EB II), while those of the second phase (EB III) were very remarkable in that their rectangular tops had been created "by sawing grooves in the top of the stone to form a rectangle, after which the stone outside was chipped away leaving the squared surface. Copper saws which could achieve this operation were used in Egypt in the period of the Third Dynasty."[14] The masonry of this room in its second phase is remarkable and unexpected for the period in Palestine. As often commented,[15] the stones were dressed at the quarry and carefully laid to look like brick. Indeed, Callaway states that the size of the stones approximated that of actual bricks found in a contemporary house in Area C I. Nevertheless, whatever the appearance of the stones, they were not meant to be seen, for a sizable piece of plaster on the north wall, finished with a thin marl layer "of exceptional quality and whiteness finished the inner surface and gave it what must have been an elegant appearance."[16]

Since the appearance of Mme. Marquet-Krause's first preliminary report in 1935, nearly all commentators and reviewers have simply followed without serious question her interpretation of the buildings in question.[17]

---

14 So Callaway, BASOR 178, p. 37.
15 Cf. B. Yeivin, "The Masonry of the Early Bronze People," PEFQSt 1934, pp. 189ff.
16 Callaway, loc cit.
17 The reconstructions of Vincent, (Note I) and of Rene Dussaud, "Note Additionnelle," SYRIA 16, 1935, pp. 346-352, cannot now be seriously considered because according to Professor Callaway's findings, they place together things that do not belong together in the same period. For recent expositions of the Vincent and Marquet-Krause views, see K. Kenyon, ARCHAEOLOGY IN THE HOLY LAND (London and New York, 1960), pp. 116, 122; and R. de Vaux, O.P. "Palestine in the Early Bronze Age," CAH², Fascicule 46, 1966, pp. 12-16.

The main exception is W.F. Albright, who without detailed discussion simply said that it could not be a palace but was a temple.[18] In favor of the temple-interpretation of Ai's main building are the following considerations:

1. For what purpose would such a large enclosed and roofed area be used? Bronze Age *palace* architecture in Asia simply did not employ this type of structure as a rule. The palace was an elaboration of the typical Bronze Age house which consisted of comparatively small living and service rooms arranged around a court. Large palaces are simply a multiplication of court complexes, as can readily be noted whether in the elaborate provincial capitals, such as at Eshnunna, Mari, Alalakh, Ugarit, or in simpler royal residences as at Megiddo, *Tell Beit Mirsim* and *Tell el-Ajjūl*.[19] The Ai building has no small living quarters around it as an integral part of the structure. Hence, a palace interpretation of the building's function is extremely doubtful.

2. It is well known that any given architectural building plan can be used for more than one purpose as occasion suited.[20] Thus, the common courtyard house can be used for sacred purposes when it is desired.[21]

---

18 See W. F. Albright, THE ARCHAEOLOGY OF PALESTINE (London: Pelican Books: 1949), p. 76. That Albright had come to this view long before 1949 is proved by this writer's article, which followed his views on the subject "The Temple in Palestine and Syria," presented during the spring of 1944 at an Oriental Institute symposium on the ancient temple, and published in *BA* 7, 1944, pp. 65-77 (reprinted without illustration in Biblical Archaeologist Reader I, Doubleday Anchor Books, 1961, pp. 169-184); see also this writer's remarks in THE BIB'E AND ANCIENT NEAR EAST (Albright Festschrift, New York 1961), p. 84 (Anchor Books, ed., 1965, pp. 100-101). Perhaps the first to call the building a fortified temple was Mme. Marquet-Krause's associate in the excavations, B. Yeivin, *loc. cit.* (see note 15). That Ruth Amiran among other archaeologists in Israel has had few doubts about the temple identification of the building may be indicated by the former's passing remark in ANCIENT ARAD, p. ii. In England M. V. Seton-Williams, "Palestinian Temples", IRAQ 2, 1949, pp. 77-89, follows Albright on the Ai large structure, but repeats the Vincent-Krause views on the "sanctuary".

19 For general discussion of the *hofhaus* type, used either as private dwellings or as temple, see W. Andrae, DAS GOTTESHAUS UND DIE URFORMEN DES BAUENS IM ALTEN ORIENT, 1930. For the structures in question see H. Frankfort, S. Lloyd and T. Jacobsen, THE GIMILSIN TEMPLE AND THE PALACE OF THE RULERS OF TELL ASMAR (Chicago 1940); A. Parrot, MARI, Pl. 81 (or see G. E. Wright, BIBLICAL ARCHAEOLOGY, Fig. 14); L. Woolley, ALALAKH (see n. 30), the palaces of Levels VII and IV, pp. 92 and 115 (or the same author's Pelican Book, A FORGOTTEN KINGDOM, 1953, pp. 71 and 102); Cl. F. A. Schaeffer, UGARITICA IV (Paris 1962), pp. 26, 28 and the large folding map inserted in the volume's pocket on the rear cover; G. Loud MEGIDDO II, Figs. 380-384 (the palaces of Strata X-VII); W. F. Albright, AASOR 17, 1938, Pl. 55 (Stratum D) (or for convenience, his Pelican Book, THE ARCHAEOLOGY OF PALESTINE, p. 91, Fig. 16); and Flinders Petrie, BETH-PELETI, London 1930, Pl. LII.

20 This has most recently been successfully argued by the distinguished archaeological architect, G. R. H. Wright, "Temples at Shechem," ZAW 80, 1968, pp. 2-35.

21 See, for example, this writer's discussion, SHECHEM, THE BIOGRAPHY OF A BIBLICAL CITY (New York and London, 1965), pp. 103-122; and forthcoming with Edward F. Campbell, Jr., "Tribal Leagues and the Significance of the Temples at Amman and Gerizim," (to appear in BA 32, Sept. 1969) and G. R. H. Wright's discussion. Since it was this writer who introduced the so-called Hittite temples into the discussion of

With regard to the large building at Ai, the first and most obvious point is that its plan is simply an enlarged and far more expensive version of the common Early Bronze I-II secular house. The one place where the largest display of EB I-II houses exists is in Arad. There Ruth Amiran found them directly under the surface soil of land not tilled or plowed between ca. 27th-26th century at the very latest and modern times.[22] In a one-period site such early structures can be displayed in a large exposure in contrast to a tell where they can be encountered only in small, deep sections where successive overbuilding of subsequent periods usually has destoyed evidence.

The typical Early Bronze house at Arad in Strata I-IV (EB II-I), says Ruth Amiran, "is composed of one large room, accompanied by a small room (kitchen or storeroom) and often a courtyard. The size of the rooms ranges from 7.30 x 5.10 m to 4.30 x 3.30 m. with the large size more common. The large room is always a 'broad room' with the entrance in the center of the long wall . . . low benches (or shelves) line most of the walls"

One building of this type has a size and thickness of walls which leave little doubt that it served a public function. Broadroom in type (11 x 5 m.), it had four pillar bases to support the roof. The excavator suggests that it was a temple because of close similarity with other contemporary temples "such as those excavated at Megiddo, Ai and (although of a somewhat earlier period) En-Gedi."[23]

The "altar" opposite the doorway of the Stratum XIX building at Megiddo makes its interpretation as a temple certain (Fig. 4,1), though the "altar" was the focus of attention, not in any modern sense, but because as a bench rebuilt many times it held the statue of the god there worshipped and perhaps votive or other offerings which were not to be burned or cooked as food on the main altar which would have been in an exterior court if preserved. The structure is precisely the Arad house in type with the four pillar bases in the center to hold up the roof. It rear wall appears to have been also a terrace wall because the building was on the eastern edge of the tell with the bedding plain rising rapidly behind it.[24] Its size approximates that of the large building which Ruth Amiran would interpret on its basis as a temple.

In an EB I context at Jericho (Stratum VII) John Garstang found a

courtyard temples,, let it be stated that one point and one only was being made: this was that, no matter the meaning of the structures as a whole, the shrines appended appear generally to have been too large to have been roofed, and the total structures, though having a multipurpose use, actually possessed open (unroofed) "cellas". If this point is proved wrong, the writer's hypotheses for interpretation at Shechem are still unaffected, because the literary evidence is too strong.

22 Ruth Amiran, ANCIENT ARAD, pp. 9-11.
23 *Ibid.,* p. ii.
24 Gordon Loud, MEGIDDO II, pp. 61-64.

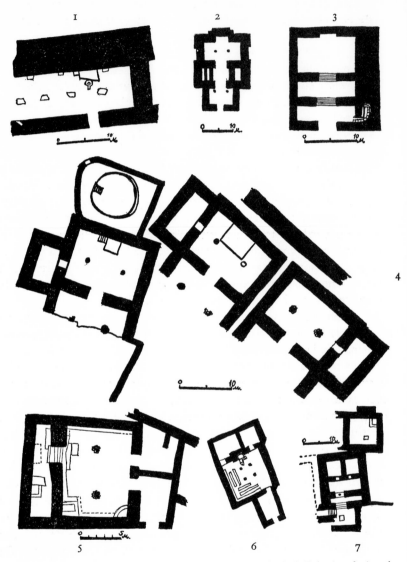

Fig. 4. Examples of the basic or most common temple-type in Syria-Palestine during the third and second millennia B.C. Basic references and dimensions are given in the text.

1 The Megiddo XIX temple, dating from the last phase of EB I.
2 The Hazor temple in Area H in its LB phase.
3 The Alalakh VII temple of MB II B.
4 The Megiddo "XV" temple complex, dating probably from EB II-III.
5 The Beth-shan VII temple, dating from the 13th cent. B.C.
6 The Lachish fosse temple in its final or 13th cent. B.C. phase.
7 The Alalakh temple of Stratum II (second half of 14th cent.). Note the two store-rooms at the rear, comparable to those of the nearly contemporary, though poorly built by comparison, Lachish temple.

similar building, broadroom in type, with benches along the interior walls. The excavator called it a "Babylonian shrine", though not indicating any substantial reason for the term. Its external dimensions are 4 m. wide x 7.5 m. long.[25] One reason for the interpretation of the building as a temple were cultic objects found in its area, especially a libation stand and a long, relatively thin, very smooth piece of stone which must have had some cultic use and which the excavator placed in the class of objects generally indicated as *măṣṣebot.*[26]

Next to be noted are the three temples of Megiddo which Gordon Loud ascribed to Stratum XV, though the altar at the rear of the easternmost building was thought to have had an earlier phase in the Early Bronze Strata XVII-XVI (Fig. 4,4). These are very well built and obviously more sophisticated examples of architecture than the preceding buildings cited above, except for that of Ai. Yet they are broadroom in type, roof supported by interior columns, and pedestals for the deity's statue located along the rear wall preserved in two of the three buildings. Of special interest is the large altar, surfaced with unhewn stones, steps ascending its top on the east — the best preserved altar of its type in the Syro-Palestinian area. Its diameter on top is ca. 8 m., its height ca. 1.15 m.

Kathleen Kenyon has suggested that the three temples were successive but surely not contemporary.[27] She thus attempts to distribute them between the mid-Early Bronze Age through the beginning of the Middle Bronze Age. Yet this attempt is not successful, because it cannot be proved.[28] The recording of objects from loci is highly suspect as to reliability in the original volume, and the architect's actual levels for the column bases in the temples are the same with a variation of only ten centimeters, or fifteen centimeters if the base of the large altar is included. This surely suggests, since the buildings were erected on a slope, that they were built as one compound on a leveled surface, presumably indicating that three different deities were here honored with "houses" to which gifts were brought.

During a careful examination of the buildings in October, 1964, the occasion being a study tour of staff and graduate students from the Hebrew Union College in Jerusalem, two of my Harvard graduate majors in archaeology and I reached two definite conclusions about the buildings. The first confirmed the original excavator's opinion that there were at least two

25 John Garstang, THE STORY OF JERICHO (London 1948), pp. 78-79 and Fig. 8. For pnotograph see AAA 23, 1936, Pl. XLIa.
26 *Ibid.,* p. 79.
27 "Some notes on the Early and Middle Bronze Age Strata at Megiddo" ERETZ ISRAEL 5, 1958, pp. 51*-60*.
28 In my "The Archaeology of the Bible," in: THE BIBLE AND THE ANCIENT NEAR EAST Albright Festschrift; ed. by G. E. Wright [Garden City, Doubleday, 1961]), I argue for an MB II A date (19th-18th cents.), precisely because the mixture of pottery in Stratum XV loci made a date impossible based on published material. In such a

majors phases visible in the great altar (4017) and in the easternmost temple (4040). The second conclusion was that the walls of all three buildings had been originally erected in earth belonging to the Early Bronze Age. Was this earth earlier fill or contemporary earth? The only way proof could now be secured would be to excavate within Building 4040, the one place where digging had not gone below the original floor of the temple. The distinguished Israeli architect, I. Dunayevski, independently had come to the same conclusions. He actually excavated a succession of floor levels in 4040, and found everything below the surface level to be Early Bronze Age, indeed contemporary with the Ai temple.[29] The only difference in form between these temples and the Ai and other contemporary or earlier EB temples mentioned above is the columned portico at Megiddo and the fact that the proportion of length to breadth is not as great.

Yet it would appear that the evidence is conclusive. The third millennium temple in Palestine was a broad-room or rectangular structure with entrance on one of the long sides. Furthermore, it was simply an enlarged and usually better built version of the Early Bronze I-II common house. Such evidence places the burden of proof on those who would claim for the Ai building some other function than that of temple or divine "house".

If this were not enough, it can be shown from evidence in both Syria and Palestine that this remains the basic temple type from northern Syria to southern Palestine during the Middle and Late Bronze Ages as well. We will not attempt to be exhaustive or present arguments about buildings, the date and form of which are inconclusive. For this reason a discussion of Byblos, for example, will be excluded.

It seems not unreasonable to suppose that at Alalakh Levels XVII-VIII are a series of temples, as suggested by the excavator, but that their date should be confined within the period of the Khabur Ware (perhaps mid-20th to the mid-18th century). In Level XII we find the familiar broadroom fronted by an elaborate portico, the whole structure forming a block ca. 15 x 12 m., a subject to which we shall shortly return.[30] In Stratum VIII, a central broadroom, ca. 13.60 x 5 m., has a narrower room to the front (a vestibule?) and another of the same dimensions at the rear (a storeroom?). The whole is on a podium, 17 m. wide by 25 m. long.[31] The same

---

situation it seemed more reasonable to assume that these fine buildings were erected in the new age of urbanization rather than in MB I (ca. 22nd-20th cent.) which thus far has failed to produce monumental architecture in Palestine. Such were the options that seemed to be open from published material at the time of the book's publication (see p. 88 and note 71).

29 Oral information from his archaeological colleagues but note I. Dunayevski and A. Kempinski, "Notes and News: Megiddo," IEJ 16, 1966, p. 142.

30 Sir Leonard Woolley, ALALAKH: An Account of the Excavations at Tell Atchana in the Hatay, 1937-1949, (London 1955), p. 48.

31 *Ibid.*, pp. 54-59.

type of broadroom continues to be built throughout the Bronze Age at Alalakh, especially clear plans being obtained in Levels VII (17th cent.?) and in IV, III, II, IA and IB. They vary in type only in the varying arrangements of porticos and courts in front of the cella (see Fig. 4,3.7).[32]

Elsewhere in Syria the Baal temple of Ras Shamra is of the same type with portico. Its proportions, however, are wider in relation to length, and in this respect it resembles the temples of Strata VII and VI at Beth-shan in LB II and of the Lachish Temple of the same period. Different though they appear, there is no doubt whatever of their architectural background (see Fig. 4,5.6).

From the Middle Bronze Age two more temples have been found in Palestine of the Early Bronze type. One at Nahariyeh on the northern coast has been excavated by I. Ben-Dor and M. Dothan.[33] It is almost precisely like the example of Garstang at Jericho (see above) in that the door on the long side is considerably off center.

The Hazor temple in Area H at the northern tip of the great enclosure, or fortified plateau, is a fine example of the long-roomed building with an elaborate portico, both erected in MB II B-C. The portico, however, having heavy supporting walls, appears to have been a tower with two or more stories and two columns in front (see Fig. 4,2).[34] Its main cult-room was ca. 10.50 m. by 5.25 m. wide, containing many cultic objects. The additional small portico in front was added only in the Late Bronze Age.

Variant Types of Syro-Palestinian Temples

It seems to this writer that the evidence cited above is definitive even though not exhaustive, regarding the *basic* temple type of the Syro-Palestinian region during the third and second millennia B.C. That is, it was a broadroom, with more or less elaboration in portico, its development being from the EB I-II common dwelling house.

There remains, however, the contention of Professor Callaway, the excavator, that the Ai building in question was a "citadel". This term requires the assumption that its primary purpose was to serve as a fortification. Yet it simply was not strong enough to serve this purpose. Its primary walls and the subsidiary walls which surrounded it are too thin to have been erected by Early Bronze people as a citadel. The great citadel was that erected directly behind (west of) it on top of the eight-meter wide city wall construction. While this is not as large as the twelve-meter wide wall near the city gate at *Tell el-Fār āh,* northeast of *Balāṭah* (Shechem),

32 *Ibid.,* pp. 59-90.
33 I. Ben-Dor, QDAP 14, 1950, pp. 1ff.; M. Dothan, IEJ 6, 1956, pp. 14ff. and: Western Galilee and the Coast of Galilee (in Hebrew), pp. 63ff.
34 Professor Yadin, to my knowledge, has not as yet published the final plans and description of the Hazor temple. A special plan seems to have been made available to M.

it demonstrates that Early Bronze people knew how to build strong fortifications, and they used mass for strength. The Ai building simply does
not fulfill the conditions suggested by Early Bronze defense planning. Since
the shape of the building belongs squarely within the main type of Bronze
Age temples, the small wall around it, with the rounded rear corners (Fig.
3), is more likely simply to set the sacred compound off from the remainder
of the city. It is unfortunate that erosion has destroyed the courtyard and
its contents from (to the east of) the structure's doorway.

Examples of temples adapted from fortifications are clearly the *migdal*
temples of Shechem and Megiddo (Fig. 5,1.2).[35] A secular *migdal*
comparable to them was found by the Beth-shan excavators, protecting the
main city gate.[36]

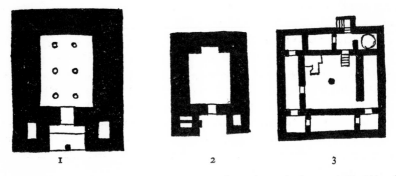

I   2   3

Fig. 5. Nos. 1 and 2 represent a different type of temple at Shechem and Megiddo, de-
riving from a fortress. Both are shown in their original MB II phases.
No. 3 is the Tenanir square courtyard temple on the east slope of Mt. Gerizim, excavated
by G. Welter in 1931 and reexcavated by Robert G. Boling in October, 1968. It is erected
on a flatbedding plane with steps leading down into it. Its mate is the temple in the
Amman airport, the court of which is just half the size of that at Tenanir.

    Noth, THE OLD TESTAMENT WORLD (Philadelphia 1966; tr. by Victor I. Gruhn from
the 4th German ed. of: DIE WELT DES ALTEN TESTAMENTS, Berlin, 1964) pl. 175,
Fig. 5: B. Detailed descriptions with photographs are published in BA 22, 1959, pp.
1-20; see also THE BIBLICAL ARCHAEOLOGIST READER 2, ed. by D. N. Freedman and
E. F. Campbell, Jr. (Garden City: Doubleday Anchor Book, 1964), pp. 215-221;
BIES 23, 1959, pp. 19-22, (Hebrew) and Pl. Aleph; and Yadin et al. HAZOR III-IV,
35 That the Megiddo temple of this type was erected in the Middle Bronze Age, roughly
in the same period as the Shechem temple, has been argued not only by this writer
(BASOR 148, p. 20, note 4; cf. also No. 169, pp. 29-30), but especially and in more
detail, using original excavation records, by Claire Epstein, "An Interpretation of the
Megiddo Sacred Area During Middle Bronze II," IEJ 15, 1965, pp. 204-221. Cf. also
B. Mazar,, IEJ 18, 1968, p. 92, note 80 and K. Kenyon, ARCHAEOLOGY IN THE HOLY
LAND (London and New York, 1960), p. 203, note I. In her latest treatment of the
subject Principal Kenyon argues for a later date: "The Middle and Late Bronze Strata
at Megiddo," LEVANT I, 1969, pp. 49ff. This detailed and acute analysis, however,
fails to convince because of the problem of knowing what pottery dates what walls.
To assume that the temple had only one floor is a major assumption considering the
methods of digging used. Miss Kenyon presents in Fig. 25 the pottery found "on"
this supposed single floor and dates it after the Thutmose III. destruction of the city,
and suggests the temple was erected then. Yet the pottery shown "on" the floor is
clearly not homogeneous. No. 11 is 12th-11th cent. in date and the rest of the group

Still another temple type, only recently recognized in Palestine, consists of only two examples found in the Amman airport, reexcavated and dated to LB II by Basil Hennessey,[37] and one of identical plan found and excavated by G. Welter in 1931 (see Fig. 5.3).[38] These buildings are square, with small rooms around a central court. In the center of the court is a non-structural podium, presumably for a sacred pillar. The Shechem, or actually the Tenanir, example was reexcavated by Robert G. Boling and ASOR staff in October, 1968, and dated to MB II C. The cultic nature of the Tenanir structure cannot be denied, and both temples exist in open areas with no cities around them.[39]

This writer has argued for the existence of a different form of courtyard temples as Shechem in MB II B before the *migdal*-temple of MB II C was erected.[40] Stratum IX of Beth-shan also has an open-air shrine with *mǎṣṣebah*, though its architectural reconstruction is most difficult.[41] Presumably, the sacred courts with rooms around them derive ultimately as temple type from royal palaces with their courts being used for a variety of functions before certain of them became specialized for cultic use.[42] On the other hand, the Amman and Tenanir square temples could very well have a background unknown to us, perhaps in desert enclosures of semi-nomadic people, otherwise unknown. The people who used the temple in the city-state capital, Shechem, were probably not the same people who used the isolated temple of Tenanir, and certainly not of the even more isolated temple in the Amman airport.[43]

Conclusions

As regards the central building at the dominant point within the fortified city of Ai, there can be no doubt, after this survey, about its nature and function as a temple. Furthermore, it is peculiar in the sense that it is

fits the 13th cent. reasonably well, though a few pieces could be either, while No. 5 and 6, unless 6 is Mycenean, could be of the same date as No. 11.

36 A. Rowe, THE TOPOGRAPHY AND HISTORY OF BETH-SHAN (Philadelphia 1930), p. 20, Fig. 2.

37 PEQ 98, 1966, pp. 155-162. See for plan the present article (Fig. 5).

38 See G. Welter's schematic plan and brief description in AA 1932, III-IV, col. 314.

39 See the forthcoming article by Edward F. Campbell, Jr. and the writer, "Tribal League Shrines in Amman and Schechem," cf. note 21. The Gerizim structure was at a site now called Tenanir. The results of Boling's excavations will shortly be published by ASOR. Cf. also G. R. H. Wright, "Temples at Shechem," ZAW 80, 1968, pp. 9-16.

40 BASOR 169, 1963, pp. 17-18, but in more detail: SHECHEM, BIOGRAPHY OF A BIBLICAL CITY (New York, 1965), Chapter 7.

41 Rowe, TOPOGRAPHY AND HISTORY OF BETH-SHAN, pp. 10-17, with plan in Fig. 1 and photographs on Pls. 16-22. The date is presumably 14th century against Rowe's original attribution to "Thothmes III."

42 Cf. the great Hittite temples of the Late Bronze Age: see Rudolf Naumann, ARCHITEKTUR KLEINASIENS (Tübingen, 1955), p. 390 and Figs. 475-476.

43 G. R. H. Wright, (n. 39) compares these temples to that connected to the royal palace of Gimilsin excavated by the Oriental Institute in the Diyala basin. Yet that

as isolated from the rest of the buildings in Early Bronze Ai as is the sacred area of Shechem in the second millennium B.C. This leads to the hypothesis that Ai was no ordinary city-state, especially as no evidence of an acropolis with royal palace exists at the site, in spite of its size and extraordinary fortification in the Early Bronze Age.

We are, therefore, left completely in the dark about the city's purpose in being — unless we use Nippur in Mesopotamia as a model of what must have been frequent among Asian city-states of the third millennium B.C. In the political development of the city-state system, as strong individuals were pressing for empires by conquest, Nippur served as the religious center of a league of city-states which had committed themselves by treaty to a unity of defense and offense, sanctioned by the deity Enlil before whom the oaths were taken. The hegemony of this god was over all parties and their temple(s) were not necessarily under the sole protection of one monarch as was to become the case in an empire ruled by one suzerain. Some such interpretation furnishes an adequate explanation of Nippur, as it does also of Ai.[44]

A by-product of this survey furnishes some interesting data about the cubit-measurement used in Syria-Palestine during the third and second millennia B.C. With the reservations to be noted below, the following rather expected results were obtained. The Babylonian cubit was used as the unit of measurement during the third millenium and throughout the second in Syria at Alalakh. In Middle and Late Bronze Palestine, with two exceptions to be noted, the long Egyptian cubit appears to have been used generally for temples. This is the one described by Ezekiel 40:5 as used in the Solomonic temple, a handbreadth longer than the short Egyptian cubit. The exceptions appear to be these: the Middle Bronze temple at *Nahariyeh* is sufficiently far north along the coast of Palestine still to employ the Babylonian cubit. The two square tribal league (?) temples of Tenanir and Amman seem to use the short Egyptian cubit, which later became

temple is unusual in early Mesopotamia, and was clearly under a royal city-state and palace protection, which the Amman temple, and probably the Tenanir temple also, were not.

44 On the individuality of Nippur in the third millennium B.C., see Thorkild Jacobsen, "Early Political Development in Mesopotamia," ZA N.F. 18, 1957, pp. 104-106. Jacobsen raises the question as to whether what he has called "primitive democracy" was ever "extended from regional application to the country of Sumer as a whole. We tend to believe that the answer should be in the affirmative." Among the evidence he cites is that from the beginning of historical times Nippur and the god Enlil held undisputed rule over all of Sumer, and the city-state kings derived their authority "from recognition in Nippur rather than from their own city and its city-god." And there is no trace of an early political dominion of Nippur; indeed, the evidence is to the contrary. During the empire of the Third Dynasty of Ur the earthly suzerain was elected to office by an assembly of gods meeting in Nippur. It was just such an assembly at Nippur which voted the end to the rule of the Third Dynasty of Ur. For another type of evidence of the special place of Nippur in the city-state league of Sumer, see William Hallo, "Sumerian Amphictyony," JCS 14, 1960, pp. 88-114.

the standard unit of measurement used by Israel.

The reservations which one must keep in mind regarding the above generalizations are as follows: (1) Excavators are too often not precise in their measurements, and even are occasionally satisfied with preliminary reports which give no measurements at all. Even when the width of a wall is given, only one measurement is taken, whereas stone walls will vary in width by several centimeters. Only by taking several measurements with the purpose of finding the average width in a cubit unit (not solely in a metric system unknown in antiquity) can one be sure of what the builders had in mind. (2) There is the problem of external or internal measurements. There should not be a problem here, but in several instances of stone bases for brick superstructures it appears certain that the bases were plastered. Since the plaster is gone, one can only estimate what the total width must have been. (3) Cases of human error must also be taken into account, as also limitations of space for the architects to work in, limitations which we usually cannot now recover.

Given these qualifications the following are some results, based upon the recent work of Professor R.B.Y. Scott of Princeton University, whose research has brought up to date older studies by the use of a large mass of new data. His calculations suggest the following approximations: the early and standard Babylonian cubit, ca. 500 millimeters; the short Egyptian cubit, ca. 445 mm.; and the long Egyptian cubit, ca. 525 mm.[45]

1. The presumed temple at Arad (11 m. x 5 m.), 22 x 10 Babylonian cubits.

2. The Megiddo XIX temple (4 m. wide by over 12 m. long; the south end, ran into the balk): 8 Babylonian cubits by ca. 30 (if 15 m. long, which it should be approximately, judging from the spacing of the column bases.)

3. The Jericho VII temple of Garstang (8 m. x 7.50 m. outside measurements) gives us 16 x 15 Babylonian cubits.

4. The Ai temple (Fig. 3), ca. 20 m. 6.60m., if thickness of two 2 m. walls and plaster are included, would run close to 48 x 22 Babylonian cubits.

5. The three Megiddo "XV" temples, contemporary with that at Ai, appear to have had identical proportions, ca. 9 x 14 m. each, which would give ca. 18 x 28 Babylonian cubits. The great altar, ca. 8 m. in diameter, yields 16 Babylonian cubits.

6. The Middle Bronze Age *Naharīyah* temple, ca. 8 x 13 m., would mean 16 x 26 Babylonian cubits.

7. The whole series of Alalakh temples from MB II to LB II B yield

an easily converted series of Babylonian cubits, the accuracy dependent entirely on the expedition's accuracy in recording. For example, the platform on which the MB II A temple VIII rests (17 x 25 m.) is 34 x 50 Babylonian cubits, and the broadroom and portico in Level XII (ca. 15 m. x 12 m.) is clearly 30 x 12 Babylonian cubits. The rooms in the temple measure 6 x 27, 10 x 27, and 6 x 27 cubits, respectively. The inner dimensions of the MB II B temple of Alalakh VII would have been ca. 23 x 11 or 12 cubits.

8. The Shechem MB II C *migdal*-temple (Fig. 5) is, on the contrary, 50 x 40 Egyptian long cubits with wall 10 cubits thick.[46] Its Megiddo contemporary (Bldg. 2048) by exterior measurements is ca. 41 x 33½ or 34 cubits of the same measurement, depending on the accuracy of the recording, and/or the plastered exterior.

9. The Late Bronze Lachish temple (Fig. 4.6) was not well built and was irregular in its outlines so that it is difficult to be sure of the architect's plan. A main room in such circumstances of 10 x 10.4 m. suggests a building whose cella was supposed to be ca. 20 long Egyptian cubits, nearly square.

10. The Beth-shan VII (13th cent. B.C.) temple (Fig. 4.5), rebuilt with minor alterations in VI (12th cent. B.C.), is wider at the north end than at the south, though like the Lachish temple is nearly square. Its main court was clearly in Egyptian long cubits, which could probably be computed precisely if walls and unknown width of plaster coating were known. Rowe's inner measurements of the cella are 8.40 m. wide by 11.70 m. long at the north and 10.57 m. at the south. This gives ca. 16 by ca. 21 and 20 long Egyptian cubits.[47]

11. The two square courtyard temples of Amman and Tenanir, on the other hand, clearly are of a different tradition, employing the short Egyptian cubit of ca. 445 mm. The inner court of the Amman structure is 10 cubits square of this measurement, while that of the Tenanir temple is exactly twice its size, 20 cubits square.

---

46 See the writer's Shechem, pp. 87-88.
47 A. Rowe, THE FOUR CANAANITE TEMPLES OF BETH-SHAN, (Philadelphia 1940), p. 8.

Abbreviations
AASOR - *Annual of the American Schools of Oriental Research*
ASOR - American Schools of Oriental Research
BA - BIBLICAL ARCHAEOLOGIST
BASOR - *Bulletin of the American Schools of Oriental Research*
BIES - *Bulletin of the Israel Exploration Society*
CAH - CAMBRIDGE ANCIENT HISTORY
IEJ - *Israel Exploration Journal*
JBL - *Journal of Biblical Literature*
JCS - *Journal of Cuneiform Studies*
PEFQSt - Palestine Exploration Fund Quarterly Statement
PEQ - *Palestine Exploration Quarterly*
QDAP - *Quarterly of the Department of Antiquities in Palestine*
RB - *Revue biblique*
ZA - *Zeitschrift für Assyriologie*
ZAW - *Zeitschrift für die alttestamentliche Wissenschaft*
ZDPV - *Zeitschrift des deutschen Palästina-Vereins*

OUR ESTEEMED FACULTY

Bernhard W. Anderson

Professor of Old Testament Theology
Princeton Theological Seminary
Princeton, New Jersey

Robert A. Bennett

Asst. Professor of Old Testament
Episcopal Divinity School
Cambridge, Massachusetts

Eugene B. Borowitz

Professor of Jewish Thought
Hebrew Union College
New York, New York

John Bright

Cyrus McCormick Professor of Hebrew
    and Old Testament
Union Theological Seminary
Richmond, Virginia

Raymond E. Brown, S.S.

Auburn Professor of Biblical Studies
Union Theological Seminary
New York, New York

Kevin J. Cathcart

Professor of Semitic Languages
University College
Dublin, Ireland

Thomas Aquinas Collins, O.P.

Professor of Hebrew and
    Old Testament
Providence College Graduate School
Providence, Rhode Island

Frank Moore Cross, Jr.

Hancock Professor of Hebrew and
    Oriental Languages
Harvard Divinity School
Cambridge, Massachusetts

Peter Gerard Duncker, O.P.

Professor of Hebrew and
    Old Testament
Pontifical Biblical Institute
Rome, Italy

Peter F. Ellis, C.SS.R.

Professor of Biblical Theology
Fordham University
New York, New York

Charles T. Fritsch

Professor of Old Testament
Princeton Theological Seminary
Princeton, New Jersey

Reginald H. Fuller	Professor of New Testament Protestant Episcopal Theological Seminary in Virginia Alexandria, Virginia
Cyrus H. Gordon	Gottesman Professor of Hebraic Studies New York University New York, New York
Harvey H. Guthrie, Jr.	Dean, Professor of Old Testament Episcopal Divinity School Cambridge, Massachusetts
Wilfrid J. Harrington	Professor of Scripture Dominican House of Studies Tallaght, Dublin, Ireland
Howard M. Jamieson	Past President, Professor of Bible Pittsburgh Theological Seminary Pittsburgh, Pennsylvania
John L. McKenzie	Professor of Theology University of Notre Dame South Bend, Indiana
George W. MacRae, S.J.	Professor of New Testament Harvard Divinity School Cambridge, Massachusetts
Eugene H. Maly	Professor of Sacred Scripture Mount St. Mary Seminary of the West Norwood, Ohio
Paul S. Minear	Winkley Professor (Emeritus) of Biblical Theology Yale University New Haven, Connecticut
John Moriarty, S.C.	Professor of Sacred Scripture St. Columban's Major Seminary Milton, Massachusetts
M. Lucetta Mowry	Professor of New Testament Wellesley College Wellesley, Massachusetts

Roland E. Murphy, O. Carm.	Professor of Old Testament Duke University Durham, North Carolina
Gerald O'Collins, S.J.	Professor of Fundamental Theology Gregorian University Rome, Italy
Jerome Murphy-O'Connor, O.P.	Professor of New Testament Ecole Biblique Jerusalem, Israel
James B. Pritchard	Curator, Biblical Archaeology, University Museum University of Pennsylvania Philadelphia, Pennsylvania
Jerome D. Quinn	Professor of New Testament, and Dean The St. Paul Seminary St. Paul, Minnesota
Leopold Sabourin, S.J.	Professor of Sacred Scripture Pontifical Biblical Institute Rome, Italy
Martin Schoenberg, O.S.C.	Professor of Sacred Scripture Crosier House of Studies Fort Wayne, Indiana
Carroll Stuhlmueller, C.P.	Professor of Old Testament Catholic Theological Union Chicago, Illinois
Alexa Suelzer, S.P.	Vice President and First Councilor Sisters of Providence St. Mary-of-the-Woods, Indiana
Bruce Vawter, C.M.	Professor of New Testament DePaul University Chicago, Illinois
John F. Whealon	Archbishop Diocese of Hartford Hartford, Connecticut
George Ernest Wright	Parkman Professor of Divinity Harvard Divinity School Cambridge, Massachusetts